# THE
# GERONIMO
# CAMPAIGN

# THE
# GERONIMO
# CAMPAIGN

ODIE B. FAULK

OXFORD UNIVERSITY PRESS
NEW YORK  OXFORD

Oxford University Press

Oxford   New York   Toronto
Delhi   Bombay   Calcutta   Madras   Karachi
Kuala Lumpur   Singapore   Hong Kong   Tokyo
Nairobi   Dar es Salaam   Cape Town
Melbourne   Auckland   Madrid
and associated companies in
Berlin   Ibadan

Library of Congress Cataloging-in-Publication Data
Faulk, Odie B.
The Geronimo campaign / Odie B. Faulk,
p.     cm.
"First published in 1969 by Oxford University Press"—T.p. verso.
Includes bibliographical references and index.
ISBN 0-19-508351-2 (pbk.)
1. Geronimo, 1829–1909.   2. Apache Indians—Biography.   3. Apache
Indians—Wars, 1883–1886.   4. Apache Indians—History.   I. Title.
E99.A6G3242     1993     973'.04972—dc20     [B]     93-2847     CIP

2  4  6  8  10  9  7  5  3

Printed in the United States of America

FOR RICHARD AND NANCY
With memories of your move
from Arizona to Oklahoma

# PREFACE

THE MEETING of Lieutenant Charles B. Gatewood and the Apache war leader Geronimo on the banks of the Bavispe River in Sonora on the morning of August 25, 1886, recapitulated almost every meeting of Indian and American in the West. Geronimo asked what terms he and his followers could expect if they surrendered. Gatewood told him that they would be exiled to Florida, giving up their ancient homeland entirely to the Americans. "Accept these terms or fight it out to the bitter end," said Gatewood, repeating the message sent by General Miles. This was the substance of what almost every Indian was told at every such meeting; there was no alternative but total surrender or a fight to the death. The cultures of the two civilizations were in direct conflict, and one had to give way totally. Because the Americans were more numerous and more technologically advanced, it was the Indians who lost. Yet neither the Army nor the civilians won either.

The great theme of Greek tragedy is the inevitability of defeat and the triumph of surviving it. Robert Louis Stevenson restated this principle when he declared, "Our business in this world is not to succeed but to continue to fail in good spirits." The final Geronimo campaign was such a tragedy. There was inevitable conflict and inevitable defeat, both sides losing in the process, but both survived. The Indians were forced to undergo decades of captivity and humiliation, and their culture was subverted. The Army, which seemingly had won the war, was torn by conflicting claims to glory. The winner was the man most shrewdly capable of playing politics, and thus he rose to become commanding general of the Army at a time when the military needed wisdom, not shrewdness and deftness at politics. And the national culture lost what the Indians might have contributed to it had there been a peaceful resolution to the clash of civilizations. The final Geronimo campaign must have pleased whatever Greek gods were still haunting Mount Olympus; it was a tragedy of which they surely would have approved. There were no victors.

In the writing of this story, I find myself most indebted to Charles B. Gatewood, Jr., who spent more than four decades collecting information relating to the campaign. Depositions from old soldiers and scouts, official documents, articles, extracts from relevant books, photographs by the hundreds, and the letters and papers of his father are included in this collection, which he donated to the Arizona Pioneers' Historical Society, Tucson. I am deeply grateful to that institution for making these papers available to me, for they have never been used to any extent to tell what happened in this tragic conflict. Dr. Andrew Wallace, former Librarian, Charles Colley, the Archivist, and Sidney Brinckerhoff, now the Director, aided in my research.

I also wish to express a deep appreciation to the Oklahoma State University Research Foundation, whose support enabled me to complete phases of the research. Dr. Homer L. Knight, Head of the Department of History at Oklahoma State University, extended many courtesies to me during the past year and made it possible for me to complete the work, while my colleagues in the Department contributed numerous ideas. I also acknowledge with sincere appreciation the help of the Library at Oklahoma State University for its support in assembling needed materials. I am deeply grateful to my wife, Laura, who, as always, has listened endlessly, given her support, and read proof. Finally, I thank the editors of Oxford University Press, particularly Mr. Sheldon Meyer, to whom I am deeply indebted.

ODIE B. FAULK

Stillwater, Oklahoma
January 1969

# CONTENTS

# THE
# GERONIMO
# CAMPAIGN

# ONE

# THE

# APACHES

In the beginning the world was covered with darkness. There was no sun, no day. The perpetual night had no moon or stars. . . . Among the few human beings that were yet alive was a woman who had been blessed with many children, but these had always been destroyed by the beasts. If by any means she succeeded in eluding the others, the dragon, who was very wise and very evil, would come himself and eat her babies. After many years a son of the rainstorm was born to her and she dug for him a deep cave. . . . Frequently the dragon would come and question her, but she would say, "I have no more children; you have eaten all of them." When the child was larger, . . . he wished to go hunting. The mother would not give her consent. She told him of the dragon, the wolves, and the serpents; but he said, "To-morrow I go."

At the boy's request his uncle (who was the only man then living) made a little bow and some arrows for him, and the two went hunting the next day. They trailed the deer far up the mountain and finally the boy killed a buck. . . . Just then the huge form of the dragon appeared. . . . The dragon took the boy's parcel of meat and went aside with it. He placed the meat on a . . . bush and seated himself beside it. Then he said, "This is the child I have been seeking. Boy, you are nice and fat, so when I have eaten this venison I shall eat you." The boy said, "No, you shall not eat me, and you shall not eat that meat." . . . Then he sped the . . . arrow with true aim, and it pierced the dragon's heart. . . .

This boy's name was Apache. Usen [the Apache word for God] taught him how to prepare herbs for medicine, how to hunt, and

3

how to fight. He was the first chief of the Indians and wore the eagle's feathers as the sign of justice, wisdom, and power. To him, and to his people, as they were created, Usen gave homes in the land of the west.

*Geronimo's Story of His Life,*
S. M. Barrett, editor (New York, 1906)

FOR THREE CENTURIES before the arrival of the Anglo-American in the Southwest, the Apaches dominated the region, striking terror not only into the hearts of surrounding Indian tribes but also into the hearts of the Spanish colonists who ventured into the area. Mexican mothers frightened their children into obeying by threatening them with the undesignated terror of the "Apaches." Their name itself came from a Zuñi word meaning "enemy"; they referred to themselves as *Diné,* meaning "the People."

Anthropologists generally believe that the Apaches migrated from northwestern Canada between A.D. 900 and 1200. Members of the Athapascan linguistic group, they still have cousins in Western Canada, Alaska, and along the coast of Washington and Oregon. These southern Athapascans—the Apaches—were scattered from West Texas, across southern New Mexico, into southeastern Arizona; north into southern Kansas and southern Colorado; and south into the Mexican states of Chihuahua and Sonora. Soon after their arrival in the Southwest, they split into a number of sub-tribes, or bands, each with a slightly different dialect. To the east were the Lipan Apaches and the Kiowa-Apaches, who roamed from West Texas northward to Kansas. In northern New Mexico were the Jicarilla Apaches, while the Mescalero Apaches and Warm Springs (Ojo Caliente) Apaches controlled the southern portion of the region. The Chiricahua Apaches lived immediately west of the present Arizona-New Mexico border and considered themselves virtually the same tribe as the Warm Springs group. Finally, there were the Western Apaches, who lived in central and east-central Arizona: the White Mountain Apaches, the Cibecue group, the San Carlos

4

Apaches (subdivided into the Pinal, Arivaipa, and San Carlos bands), and the Coyotero Apaches. To single out any one group, or band, as the most fearsome would be a difficult—and fool-hardy—task, but certainly the Chiricahua and Warm Springs bands ranked high.

At the time the Apaches moved into the Southwest they existed by hunting and gathering, living on small game and wild plants. In their new environment, however, the eastern groups became buffalo hunters, lived in Plains-Indian tepees or brush dwellings built on tepee frames, and adapted themselves to the horse. The western groups continued to live in brush shelters, known as wickiups, borrowed enough from the Pueblo tribes to weave baskets and make pottery, and even did some farming. Although they too had horses, they never really became "horse Indians." They could—and did—travel much farther on foot over rugged mountains and harsh desert than could Spanish, Mexican, or American cavalrymen. One group of Athapascan-speaking Apaches in the Southwest adopted a radically different mode of life, so different that they came to be regarded separately—the Navajo. They became raisers of sheep after the arrival of the Spaniards.

All the Apache bands, including the Navajo, were distinguished from neighboring southwestern tribes by one other feature—their ferocity as warriors. Perhaps because they felt threatened by the Indians whom they had dispossessed when they moved into the region, they became remorseless warriors and guerrilla fighters. Inhabitants of a hard, cruel land, they became, like it, hard and cruel to everyone except themselves. They warred endlessly against the Pueblo Indians of New Mexico, the Pimas and Papagos of Arizona, and the Comanches in Texas. They were nomadic wanderers across their desert-mountain homeland, although each band had an ill-defined region it considered its own. Each group had hereditary chieftains to whom nominal allegiance was given; however, on the warpath the men followed whichever leader inspired their confidence by his success as thief and murderer. In fact, their economy, beyond some hunting and gathering, was based on booty gathered in raids. And while the Plains Indians worried about "counting coup" and gaining honor, the Apaches fought principally for material gain. The sudden raid by small bands, swooping down on unsuspecting villages, taking whatever plunder was available, was the hallmark of Apache warfare, after which they would retreat to mountain hideouts. In most of these forays, they rode to the scene of battle, then made their attack on foot, which meant that the women and children were left behind when they went on the warpath.

The Spaniards who colonized New Mexico beginning in 1598 and Arizona a century later came with the cross in one hand and the sword in the other. But at first the cross was in the right hand; the emphasis was on converting the Indians to Christianity, civilizing and Hispanicizing them in the process. The instrument of this policy was the mission—but with the Apaches it failed. Lordly warriors, they had no inclination to become farmers of the mission fields and vineyards or herders of the mission cattle and sheep. So in the last half of the eighteenth century the sword was shifted to the Spaniard's fighting hand. The Apaches were to be made receptive to the exhortations of the priests. Presidios (forts) were erected across the northern frontier in haphazard fashion until 1772; in that year the Spanish monarch Charles III issued the royal regulations which decreed that presidios be stretched in a regular cordon from the Gulf of California to the Gulf of Mexico. New methods of supply, of training of the soldiers, and of administration were embodied in these regulations in the belief that the Indians could be forced into submission.

By 1786 the continued decline of the northern frontier proved that Spanish arms could not do the job that Franciscan and Jesuit missionaries had failed to do—bring the Apaches to heel. That year a new system was inaugurated. Vigorous warfare was to be conducted against the Apaches, as well as other tribes not at peace with Spain. When the Indians asked for peace, they were to be settled in the shadow of a presidio. There they would be given presents regularly, along with inferior firearms and alcoholic beverages. Spanish officials reasoned that with presents of sufficient value the Indian would prize peace more than war. Most of the Apaches could not be reduced so readily, however, and for them the system was different: trading posts were to be established near their villages and from such posts the Apaches would receive the annual distribution of presents; the traders could keep a watchful eye on the activities of the Indians, get news of impending raids, and work to keep them friendly toward Spain.

This plan of conciliation and bribery accomplished what neither cross nor sword had been able to do. It brought peace to the northern frontier, a peace that lingered into the Mexican era of the Southwest's history. Then in 1831, when the annual distribution of presents had ceased, the Chiricahuas and other Western Apaches rose in concerted rebellion against Mexico, striking the frontier settlements in Sonora and Chihuahua with great fury. Following mountain paths, the Indians would move quickly and quietly to the south in small bands. Leaving the Sierra, they would attack settlements in the interior, burning and looting the buildings, killing the men and capturing as many women and children as was convenient, and drive off the livestock. Returning to their mountain trails, they would flee northward to their homes. Pursuers were discouraged by ambushes laid along the way. If necessary, loot and prisoners were abandoned, but rarely would the Apaches fight unless they had both superior numbers and the element of surprise in their favor.

The Mexican response to these bloody raids was first to reactivate the old cordon of presidios. The Royal Regulations of 1772 were reprinted in 1834, even to the signature *Yo, el Rey* (I, the King). Organized military resistance proved a failure, however, because the national government in faraway Mexico City was paralyzed by political intrigue and instability. Therefore the governments of the two states most affected, Sonora and Chihuahua, turned to the use of militia and treaties. These likewise failed, for the militia was incapable of military victory over the Apaches, and the Indians signed treaties only when convenient, with the young warriors breaking them at will. The two states then turned to the old Spanish method of paying bounties for Apache scalps. This program committed the states to a policy of total extermination, for bounties were offered for the hair not only of warriors but also of women and children. Enterprising Mexicans soon took the field as "backyard barbers," to be joined quickly by Americans, runaway American slaves, and even other Indian tribes such as the Delawares from the United States and the Tarahumaras of Mexico. The bounty system had the entire border country aflame with hatreds and suspicions within a short time, however, for it proved impossible for examining committees to tell the difference between the hair of friendly Indians and that of the hostiles; in fact, it was difficult to tell the hair of an Indian from that of a Mexican, and whole villages of unsuspecting Mexicans were exterminated for their scalps. By the end of the Mexican War and the conquest of the Southwest by the United States, no solution to the Apache problem had been found.

When the first American pioneers arrived in Arizona in the mid-1850s, the Apaches, aware of the recent war between the two nations, welcomed them as allies. The leader of the Chiricahuas at this time was Cochise, born about 1823. He had succeeded his father, Nachi, as hereditary leader of the band; in addition, by his ferocity on the battlefield he had become the acknowledged war chieftain as well, and was widely trusted by both soldiers and civilians in Arizona. Charles D. Poston, who came to the territory in 1856 as general manager of a mining firm operating from Tubac, declared in 1859: "The Apaches have not up to this time given us any trouble; but on the contrary, pass within sight of our herds, going hundreds of miles into Mexico on their forays rather than break their [friendship] . . . with the Americans."

8

The first breach of these good relations came in the fall of 1860 when some thirty Mexicans rode into Tubac with information that the Apaches had raided their ranches in Mexico and were returning to their Arizona haunts by way of a crossing on the Santa Cruz River, a few miles downstream from Tubac. The Mexicans asked the men at Tubac to help ambush the Apaches, promising them in return half of the three hundred horses and mules which the Indians had stolen and were driving north. Poston refused to allow any of his men to participate. Thereupon the Mexicans rode a dozen miles north to Canoa, which was the headquarters of a company of lumbermen from Maine. They were whipsawing lumber out of the nearby Santa Rita Mountains and were always in need of additional horses and mules. The Mexicans made the lumbermen the same offer—half the stock in return for their aid in ambushing the Chiricahuas—and the lumbermen foolishly accepted. The ambush succeeded admirably. The Apaches were caught in a murderous crossfire and abandoned the stock.

"About the next full moon after this event," later wrote Poston, "we had been passing the usual quiet Sunday in Tubac, when a Mexican vaquero came galloping furiously into the plaza crying out, 'Apaches! Apaches! Apaches!'" From him Poston learned that the Apaches had attacked the lumbering camp and had exacted a bloody revenge. Poston and a group of his men went to Canoa to be greeted by a scene of massacre and destruction: "The place looked as if it had been struck by a hurricane. The doors and windows were smashed, and the house was a smoking ruin. The former inmates were lying around dead, and three of them had been thrown into the well, head foremost. We buried seven men in a row in front of the burned house." Dragoons from nearby Fort Buchanan, established in 1857, went in pursuit of the raiders but never caught them.

Cochise did not turn on all Americans as a result of this event, however. His violent hatred of them dated from a few months later and stemmed from an even more needless incident.

9

In the Sonoita Valley, some twelve miles from Fort Buchanan, lived a rancher named John Ward with his common-law wife—who had been a captive of the Apaches for several years—and his stepson, who had been sired during that captivity. During a drunken fit Ward beat the stepson so badly that the lad ran away to live with his mother's relatives in Sonora. When sober Ward, unaware of the boy's destination, went to Fort Buchanan and complained that Cochise and the Chiricahuas had stolen the boy and some cattle. Some three months later, the commanding officer, Lieutenant Colonel Pitcairn Morrison, detached Second Lieutenant George N. Bascom and approximately sixty men to recover the boy and the cattle, and to use force if necessary. Ward went along with them.

Bascom led his detachment eastward to Apache Pass in the knowledge that Cochise lived in the vicinity. Arriving there on February 4, 1861, Bascom paused at the Butterfield Overland Mail Company's corral in the Pass, then went eastward along the road about three-quarters of a mile and made camp. This ruse was designed to give the Indians the impression that the soldiers were merely on their way to New Mexico, such travel being common. Cochise soon came into the camp voluntarily, accompanied by several of his relatives and friends. Bascom invited the Chiricahua chieftain into his tent, and he and seven followers entered. Thereupon Ward and a group of soldiers surrounded the canvas meetinghall. Lieutenant Bascom bluntly demanded the return of the boy and cattle, declaring that Cochise and his party would be held as hostages until both were brought in. Cochise protested his innocence to no avail. Then, sensing that the lieutenant meant what he had said, Cochise drew his knife and slit an opening in the side of the tent. Through this he plunged, landing outside in the midst of some very startled soldiers. Without pausing, Cochise dashed away, making good his escape. The Indians with Cochise in the tent were not so fortunate. One warrior followed his chief through the hole in the tent, but was clubbed by one soldier and bayoneted in the stomach by an-

10

other. The other six, mostly relatives of Cochise, were seized as hostages.

Cochise quickly rallied his warriors and struck the unsuspecting employees of the Butterfield Overland Mail. One was killed and another made prisoner. That evening a wagon train entered Apache Pass on the Butterfield road; on it were two Americans and eight Mexicans. Cochise captured the train, held the two Americans prisoners, and ordered the Mexicans tied to the wagon wheels and burned. Then under flag of truce, he offered to trade his three Americans for the six Apaches held by Bascom, but this was refused.

Lieutenant Bascom realized his precarious position in the Pass and sent runners to Fort Buchanan for aid. On February 14 Lieutenant Isaiah N. Moore and seventy dragoons arrived to find that the Indians had seemingly melted away at their approach. During a scout of the vicinity, the bodies of the three Americans held hostage by Cochise were found; they were filled with lance holes and mutilated beyond individual recognition. Bascom's official report tells what then took place: "Finding no fresh sign of Indians, we returned to the [Butterfield] Station and on the next day started for Fort Buchanan; when near the scene of the macsacre [sic] and about three hundred yards from the burnt train, I took the six warriors I had prisoners to the grave of [the] murdered men, explained through the interpreter what had taken place, and my intentions, and bound them securely hand and foot, and hung them to the nearest trees. . . ."[1]

The "Bascom Affair," as this tragic and needless episode came to be known, so enraged Cochise that he launched a long and terrible war, intending no less than the total extermination of all Americans in Arizona. Compounding the misery this engendered was the abandonment of the territory by the Army; the outbreak of the Civil War in the spring of 1861 caused all troops to be withdrawn to the Rio Grande, leaving Arizona totally without military protection. Mining came to a standstill; ranchers abandoned their stock; farmers fled their fields; and all moved to

Tucson or left the territory entirely. The arrival of the California Column in 1862 brought little respite, for most of these troops went on to New Mexico, and Cochise continued to exact his revenge.

In 1865, because of the intensity of the Indian depredations in the Territory, the district of Arizona, a part of the Department of California, was placed under the command of Brigadier General John S. Mason, who came east from California with 2800 men to regarrison the old posts and to establish new ones. But little was accomplished by these troops, as the Apaches continued to raid at will. Then on April 15, 1870, the district was detached from California and made a separate department. Brigadier General George Stoneman was sent to take command. Following orders from Washington, Stoneman sought to implement the "peace policy" of President Grant, a policy based on the theory that the Indians would best respond to kindness, religious instruction, and training in agrarian methods. Army officers were deprived of the right to act as Indian agents, these jobs going instead to members of the various religious denominations. Peace treaties with the Indians would remove them to reservations where they would get an annual distribution of presents, a regular issue of food, and gifts of farm implements and seed so they could become farmers.

Stoneman followed his orders by making treaties and establishing reservations with those Indians who would accept them and by feeding the Indians when they did. Arizonans were enraged at this practice, believing such reservations to be nothing more than feeding stations for Apaches who slipped away regularly to kill and loot. On April 30, 1871, a citizen army from Tucson, composed of approximately fifty Americans and almost one hundred Papago Indians, attacked a reservation for the Arivaipa Apaches near Camp Grant, Arizona, killing one hundred and eight of the Indians—only eight of them men—and carrying off twenty-nine children into captivity. The perpetrators of the "Camp Grant Massacre," as eastern newspapers headlined it, were arrested and brought to trial in Tucson, but a local jury exonerated them at once; Arizonans simply would not convict a man for killing an Indian, even though the Indian might be a child. "Nits make lice," they said. Beyond this, it was good business for merchants in the Territory when there were Indian troubles. More troops would come, which meant rations would be bought locally for them and their horses. The group of merchants in Tucson who actively promoted incidents and Indian scares were labeled the "Tucson Ring," and proved quite successful. Beyond this, they connived with Indian agents to furnish sub-standard rations at standard prices, splitting the profits; and often, with the aid of a reservation agent, they furnished no rations at all and pocketed the money.[2]

As a result of the national attention focused on the Apache problem in Arizona by the Camp Grant Massacre, President Grant sent a peace commission to Arizona. Headed by the mild-mannered Quaker, Vincent Colyer, this commission was charged with arranging treaties with the various Apache bands and putting them on reservations. Governor A. P. K. Safford reflected public sentiment in the Territory when he issued a proclamation asking the people to co-operate with the commission, despite its members' "erroneous opinions upon the Indian question and the condition of affairs in the Territory." One local newspaper editorialized that Arizonans "ought, in justice to our murdered dead, to dump the old devil [Colyer] into the shaft of some mine, and pile rocks upon him until he is dead. A rascal who comes here to thwart the efforts of military and citizens to conquer a peace from our savage foe, deserves to be stoned to death, like the treacherous, black-hearted dog that he is." Despite such opposition, engendered by the Tucson Ring and its cohorts, Colyer proceeded to get some four thousand Indians onto reservations. When he departed, the only major tribe of Apaches not on reservations was the Chiricahuas, still led by Cochise.

While Colyer was at work, Lieutenant Colonel George Crook had arrived in the Territory, and on June 4, 1871, he took command of the Department from Stoneman. Before he was allowed to undertake a field campaign to force the renegades to reservations, however, another peace commission arrived, this one headed by Brigadier General Oliver Otis Howard, a one-armed veteran of the Civil War known to the troops as "Bible-Quoting Howard." He likewise encountered heavy local resistance, but proceeded with his work. He inspected the military posts in the Department, arranged conferences with the Pimas, Papagos, and other tribes, and moved the Camp Grant agency northward to the Gila, where it was renamed San Carlos. Thereafter San Carlos would be the major reservation for Apaches. Finally, with the assistance of Thomas J. Jeffords, a white man who had won the friendship of Cochise, Howard met the aging Chiricahua chieftain in a dramatic confrontation; arriving unarmed and accompanied only by Jeffords, Howard persuaded Cochise to accept a peace treaty.[3] The Chiricahuas, by this treaty, were given a reservation approximately fifty-five miles square in southeastern Arizona, including the Dragoon and Chiricahua mountains and the Sulphur Springs and San Simon valleys—the traditional homeland of the Chiricahuas—with Tom Jeffords as their agent. Until the death of Cochise in 1874 the Chiricahuas honored this agreement, despite visits from their New Mexican cousins, the Warm Springs Apaches who wanted them to go on the warpath. Cochise through force of personality, as well as his position as hereditary chief, was able to keep all but the most impatient young warriors from raiding into Mexico.

After Cochise's death on June 8, 1874, his oldest son, Taza became the titular head of the Chiricahuas. There followed two years of great hardship, unrest, and disaster. Jeffords was too openly sympathetic to his charges, and too popular with them, either to suit jealous functionaries in the Indian Bureau or local citizens in Arizona. Through pressure, the Tucson Ring persuaded officials in Washington first to cut the ration of beef to the Chiricahuas, then in February 1876 to halt it entirely. Jeffords notified the Chiricahuas that they would have to supply

14

*Thomas Jeffords, blood brother to Cochise and agent for the Chiricahua Apaches.* Courtesy Arizona Pioneers' Historical Society.

their own meat by hunting. Taza, who had never exercised the kind of strong leadership his father had, was unable to prevent a split from developing within the tribe. On a hunting expedition away from the reservation, a fight developed in the mountains, during which shots were fired, killing two men and a young grandson of Cochise. Taza thereupon led most of the tribe back to the reservation, but Skinya and some fifty malcontents remained in the mountains. Four of this group, along with three Coyotero Apaches, determined to conduct a raid into Mexico, later returning with some one hundred dollars in gold dust and silver. On April 6 the station keeper at Sulphur Springs, named Rogers, sold the renegades whiskey at ten dollars a bottle in exchange for their promise to leave. The next day the Indians wanted more whiskey, but Rogers refused, whereupon the Indians killed Rogers and his cook, Spence, stole horses and ammunition and fled to their camp in the Dragoon Mountains. The next day, April 8, other renegades of Skinya's band killed another white man and stole four horses.

Immediately upon hearing of these incidents, Jeffords called for soldiers from nearby Fort Bowie and set out in pursuit of the renegades, after assuring Taza and his peaceful followers that they would not be harmed. However, Skinya and his hostiles could not be dislodged from the Dragoons, so the troops returned to the fort. Then on June 4 Skinya slipped into Taza's camp and tried to persuade the entire Chiricahua band to go on the warpath under his leadership. They refused, and a fight developed in which Skinya and six of his followers were killed.

The Indian Bureau used these disturbances as an excuse to order the Chiricahua reservation closed and the Indians there moved to the San Carlos Agency. In fact, on May 3, more than a month before, Agent John Philip Clum of San Carlos had received instructions from Washington to go to the Chiricahua reservation, suspend Jeffords, and, if possible, move the Chiricahuas to San Carlos. Clum had become agent at San Carlos on August 8, 1874—at that time he was a month short of being twenty-three years old. Nominated by the Dutch Reformed Church for the position, he was filled with "brass and impudence," according to the Prescott *Arizona Miner*. Within a year, however, he had organized a force of Indian police, had established a court where offenders were tried before an Apache judge and juries, and had forced the Army entirely from the reservation.

Clum's orders to close the Chiricahua Agency came not only because of the activities of Skinya and his followers, but also because that reservation had become a refuge for renegades from both sides of the international boundary. In addition, the Warm Springs Apaches of New Mexico frequently visited there, usually conducting small raids as they moved east or west. Another reason for the closing of the Chiricahua reservation was Jeffords's steadfast refusal to enter into connivance with the Tucson Ring to cheat his charges, and the Ring in turn had brought pressure to bear in Washington to have it closed.

Clum arrived at the Chiricahua Agency and held a conference with Taza on June 6 during which Taza agreed to remove his followers to San Carlos. On June 12 Clum started on the trip, accompanied by Taza and 325 Chiricahuas, only sixty of whom were warriors, the rest women and children. Some four hundred bronco Chiricahuas had refused to make the move and had fled into Mexico under the leadership of Juh, Nolgee, and a rising war leader named Geronimo.

The removal of the Chiricahuas to San Carlos and the closing of their separate reservation was a disastrous mistake. The various Apache groups at San Carlos hated each other, and they were living in what, to them, seemed very cramped quarters— four thousand were crowded onto land that originally had been the home for only eight hundred Apaches. In addition, most of the bands there were homesick. Shortened on rations, forced to farm, angry and resentful, the Apaches at San Carlos all too often were willing recruits for a warrior promising loot and adventures off the reservation. But still more Apaches continued to be crowded in as more renegades were caught and brought to San Carlos.

On March 20, 1877, Clum received orders from the Commissioner of Indian Affairs to arrest Geronimo, a rising war leader, and his Membraño renegades and confine them at San Carlos. Geronimo had used the months between June 1876 and March 1877 to steal horses, mules, and cattle in Sonora and drive them north to New Mexico for sale to ranchers not bothered by a lack of title. Their hideout for this operation was the Hot Springs Agency in New Mexico (located some thirty-seven miles northwest of the present Truth or Consequences, New Mexico), which was headquarters for the Warm Springs Apaches. Using his Indian police and Apache volunteers, Clum planned to coordinate

17

his movements with troops from the Ninth Cavalry, the rendezvous to occur on April 21 at Ojo Caliente. The troops failed to
arrive at the appointed hour, but Clum went ahead with the arrest. On April 22 he and his force met Geronimo and his 110 followers. Clum's police, who had been hidden, appeared at his signal, and the agent had trapped Geronimo. "I have seen many
looks of hate in my long life," Clum later wrote of that moment,
"but never one so vicious, so vengeful. . . . When I took his
rifle from him, his lips tightened and [his] . . . sneer was ac-
centuated. The old scar on his right cheek was livid." Before
Clum could leave with the prisoners, he received word from
Washington to take all the Warm Springs Apaches to San Carlos,
including their leader Victorio—a total of 343 Indians. All arrived at San Carlos on May 20. A few months later, on August
15, 1877, Clum resigned his post because of disputes with Army
officers and Indian Bureau functionaries.[4]

The Chiricahuas were dissatisfied at San Carlos, crowded as
they felt themselves to be and discontented as they were with the
administration of the Agency. In addition, Taza was not a leader
to inspire confidence, nor was his younger brother Nachez (also
spelled Natchez, Nachite, and Naiche), who became the nominal
leader following the death of Taza on a trip to Washington with
Agent Clum in June 1876. Britton Davis, an Army officer in
Arizona during the Indian-fighting era, later wrote, "Nachite
was a good warrior with no peace scruples; but he was fond of
the ladies, liked dancing and a good time generally, and was not
serious enough for the responsibilities of leadership." Nachez
wanted his tribe restored to their old homeland in southeastern
Arizona, and he thought this could be achieved by following the
advice of the two leading warriors in the tribe, Juh and Geronimo. Juh (also spelled Ju and Woo, and pronounced "Ho") was
married to Geronimo's favorite sister, and he and Nachez were
on good terms with each other. Juh also had a good chance of
succeeding Nachez as tribal leader, whereas Geronimo was not
related to Chiricahua chieftains. But it was Geronimo who would

*Nachez, son of Cochise, was the chief of the Chiricahua Apaches during the final Geronimo Campaign.* Courtesy Arizona Pioneers' Historical Society.

gradually exercise all the prerogatives of leadership and who would become the best known of all Chiricahua warriors and chieftains.[5]

According to his own biography, dictated to S. M. Barrett in 1906, Geronimo was born in No-doyohn Canyon, Arizona, in June 1829. His grandfather, Maco, had been the chief of the Mimbreño Apaches, but his father had married a Bedonkohe Apache, thereby forfeiting what hereditary rights he had as a Mimbreño, for these Indians were matrilineal in their family relationships. Thus on Maco's death, Mangas Coloradas had become the chief, while Geronimo became one of the Bedonkohes. He, his three brothers, and four sisters grew to adulthood in a peaceful era, for the Mexicans were exerting no real pressures on the Apaches of Arizona. 'I was warmed by the sun, rocked by the winds, and sheltered by the trees as other Indian babes," he reminisced in 1906. His mother taught him the legends of his people and to pray to their god Usen; his father told him of "the brave deeds of our warriors, of the pleasures of the chase, and the glories of the warpath." His childish games were those that would aid him as an adult: practicing stealth and concealment, hunting bear, deer, and eagles, and perfecting his skill with weapons.

Geronimo's father died when the lad was still young, and he had to assume the care of his mother. At the age of seventeen he was admitted to the council of warriors, which meant that he was ready to go on the warpath and to share in the booty taken. It also meant that he was free to marry, and he had picked out his bride, "the fair Alope," daughter of No-po-so, "a slender, delicate girl." Geronimo immediately approached her father, who "asked many ponies for her." A few days later Geronimo appeared outside No-po-so's dwelling with the stipulated number of horses and took away his bride, that being the only ceremony necessary. He built a wickiup for her near that of his mother, and in the years that followed three children were born to them, "children that played, loitered, and worked as I had done."

Apaches usually received their names for some personal characteristic, and Geronimo at this time must have been indolent,
even good-natured, for he was called Goyakla, "He Who Yawns."

Then came the fateful summer of 1858 that was to change his
name and turn him into a bloody fighter asking and giving no
quarter. That year, as was their annual custom, the Bedonkohe
Apaches journeyed southeast into the Mexican state of Chihuahua to trade for the goods they needed. Sonorans were considered the eternal enemies of the Bedonkohes, and thus subject to
raiding, while Chihuahua was considered a safe refuge. Arizona
at that time had only two settlements, Tubac and Tucson,
neither of which was capable of or willing to supply the Apaches
with goods. The band encamped outside the town of Janos, and
every day the men would go into town to trade and drink while
the women and children remained in camp under the protection
of a token guard. Late one afternoon, as the men were returning
to camp, they were met by a few of the women and children.
From them they learned that Mexican irregular troops from another town had attacked, killed the warriors on guard, taken the
arms and supplies, and murdered many of the women and children. The dead had been scalped, the grisly pelts to be turned
in for the bounty on them. The men and surviving women and
children concealed themselves until dark, then warily stole into
the camp to seek their relatives. Geronimo discovered that his
mother, his wife, and his three children were among the dead. "I
stood . . . hardly knowing what I would do—I had no weapon,
nor did I hardly wish to fight, neither did I contemplate recover-
ing the bodies of my loved ones, for that was forbidden," Geronimo later stated of that night. "I did not pray, nor did I resolve
to do anything in particular for I had no purpose left."

The survivors made a forced march to Arizona and their settlement there. Geronimo burned all traces of his dead, all their
possessions, as was the Apache custom. After the first numbing
shock wore off, he swore vengeance on the Mexicans. He was sent
by his tribe to seek the aid of the Chiricahuas in the contem-

plated war on Mexico, for the Chiricahuas were cousins of his tribesmen. Successful in his diplomatic venture, he joined the combined tribe in the summer of 1859 in raids into Sonora, where he distinguished himself in many ways. "I could not call back my loved ones, I could not bring back the dead Apaches, but I could rejoice in . . . revenge," he said. The next fifteen years saw Geronimo steadily rise in fame as a war leader always ready to raid into Mexico, whether as follower or leader he cared not. Sometimes he was unsuccessful on these raids, but usually he brought home booty and tales of dead Mexicans. Then in April of 1877 he was arrested by Agent John Clum and taken to San Carlos with his 110 followers, along with the Warm Springs Apaches led by Victorio.

Trouble brewed quickly at San Carlos. Early in September 1877, some 310 Warm Springs Apaches under Victorio fled the reservation toward the east. Rapid pursuit by the Army, guided by White Mountain Apache scouts in government employ, forced the renegades north into the badlands south of Fort Wingate, New Mexico. There they killed a dozen ranchers, stole horses, and created widespread alarm among civilians in the region. Forced to surrender eventually, the Warm Springs Apaches were taken to their old reservation at Hot Springs, New Mexico. Then on October 8, 1878, on orders from Washington, troops arrived to escort Victorio and his band to San Carlos once again. Victorio refused to go, and with almost one hundred of his warriors he became a renegade. In the fall of 1879 he was joined by discontented Chiricahua and Mescalero braves. The Victorio campaign of 1879-80 involved thousands of American troops, who followed him relentlessly, but it was Mauricio Corredor, a Tarahumara Indian scout, who killed the wily Apache on October 15, 1880. The state of Chihuahua paid Corredor the 3000-peso bounty offered for Victorio's scalp, and presented him with a nickle-plated rifle.

To most New Mexicans and Arizonans, the death of Victorio and the return of his followers to San Carlos seemed to signal

*Geronimo in 1884.* Courtesy Arizona Pioneers' Historical Society (Gatewood Collection).

the end of Apache hostilities. The year 1881 started peacefully
enough. Then in June of 1881, Nakaidoklini (also spelled Noch-
ay-del-klinne), a medicine man, stirred the White Mountain
Apaches with a new religion. A mystic who had attended a Chris-
tian school in Santa Fe, Nakaidoklini preached the resurrection
of the dead and a return to the "good old days." To achieve this
desired result, his followers were told to perform an unusual
dance (a "ghost dance" similar to that later introduced among
the Sioux and other tribes). On August 15 San Carlos Agent J. C.
Tiffany informed Colonel Eugene A. Carr, commander of the
Department of Arizona, that he wished Nakaidoklini "arrested
or killed or both." Carr led seventy-nine soldiers, twenty-three
scouts, and nine civilians to Cibecu Creek, and on August 30 arrested the prophet of the new religion. At their encampment that
evening, however, they were attacked by some one hundred followers of Nakaidoklini; in the fighting the medicine man was
killed by his guard. Carr and his soldiers were barely able to
reach Fort Apache the next day, only to be attacked there on
September 1 by angry White Mountain Apaches, one of the few
direct attacks on an Army post by Arizona Indians. Natiotish assumed the mantle of leadership of the White Mountain Apaches,
and a battle was fought between them and the soldiers at Cheva-
lon Creek on July 17, 1882. Called the Battle of Big Dry Wash, it
resulted in the death of twenty-two Apaches and the surrender
of the rest. It was the last real battle between Indian and soldier
fought on Arizona soil.

While the ghost-dance craze was sweeping the White Mountain
Apaches, the Chiricahuas had taken advantage of the diversion.
Nachez, Juh, Geronimo, and their followers fled into Mexico at
the end of September 1881, and eluded capture for almost two
and one-half years, raiding north and south of the border, then
fleeing into mountain hideouts. Their activities were severely
restricted, however, by a treaty signed on July 29, 1882, between
the United States and Mexico which allowed the soldiers of
either nation to cross the international boundary in pursuit of

marauding Indians. Always before, when being pursued, the Apaches could escape by crossing the border one way or the other. The pressure of Mexican and American soldiers forced the renegade Chiricahuas gradually to return to San Carlos; Geronimo and his followers surrendered in January 1884. But he was sullen and unhappy because the Indians' horses and cattle were taken from them. ". . . These were not white men's cattle, but belonged to us, for we had taken them from the Mexicans during our wars. . . . We did not intend to kill these animals, but . . . wished to keep them and raise stock on our range." Geronimo hated and distrusted the soldiers guarding him on the reservation and was looking for an opportunity to escape and return to his mountain haunts in Sonora whenever an opportunity presented itself. He also needed an incident that would convince his followers to leave the reservation with him. That incident came in May 1885.

# TWO

# THE

# ARMY

It is with painful reluctance that the military forces take the field against Indians who only leave their reservations because they are starved there, and who must hunt food for themselves and their families or see them perish with hunger. . . . I desire to say with all emphasis, what every Army officer on the frontier will corroborate, that there is no class of men in this country who are so disinclined to war with the Indians as the army stationed among them. The Army has nothing to gain by war with Indians; on the contrary it has everything to lose. In such a war it suffers all the hardship and privation; and, exposed as it is to the charge of assassination if Indians are killed; to the charge of inefficiency if they are not. . . .

General John Pope, "Report of the Secretary of War, November 22, 1875," *House Exec. Doc. 1,* 44 Cong., 1 Sess.

THE END OF THE CIVIL WAR brought drastic changes in the United States military forces. No longer was soldiering a glorious occupation. No longer were the troops a part of the Grand Army of the Republic, patriotically preserving the Union. They had become a peacetime force with little public understanding or appreciation. Nor was a large army needed. An economy-minded Congress in 1866 ordered the regular Army reduced to 54,302 men, consisting of ten regiments of cavalry, forty-five of infantry, and five of artillery. A majority of these men were stationed in the conquered South to enforce Reconstruction, leaving only a small number available for fighting the Indians—and all across the American West there were bloody uprisings to suppress. Nor were more men sent West when Reconstruction ended; the Army was reduced in strength as Southern states regained control of their own affairs. On March 3, 1869, the Army was reduced to 45,000 men; on July 15, 1870, to 30,000 troops; and on July 16, 1874, to 25,000 enlisted men and officers.[1] However, the Army was 10 per cent over its authorized strength during much of this period. Not only was the Army severely under-strength to fight the Indian wars, it also had poor equipment. Congress in 1866 decreed that the Army had to exhaust Civil War surpluses before ordering new materials. Thus the soldiers were sent to do battle with obsolete weapons and equipment, as well as in under-strength numbers.

All of the men in the Indian-fighting Army were volunteers, both officers and enlistees, for the unpopular conscription laws had ended with the Civil War. The average age for common soldiers was twenty-three, many of whom were recent immigrants, and most of them were from the bottom of the economic ladder. The three decades following the Civil War were years of economic unrest, where the ordinary worker had no union to protect him from the hardships of recurring financial panics, from the whims of the captains of industry, or from cyclic unemployment. Some volunteers were attracted by the steady employment offered by the Army, with its pay of thirteen dollars a month for privates, its regular rations, and its side benefits, such as free medical care. Others came to "see the elephant," lured by tales of adventure in the American West. Still others were rootless veterans of the Civil War—Confederates who had lost everything, ex-slaves who had nothing to start with, and former Union men who had returned home to find conditions so changed that they preferred to stay in the Army. Finally, the military life attracted criminals and other undesirable elements who found it expedient to travel and who knew they could not be traced in that era before photographs and fingerprints were part of a man's service record.

When he enlisted for a five-year term, the new soldier was sent to a recruit depot for three or four weeks to learn to follow orders and to drill. Three recruit depots served the entire Army; cavalry recruits went to Jefferson Barracks, Missouri, and infantry recruits to David's Island, New York, or Columbus Barracks, Ohio. There the enlistee received his uniforms (which until about 1875 were leftovers from the Civil War and of inferior quality), suffered endless hazing, and got his first taste of Army food. A typical daily menu started with a breakfast of salt pork, fried mush, and strong black coffee; lunch usually consisted of dry bread and "slumgullion stew"; and the evening meal normally was more dry bread and more coffee, with occasionally three prunes for dessert. From this recruit depot, the young soldier was sent west to join the regiment to which he was assigned. This travel was, for the most part, by land-grant railroads, which were obligated to furnish transportation to the Army. The recruits generally considered the ride a real adventure—for most it was their first trip by rail—even though the railroads invariably furnished only day-coaches in which to ride. The soldiers were fed in the coaches, with barrels of water supplying their drinking needs.

Once he joined a regiment, the soldier rarely transferred out of it, no matter how long he remained in the Army. In fact, he usually did not transfer out of the company to which he was assigned. Until 1876, each company had sixty-four privates, after which time it was supposed to have one hundred, but most were under-strength at any given moment. The recruit soon learned that he had little contact with men outside his company, even at small posts consisting of only two companies, and therefore made his friends—and enemies—within it. These were self-contained social as well as military units. He associated, in the cavalry, primarily with his "set of four," the men he rode with, or, in the infantry, with his squad. When campaigning, soldiers usually

28

carried only one blanket. At night two men would pool their blankets, one for the ground and one for cover, leading to the term "bunky" to describe one's best friend.

In his company the recruit found himself completely at the mercy of his non-commissioned officers. He could not even speak to an officer without the permission of his first sergeant, who actually ran the company. Officers not only knew this; they expected it. And an ability with fists was one of the first requisites for promotion to non-commissioned officer status. The Army Regulations forbade the beating of an enlisted man by the non-commissioned officers, but punishments for that offense were rare —and then usually light. Army regulations also stipulated that officers were to exercise their authority firmly but with "kindness and justice." Because of isolation and ignorance, however, few soldiers knew how to complain of injustices and unkindness, and discipline ranged from kind and just to unkind and unjust, depending more upon the character of the officer involved than on the Army regulations. All major punishments were meted out by court-martial held within the company or regiment. This meant that the soldier was tried by his own officers, or by their friends within his regiment.

Punishments ranged from marching double-time around the parade ground to the brutal and sadistic. Deserters were branded with a D and thieves with a T. Men were suspended by their thumbs, wrists, or arms in the guardhouse for as long as a full day at a time, for officers could impose harsh or unusual punishments with relative impunity. Soldiers could also be confined in the post guardhouse for periods from a few days up to six months. The guardhouse was not supplied with such niceties as furniture; prisoners brought their blankets, and they ate and slept in an unheated, unventilated cell measuring four by four by five feet in which they could not fully stand or lie down. Some had no windows and only a crack at the bottom or top of the door, which meant almost total darkness inside. In view of these circumstances, it is not surprising to find that desertion was the most common crime in the service. In 1891 Secretary of War Stephen B. Elkins reported that losses through desertion between 1867 and 1891 averaged one-third of all enlistees.

The non-commissioned officer did enjoy many privileges, including higher pay and less physical labor. A sergeant received twenty-one dollars a month, and an infraction on his part would most likely result in a reduction in rank rather than a trip to the guardhouse. Competition for promotion was great, but since promotions also came within the company, none was available until a vacancy occurred either through discharge, death, or disciplinary reduction in rank. Non-commissioned officers usually were men with long years of service.[2]

A wide gulf separated enlisted men from their officers. The caste system was rigid, imposed both by regulations and by the backgrounds of the individuals concerned. Most officers in the Indian-fighting Army were graduates of the Military Academy at West Point—and thus mostly men with a genteel background of wealth and family position. The isolation of frontier military service brought out the best or the worst in this kind of officer. There he could indulge himself as a petty tyrant, or he could strive to improve the lot of his men. Each generally was given a nickname by the troops under him: "Bull-Dozer" for an overbearing officer, "Jack of Clubs" for one who had sympathetic feelings for the enlisted soldiers. George Armstrong Custer, who drove his troops mercilessly, was known as "Hard Backsides"; at least, that was the way reporter Mark Kellogg put it in his dispatches.

Soldiering was difficult, even for officers. Isolated from polite society, the officer could associate only with his fellow officers, as fraternization with the enlisted men was forbidden. He thus had a very limited circle from which to draw his friendships. His pay was small, a lieutenant drawing only forty dollars a month, with which he had to pay for his mount, his equipment, his clothing, and support his family, if he had one. Moreover, his isolation on the frontier meant that, if still single, he had few chances for meeting a suitable mate except on leave. And to marry an eastern girl and bring her to the raw conditions prevalent in the West was to invite marital diaster. Only through a private income could he improve his lot, for promotion for him had to take place within the regiment to which he was assigned. Transfers rarely occurred below the rank of lieutenant colonel. Many a young second lieutenant was assigned to a post he considered "the end of the world"; there he found no friends to his liking and the duty dull and uninteresting. Many of them took to liquor and became alcoholics in the process, which contributed to the public impression that soldiering was an unfit and ignoble profession.

At the upper ranks of the Army, lieutenant colonel and above, competition for promotion was even more bitter than below. The end of the Civil War and the reduction in the size of the Army had produced a top-heavy officer corps. Brevet major generals who wished to stay in the Army, such as George Armstrong Custer, had to accept a lieutenant colonelcy and command of a regiment in order to get a regular commission. A reduction of three or four grades was common for those who did stay in the regular Army, and such officers strongly desired to rise again in rank. Jealousies, intrigues, politics, and "wire-pulling" were normal, even expected, in order to gain a rung up the ladder of promotion. Few officers hesitated to use their relatives, their in-laws, their friends, or even friends-of-friends. Some did wait passively for length of service or merit to secure advancement. A few others, who were without the important connections, sought promotion through some spectacular feat on the battlefield. Custer's blunder at the Little Big Horn is usually explained in this manner; he believed that a victory over the Sioux would win him praise in the newspapers and popular adulation that would force officials in Washington to give him back his "star." A few men did win promotion for success in the field without Custer's blundering, men such as George Crook, who bore most of the responsibility for the Apache wars of the Southwest.

Crook was born on a farm near Taylorsville, Ohio, on September 8, 1828. He might have remained an Ohio farmer had not the Whig Congressman from his district, Robert P. Schenck, needed to fill a vacancy at West Point and inquired of Crook's father if he had a son who would like to attend the Military Academy. Crook was appointed to the Academy in 1848 and four years later he graduated thirty-eighth in a class of fifty-six. There followed nine years of quiet duty in California. The Civil War offered him an opportunity to rise quickly, however. He became colonel of the Thirty-eighth Ohio Volunteers and captain of the Fourth Infantry. By March 1865 he had risen to command of the Army of the Potomac and brevet major general of volunteers. After the war he was reverted to the rank of lieutenant colonel and sent to Idaho Territory for duty. There he remained until June 4, 1871, when he took command of the Department of Arizona.

Crook was unorthodox in many ways, not the least of which was his dress. By the time of his arrival in Arizona, he usually wore a weatherbeaten canvas suit and a Japanese summer hat, but no military trappings of any style, not even a symbol of his rank. Because of this, and his peculiar whiskers, the Indians of the Southwest dubbed him "Gray Fox."

In Arizona, Crook soon discarded standard Army tactics—which were based in large measure on the experience of the Civil War and were predicated on an enemy that stood and fought in large numbers—in favor of radical innovations. A study of conditions in Arizona convinced him that only an army capable of rapid pursuit could cope with the Indians, and he began training his men in this fashion, employing mules to carry their provisions and operating in extremely mobile, small units. He also decided that the best trackers of Apaches were other Apaches; he enlisted Indians into units designated the Apache Scouts. Recruitment was easy since great hatreds existed between the various bands; when enlistees were needed they were drawn from the enemies of the renegades and were told that they were

32

*Brigadier General George Crook in 1885 near Fort Bowie, Arizona.*
Courtesy Arizona Pioneers' Historical Society.

being offered an opportunity to repay old debts and settle old hatreds.

Crook's troopers responded to these challenges, for they learned to respect the forty-three-year-old veteran; he knew how to pack a mule, mend a saddle, or throw a lariat, as well as cook a meal in the field. He ate with the men having charge of the pack trains when engaged in field operations, taking no special supplies for himself. Not only did he study the over-all strategy of any campaign, but also he looked to the small details. On one occasion, a man who had never seen Crook was employed to take charge of a pack train, with authority to employ the assistants he needed. While the man was busy hiring these assistants, Crook wandered over to see how the fellow was progressing and to check on him. The packer, noticing the newcomer, dressed in an ordinary manner and apparently able-bodied, asked him, "Say, mister, do you understand packing mules?"

Crook responded, "I think I do."

"Have you had experience in that line?" the packer wanted to know.

"Well, considerable, here and there," Crook replied.

The packer was satisfied. "Well, I'll give you forty dollars a month and grub to help us in this campaign."

"I am much obliged for the offer," Crook said with a straight face, "but I already have a job." He elaborated no farther.

After a moment's wait, the packer asked, "Is that so? What is the job?"

"Well, my friend, I am at present commanding this Department." With that Crook walked off, leaving the packer to face the amusement of those who had witnessed the episode.[3]

Crook had not been allowed to test his theories in the field immediately upon taking command of the Department. However, when both Colyer and Howard completed their peace missions, he was told to drive all renegades in Arizona onto reservations. During the winter of 1872-73 he and his men took to the field, pressing the hostiles hard during the months when they normally could rest, hitting them in winter hideouts they had considered safe refuges and demoralizing them. The most spectacular battle of the campaign occurred on December 28, 1872, at Skull Cave, where approximately seventy-five Yavapais were killed. The following April 6 the Yavapais surrendered at Camp Verde, by which time the remaining Apaches had quit fighting—bringing a period of relative peace to the Territory. Crook was rewarded for his success by a startling promotion from lieutenant colonel to brigadier general.

When the battles were over, he continued his innovations. On the reservations he issued every Indian a numbered tag so that a quick count could be taken and reservation-jumpers identified easily. He was hard in battle but just in peace—so much so that the Indians grew to trust him. As long as he remained in the Territory he strongly opposed concentrating all the Apaches at San Carlos, and he fought to keep the Indian agents honest. Then in 1875 he was transferred north where he had to fight the Sioux.

His successors in the Department of Arizona proved as unsuccessful as Crook had been successful. From 1875 to 1878 the commander was Brevet Brigadier General August V. Kautz. Despite his keeping troops in the field almost constantly, the Apaches jumped the reservation virtually at will—which was frequently. Public criticism led to Kautz's removal in March 1878, to be replaced by Brevet Major General Orlando B. Willcox. Under his disastrous management the Apaches fled to Mexico in 1881 and the bloody Cibecu Creek Affair occurred. On September 4, 1882, Crook returned to take command of the Department.

His major problem, once back in Arizona, was to regain the confidence that the Apaches had placed in him earlier. They no longer seemed willing to believe the words of a government official, not even those of the commanding general. To combat this attitude he first sought the removal of several Indian agents who were hampering his work. In this he was successful, replacing them with Army officers. Once the Indians on the reservations began receiving regular rations, they began to look on Crook as a man interested in their welfare. Next, he sought to force the Chiricahuas in Mexico to return to their reservation; in order to accomplish this, he had to penetrate their mountain hideouts in the Sierra Madre of Sonora. Meanwhile the treaty between the United States and Mexico that allowed troops of either nation to cross the international boundary when in pursuit of hostiles had been signed. Just as Crook was preparing a campaign in Sonora in March 1883, the renegades stormed out of Mexico on a raid, led by Chatto.

Chatto's group came into southern Arizona and New Mexico searching for ammunition. Along the way they murdered Judge H. C. McComas and his wife and carried off their six-year-old son Charles. Later the boy was found dead. This incident created a national sensation because of the prominence of the judge, and a cry was raised in the newspapers for the punishment of the guilty Indians. One Chiricahua, known as Tso-ay by the Indians and Peaches by the Americans, deserted Chatto's group during the raid, however, and tried to return to the reservation. Captured and taken to Crook for questioning, Peaches agreed to lead the soldiers to Chatto's hideout in Mexico. With forty-five cavalrymen and 193 Apache Scouts, Crook crossed into Sonora and surprised the hostiles at their village high in the Sierra on May 15. Eight days later, he started home with 285 prisoners, who said they were tired of war. Eventually all other hostiles in Mexico came in and surrendered, including Geronimo and his followers in January 1884. Once again peace had been restored in Arizona, and Crook was the hero of the hour.[4]

Crook realized that his success in this campaign, as well as a decade earlier, had been due in large measure to his Apache Scouts. To command them he selected only the finest officers in his Department. In over-all charge of the Apache Scouts after Crook's return to the Department in 1882 was Captain Emmet Crawford. Crawford, born in Philadelphia on September 6, 1844, had enlisted in the California Volunteers at the outbreak of the

Civil War and had risen to the rank of first lieutenant of volunteers. Deciding to make the Army his career, he accepted a commission as second lieutenant when the war ended. In December 1870, by then a first lieutenant in the Third Cavalry, he had come to Arizona; early in 1872 his regiment had been transferred north to fight the Sioux, and a decade passed before he returned to the desert Southwest. By then he was a captain and was detached from his regiment as military commandant at San Carlos. Crawford led his Scouts into Sonora in 1883 and aided in forcing the Chiricahuas back to the reservation. At San Carlos he concentrated on teaching his charges how to farm, and in the process they learned to trust him.[5] Britton Davis, a lieutenant serving under Crawford, later wrote of him:

> Crawford was born a thousand years too late. . . . Mentally, morally and physically he would have been an ideal knight of King Arthur's Court. Six feet one, gray-eyed, untiring, he was an ideal cavalryman and devoted to his troop, as were the men of it to him. He had a keen sense of humor but something had saddened his early life and I never knew him to laugh aloud. . . . Modest, self-effacing, kindly, he delighted in assigning to his subordinates opportunities and credit he might well have taken to himself—a very rare trait in an officer of any army. His expressed wish was that he might die in the act of saving the lives of others.[6]

Serving under Crawford as commander of Apache scouting battalions were several lieutenants. At the White Mountain Apache Agency at Fort Apache was Lieutenant Britton Davis. Born on June 4, 1860, at Brownsville, Texas, he was from a family with a military tradition. His paternal grandfather, Godwin Davis, had been killed in the Revolutionary War; his maternal grandfather, Forbes Britton, had graduated from the Military Academy in 1834 and had written some of the songs of West Point. And his father, Edmund J. Davis, although a Texan, had served as a brevet brigadier general of volunteers on the Union side in the late conflict between North and South, and had served as the Radical Republican governor of Texas during Reconstruction. Davis had graduated from the Academy in 1881. Assigned to the Third Cavalry, he served briefly in Wyoming, then was transferred to Arizona Territory to command companies B and E of the Apache Scouts. Both he and Crawford were kept in Arizona at Crook's insistence when the Third Cavalry was sent to Texas in 1885.

Another officer, similar to Crawford in being modest and unassuming, was Lieutenant Charles Baehr Gatewood. Born in Woodstock, Virginia, in 1853, Gatewood, too, was from a military family. Appointed to the Military Academy in 1873, he graduated four years later and was assigned to the Sixth Cavalry. From then until the fall of 1886 he was almost constantly on field duty in New Mexico and Arizona. He saw combat in the Victorio campaign of 1879-80 in Mexico, and received a special commendation from Colonel A. P. Morrow for his efforts. He also was a member of Crook's expedition into Sonora in 1883, which resulted in Chatto's surrender, serving in Crawford's command. For this he was mentioned in War Department orders. In 1885 in published General Orders in Arizona, he was described as having "seen more active duty in the field with Indian Scouts than any other officer of his length of service in the Army." He still had not been promoted beyond first lieutenant, however.

The son of a Confederate soldier, Gatewood stood about five feet, eleven inches tall, had gray eyes, and a dark complexion. His most prominent feature was his nose, which was quite large. At West Point his fellows had dubbed him Scipio Africanus because his profile was said to resemble that of a Roman general. The Indians were not so classical and referred to him as "Nanton Bse-che," translated as Big Nose Captain. His wife was from Frostburg, Maryland, the daughter of T. G. McCullough, a local judge with only minor political connections. To Gatewood and his wife three children were born while they lived in the Southwest; one child died and was buried at Fort Wingate, leaving a son and daughter to grow to maturity. Through all the hardships encountered, the disappointments, even the death of their

*Lieutenant Charles B. Gatewood.* Courtesy Arizona Pioneers' Historical Society (Gatewood Collection).

child, his wife never complained. Nor did he. Apparently he personified the motto of the Academy, "Duty, Honor, Country." Even his spare time was spent on a history of artillery, which he hoped would be published. Unpretentious and unassuming, he never sought to glorify himself, doing extraordinary deeds of valor as if they were commonplace.[7] While he was in the East on leave in early 1885, the newspaper in his wife's hometown, the Frostburg *Mining Journal,* carried a story about him entitled "A Gallant Young Officer":

Lieutenant Charles B. Gatewood, of the Sixth Cavalry, is perhaps the most expert scout, trailer, and mountain man of his years on the frontier. Twelve years ago this officer was a young country lad in the Virginia mountains. He heard stories told at his father's hearth of the great [Civil] War, until his heart was full of a nameless longing to see the world, and be a soldier as his ancestors had been. But how should he do this? A good genius guided his steps, and he was gazetted to West Point. He was a boy then, and rather an ungainly one at that, for he had the long figure of his mountain race, not yet filled out to manhood's growth. After four years of training at our military school you would not have known him. Tall, perfectly straight, with a steely gray eye that looked at you in frank honesty, you felt that he would be a friend upon whom you could lean in time of need as against a rock, or an enemy that would never forget or condone an intentional wrong. Though Lieut. Gatewood has been in the service as a commissioned officer only eight years, he has made a reputation in this brief period of [time a man] of thrice his service might be proud to own. He is the commander of a battalion of five companies of Apache scouts—the hardest service a soldier can have.

On men such as these—Crawford, Davis, Gatewood—Crook relied to keep the peace. And when war came, he turned to the same men to recruit and lead Apache Scouts to track down the renegades. Because they were field soldiers, quiet men and modest, they were rewarded for their service only so long as the general in command of the Department was sympathetic. Otherwise they lost their chances for promotion and medals, while others who performed less valiantly received both.

Also under Crook's command were men from the Fourth, Sixth, and Tenth cavalry. Of these, the troops in the Tenth had perhaps the fewest illusions about winning popular adulation and appreciation, for it was one of two Negro cavalry regiments in the Army. Bitter rivalries marked relations between the Fourth and Sixth cavalry, just as it did between all regular Army units at that time, to the extent that otherwise honest men were willing to conceal the truth about any matter that might not reflect more credit on their own regiment than on another. Such were the conditions that prevailed in May 1885 when the Chiricahuas made their final bid for freedom south of the border.

# THREE

# CAUSES OF

# THE OUTBREAK

. . . San Carlos won unanimously our designation of it as "Hell's Forty Acres." A gravelly flat in the confluence of the two rivers rose some thirty feet or so above the river bottoms and was dotted here and there by drab adobe buildings of the Agency. Scrawny, dejected lines of scattered cottonwoods, shrunken, almost leafless, marked the course of the streams. Rain was so infrequent that it took on the semblance of a phenomenon when it came at all. Almost continuously dry, hot, dust- and gravel-laden winds swept the plain, denuding it of every vestige of vegetation. In summer a temperature of 110° in the shade was cool weather. At all other times of the year flies, gnats, unnamable bugs,—and I was about to say "beasts of the air"—swarmed in millions. Curiously, in the worst heat of the summer most of the flies disappeared; left, evidently, for the mountain resorts.

Everywhere the naked, hungry, dirty, frightened little Indian children, darting behind bush or into wikiup at sight of you. Everywhere the sullen, stolid, hopeless, suspicious faces of the older Indians challenging you. You felt the challenge in your very marrow—that unspoken challenge to prove yourself anything else than one more liar and thief, differing but little from the procession of liars and thieves who had preceded you.

> Britton Davis, *The Truth About Geronimo*
> (New Haven: Yale University Press, 1929)

SINCE THE DEPARTURE OF JOHN CLUM from San Carlos in 1877, relations between agents and Apaches had deteriorated badly. Then in the early 1880s, as the Chiricahuas were forced back on this reservation, functionaries in the Indian Bureau decreed that these proud warriors become farmers, despite the recommendations of such knowledgeable officers as Crawford, Davis, and Gatewood that they be encouraged in pastoral pursuits. To the San Carlos Agency came a dozen light wagons, double harness for each, a dozen plows, two dozen picks and shovels, and a few bags of corn and wheat for seed. When the Apaches tried to hitch their horses to the wagons, they discovered that the harness was designed for draught animals twice the size of their small ponies. Even when finally hitched, the animals, never broken to this type of work, ran away, with peril to the life of those trying to drive the wagons. Also, their horses were unaccustomed to the slow gait necessary to plowing and tried to run with these, so that the plow point was more frequently above ground than below it. Both Army personnel and Indians laughed endlessly at these efforts, as if they were at some "circus." But it was black humor, for thereby the proud Apaches were reduced to living on rations provided for them by the Indian Office through the resident agent at each reservation—a system inviting graft, one allowing the Tucson Ring to get rich through connivance.

One of Crook's aides, Captain John G. Bourke, later wrote, "The 'Tucson Ring' was determined that no Apache should be put to the embarrassment of working for his own living; once let the Apaches become self-supporting, and what would become of 'the boys'?" The Indians were aware of this system, too, knowing that rations intended for their consumption were being openly sold in neighboring towns, that they were being shorted on their allotments. The principal items of issue to them were flour and beef, but their week's ration of flour would barely suffice for a day. The cattle sent them were held without water by the con-

42

tractor until they crossed the river just before being weighed; "The Government was paying a pretty stiff price for half a barrel of Gila River water delivered with each beef," wrote Britton Davis of this practice. In addition, the scales used were incorrect in favor of the contractors. And "There was not enough fat on the animals to fry a jackrabbit, many of them being mere skin and bones," Davis asserted. He once accused the herders of actually carrying some of the cattle to the Agency on horseback, but the herders swore that all had walked.

The Tucson Ring likewise profited when the Apaches left the reservation. Lucrative contracts could be had supplying grain, hay, and provisions for the soldiers sent to quell uprisings. Sometimes they even wanted to benefit both from Indians on the reservation and from more soldiers; the "boys" would generate an Indian scare through their newspapers, then bombard Washington with requests for "protection." As Captain Bourke phrased it, "They had only to report by telegraph that the Apaches were 'uneasy,' 'refused to obey the orders of the agent,' and a lot more stuff of the same kind and the Great Father would send in ten regiments to carry out the schemes of the ring, but he would never send one honest, truthful man to inquire whether the Apaches had a story or not."[1]

One agent involved in the schemes of the Tucson Ring, and profiting from them, was J. C. Tiffany, who was in charge of the San Carlos reservation during the fitful uprising by the medicine man Nakaidoklini and the subsequent Cibecu Affair. Tiffany had recommended that the medicine man be arrested "or have him killed without arresting." Soon after Crook returned to Arizona in 1882, Tiffany's methods and his cruelty came to light when eleven Apaches who protested against him were brought to trial in Federal court. His recommendation of their trial led to a Federal Grand Jury investigation, at the end of which an indictment was returned—against Tiffany. Printed in the Tucson *Star* of October 24, 1882, it stated that the Agent had released guilty Indians without permission and had "held in confinement these eleven men for a period of fourteen months without ever presenting a charge against them, giving them insufficient food and clothing, and permitting those whose guilt was admitted by themselves and susceptible of overwhelming proof, to stalk away unblushingly and in defiance of law."

Even more startling than this accusation by the Grand Jury was its indictment of the corrupt agents in the Indian Bureau service—something almost unique on the frontier, where white men rarely saw any wrong in anything a fellow white did to an Indian:

> . . . We nevertheless feel it our duty, as honest American citizens, to express our utter abhorrence of the conduct of Agent Tiffany and that class of reverend peculators who have cursed Arizona as Indian officials, and who have caused more misery and loss of life than all other causes combined. . . . The Grand Jury little thought when they began this investigation that they were about to open a Pandora's box of iniquities seldom surpassed in the annals of crime. With the immense power wielded by the Indian agent almost any crime is possible. There seems to be no check upon his conduct. In collusion with the chief clerk and storekeeper, rations can be issued *ad libitum* for which the Government must pay, while the proceeds pass into the capacious pockets of the agent. Indians are sent to work on the coal-fields, superintended by white men; all the workmen and superintendents are fed and frequently paid from the agency stores, and no return made thereof. Government contractors, in collusion with Agent Tiffany, get receipts for large amounts of supplies never furnished, and the profit is divided mutually, and a general spoilation of the United States Treasury is thus effected. While six hundred Indians are off on passes, their rations are counted and turned in to the mutual aid association, consisting of Tiffany and his associates. Every Indian child born receives rations from the moment of its advent into this vale of tears, and thus adds its mite to the Tiffany pile. In the meantime, the Indians are neglected, half-fed, discontented, and turbulent, until at last, with the vigilant eye peculiar to the savage, the Indians observe the manner in which the Government, through its agent, complies with its sacred obligations. This was the united testimony of the Grand

Jury, corroborated by white witnesses, and to these and kindred causes may be attributed the desolation and bloodshed which have dotted our plains with the graves of murdered victims.[2]

George Crook was as aware of the cause of Indian displeasure as the Grand Jury, and he sought to change the system in favor of the Apaches. He appealed to the vigorous, honest, blunt Secretary of the Interior in the Chester A. Arthur administration, Carl Schurz, who fired the Commissioner of Indian Affairs, the Inspector-General of the Indian Bureau, and Agent Tiffany, along with several dozen other agents. Tiffany's replacement at San Carlos was P. P. Wilcox, who for a time seemed honest, and who was directed to be more co-operative with the military. Crook next placed Captain Crawford in over-all military command of the reservations where Apaches were lodged, with Lieutenant Gatewood in command of the Apache Scouts at Fort Apache (the White Mountain Agency) and Lieutenant Davis in charge of the Scouts at San Carlos. He also issued General Order No. 43 on October 5, 1882, in which he declared: "Officers and soldiers serving this department are reminded that one of the fundamental principles of the military character is justice to all— Indians as well as white men—and that a disregard of this principle is likely to bring about hostilities, and cause the death of the very persons they are sent here to protect."

Yet every positive measure Crook applied was hampered by bureaucratic inefficiency in Washington, where the Tucson Ring had influence. For example, on January 22, 1885, Crook wrote a confidential letter to Lieutenant Gatewood from Prescott, in which he stated:

> Your letter of 13th inst. just received. From its general terms you seem to consider that I have no troubles beyond myself in dealing with the Indian problem. To give one instance, it took over one month's vigorous telegraphing to get authority to buy Indian produce [for the Army] direct, although I thought the whole matter had been arranged. This was with the War Dept. where everything is comparatively plain sailing, but this difficulty is in-

creased tenfold where the Interior Dept. is concerned. Whenever your people [the Apaches] do anything that can be used against me it is at once taken advantage of and worked for all it is worth. I was officially informed several months ago that the annuities for Chiricahuas and White Mountains would be given to them at once and notwithstanding my constant prodding they haven't got these yet. It is always safe not to promise Indians anything which is not in your power to grant.[3]

In addition to his work in behalf of the Apaches, Crook took defensive steps. He reinstituted the system of each Indian wearing a number, and a head count was taken regularly. Indian police again were enlisted to enforce law and order on the reservations, and the various sub-tribes were allowed to spread out on the reservations in search of better farmland. Gradually, through such methods, Crook was able to regain some of the trust he once had enjoyed from them.

It was during these same two years after his return to Arizona that Crook also was engaged in tracking down renegade Chiricahuas in Sonora led by Chatto, Nachez, Juh, and Geronimo. And just as he had found the reservation Apaches changed, so also he found the renegades different. They had not been slow to learn from the whites; they now were armed with the best rifles and revolvers—better than those Congress provided for American soldiers. The telegraph line, which once had commanded their awe, no longer was mysterious. By 1882 the Apaches had learned its function and its method of operation; when they jumped the reservation, they would cut the lines and remove long sections of wire, or they would remove a short piece of wire and replace it with a thin strip of rawhide, so cleverly splicing the two together that the line would appear intact and the location of the break would take days of careful checking to discover. In addition, they had learned the value of field glasses, and almost every warrior carried a pair.

Thus by the time Geronimo and his band surrendered in January 1884, the Apache had become a deadly warrior indeed.

With his modern arms and his newly acquired knowledge, he had become a near-even match for the troops. In ambushes, he no longer fled swiftly after the first blow to escape superior firepower and weapons; now he could stand his ground and make the soldiers retreat.

In 1884 the basic problem of what to do with the Indians on the reservations still had not been solved; they were still being forced to "take the white man's road," and were not free to be themselves. Because of the many broken promises, there were more sullen individuals among them than ever before, warriors who smarted under real and fancied wrongs, warriors who knew that their facility with modern arms made them the equal or superior of the soldiers; warriors in the mood for reckless, even suicidal, deeds. They were the surviving members of the Chiricahua and Warm Springs Apaches, now united as one group, and Geronimo was ready to be their war leader.

When Geronimo surrendered in January 1884, Lieutenant Britton Davis was directed to take the Chiricahua and Warm Springs Apaches, numbering 550 men, women, and children, to Turkey Creek, a part of the San Carlos reservation some seventeen miles southwest of Fort Apache. There an undefined portion of the reservation had been designated for their use by General Crook. Davis was told to instruct them in agrarian methods, the usual seed, plows, and implements to be furnished by the Indian Bureau. But from the outset the experiment was doomed to failure. The warriors deemed farming beneath their dignity, preferring to hunt, gamble, or loaf, leaving the work to their squaws. Trouble brewed between the various subgroups within the tribe, usually over a young squaw, a game of chance, or when drunk on *tiswin,* a crude beer brewed by the Indians from partly fermented corn. Since *tiswin* caused so much trouble, Crook finally prohibited its manufacture or its consumption. But *tiswin* drowned many an insult and sorrow, and the Apaches continued to make and drink it in secret.

During the summer of 1884 at Turkey Creek, Lieutenant Davis

*Lieutenant Britton Davis, taken at the time of his graduation from West Point.* Courtesy Arizona Pioneers' Historical Society (Gatewood Collection).

barely avoided trouble. He relied heavily on his Scouts, particularly on Chatto, who had enlisted after being tracked down by Crook in 1883, and Dutchy, who reportedly had proven his loyalty by tracking down, killing, and bringing in the head of his father when his father had killed a white man. Serving as Davis's interpreter was Mickey Free, the stepson of John Ward who had run away in 1860 and thus helped precipitate the Bascom Affair; Free in 1885 was employed officially as an interpreter, but was also used by Davis as a spy. The trouble-makers at Turkey Creek included Geronimo, Nachez, Chihuahua, Nana, and, especially, Kayetenay (also spelled Ka-ya-ten-nae). Kayetenay, according to the reports Davis was receiving from his Scouts, was

48

*Mickey Free at the time he served as interpreter for Lieutenant Davis.*
Courtesy Arizona Pioneers' Historical Society.

telling the Chiricahua and Warm Springs Apaches they had been foolish to surrender, was secretly making and drinking *tiswin,* and was beating his wives. The Indians claimed the right of a husband to beat his wife as an ancient and accepted tribal custom, but some of the beatings, administered with a heavy stick, were so brutal that Crook had prohibited the practice. Kayetenay had a following of thirty-two of the most unreconstructed warriors, and his influence would grow unless checked.

Davis responded by calling a conference of the chiefs and explained to them that disobedience to Crook's orders regarding *tiswin* and wife-beating would result in punishment. The chiefs protested, saying that in surrendering they had agreed only to keep the peace, but they had made no agreement concerning their families. Therefore they would continue their family customs. Furthermore, they pointed out that officers, soldiers, and civilians regularly drank something "to make them feel good." Why, they wanted to know, should the same right be denied to Indians? The meeting broke up with no decisions being reached. Kayetenay afterwards was reported to be advising resistance to any attempt to arrest an Indian for drinking or wife-beating.

A few days later Davis received information that Lieutenant Frank West, a friend stationed at the San Carlos Agency headquarters, was coming out to have Thanksgiving dinner with him, and so he went hunting for a wild turkey. Half way up a mesa, he heard a turkey gobble in the creekbed below and turned back to shoot it. Later, from his spies, he learned that atop the mesa he had been climbing Kayetenay and his warriors had been drinking *tiswin* and, seeing Davis approaching, had determined to kill him. Davis had avoided the ambush only because he had heard a turkey gobble below.

The lieutenant determined to arrest Kayetenay and sent for four troops of cavalry from Fort Apache. Then he called another council with the chiefs in the ordinary manner. Kayetenay arrived with his warriors, all armed and ready for battle; apparently Kayetenay sensed something out of the ordinary. Davis explained to the gathering that he was arresting Kayetenay, who would be tried in proper fashion. A tense moment passed, and then Kayetenay surrendered without a fight; later he was tried by a jury of Apaches, convicted, and sentenced to three years' confinement, half of which he served at Alcatraz in San Francisco Bay, before being released on orders from Crook.

The arrival of winter forced the removal of the Chiricahua and Warm Springs Apaches from Turkey Creek. They were located some three miles from Fort Apache. With this move, even the little pretense of farming ceased, the Indians drawing their rations, gambling, quarreling, and loafing. The arrest of Kayetenay had removed the major source of irritation from within the band, however, and the cold months passed without major incident. But during those same months came a series of disastrous events. First, Agent P. P. Wilcox, who had been somewhat honest in his relations with the Apaches and who had allowed the military to retain all police powers, was relieved in November 1884. C. D. Ford, his replacement, was an unfortunate choice of the old type. Ford had no knowledge of the Apaches, but he was determined to assert absolute military control over them himself, an attitude that brought him into conflict with Captain Crawford. Shortly after his arrival, the agent showed this desire by reactivating the office of chief of police, which had been vacant since 1882 and whose function had been exercised by Crawford. Ford's Apache appointee to the post began shielding Indians that Crawford wanted arrested and hampered the captain's policies in general. The Apaches were quick to take advantage of this dichotomy, appealing to the agent when a request was denied them by the military and to the military when a request was denied them by the civilian. The Chiricahua and Warm Springs Apaches had always been masters of diplomacy, and this situation was very exploitable. Crawford protested to Crook, and Crook protested to Washington, but the in-coming administration of Grover Cleveland was hostile to Crook, and Ford was sustained.

51

Newspapers controlled by the Tucson Ring took advantage of the new administration in Washington to editorialize bitterly against Crook and Crawford, wanting to see the farm policy fail for fear the Indians might become self-sustaining. Crawford responded to these attacks by calling for a Board of Inquiry to investigate his conduct—and was completely exonerated. However, in the process he became so embittered that he requested transfer to duty with his regiment in Texas. Crook reluctantly agreed, and Crawford was replaced at San Carlos by Captain Francis C. Pierce of the First Infantry, who came to the post from duty with the Walapais of northern Arizona. Unfortunately, experience with one tribe of Indians did not qualify Pierce to work with another tribe; he had no knowledge of the Apache character, and his appearance at a time when Agent Ford was reasserting the old ways was "fatal," at least according to Britton Davis.

During the political changes, the Apaches renewed their *tiswin* parties, their wife-beating, and even their practice of biting off the nose of an adulterous squaw. Crook had ordered nose-biting halted in 1873, and for nearly twelve years there had been few cases of it. Britton Davis had orders to halt all these practices, however, and worked to impose the regulations. Vigorous protests came from chiefs Mangus and Chihuahua, both of Warm Springs extraction. According to Davis, Mangus wanted the right to make *tiswin,* and Chihuahua, "who loved his toddy," to drink it. On May 15, 1885, the situation came to a head. The Indians had determined on a confrontation.

When Davis emerged from his tent on that warm spring Thursday morning, he found a large group of chiefs and sub-chiefs waiting with their followers. Most were armed, and all appeared serious. Davis invited the chiefs into his tent, where they squatted in a semicircle. Chihuahua took the lead, arguing for the right to beat wives and drink *tiswin*. Davis responded by reminding them of Crook's orders, but Nana interrupted. With Mickey Free interpreting, he said: "Tell *Nantan Enchau* (Fat Chief) that he can't advise me how to treat my women. He is only a boy. I killed *men* before he was born." With that, he stalked from the tent.

Chihuahua then spoke. "We all drank *tizwin* last night, all of us in the tent and outside . . . and many more. What are you going to do about it? Are you going to put us all in jail? You have no jail big enough even if you could put us all in jail."

Clearly the Chiricahua and Warm Springs Apaches were flaunting their guilt to test the Army's response. Clearly they believed that if all the Indians drank *tiswin,* none would be punished. Such a confrontation demanded answers that Lieutenant Davis could not give, and he responded to the chiefs by saying he would wire General Crook at once for instructions.[4] Under military procedure such a telegram had to pass through channels, first to Davis's immediate commanding officer, then up the chain of command to Crook; thus the telegram sent by Davis was addressed to Captain Pierce; it contained only a bare outline of the facts, as Crook had ordered:

Captain Pierce,
    Commanding San Carlos, A. T.
There was an extensive *tiswin* drunk here last night and this morning the following chiefs came up and said that they with their bands were all concerned with it; Geronimo, Chihuahua, Mangus, Natchez, Tele, and Loco. The who[le] business is a put up job to save those who were drunk. In regard to the others, I request instructions. The guard house here is not large enough to hold them all, and the arrest of so many prominent men will probably cause trouble. Have told the Indians that I would lay the matter before the General, requesting, at the same time, that their captives in Mexico be withheld. I think they are endeavoring to screen Natchez and Chihuahua.

                                    (Signed)  DAVIS, Lieut.[5]

Captain Pierce received the telegram that morning and, new at his job, wondered what he should do with it. If it were important, it should be forwarded at once to General Crook; yet if it were unimportant, he would look foolish to the Departmental

*Al Sieber, seated in the front row, with four Tonto Apache Scouts, taken at the San Carlos Reservation in 1883; standing behind Sieber is "Squaw Mack," who lived with the Indians.* Courtesy Arizona Pioneers' Historical Society (Gatewood Collection).

commander for forwarding something he should have handled himself. For help, he turned to Al Sieber, his civilian chief of scouts. Sieber had spent the previous night drinking and gambling, and was sleeping off a hangover when Pierce awakened him, thrust out the telegram, and commented, "From Davis. What about it?" Sieber read it and grunted, "Oh, it's nothing but a *tiswin* drunk. Davis will handle it." He then rolled over and went back to sleep. Pierce accepted Sieber's words as final and pigeonholed the message.[6]

This lost telegram led directly to the events that followed. Crook, who did not receive the message until September 23, later said, "I am firmly convinced that had I known of the occurrence reported in Lieutenant Davis's telegram . . . the outbreak . . . would not have occurred."[7] Had Crawford been at San Carlos, he would have realized the significance of the telegram and how critical Davis's position was and would have acted swiftly; had Al Sieber been sober, he too would have known the urgency of the telegram. But no action was taken. The telegram was "lost," and the die was cast.

At Davis's camp, Friday and Saturday passed with no word from Crook, the Indians growing more and more apprehensive as each hour passed. Then on Sunday afternoon, May 18, Davis was asked to umpire a baseball game between two post teams. The game was never finished, however. About four o'clock, Chatto and Mickey Free, two of Davis's spies, as well as Scouts, reported that Geronimo and a number of Chiricahua and Warm Springs Apaches—they did not know how many—had fled the reservation. Davis attempted to send another telegram to Captain Pierce immediately, but found that the telegraph wires had been cut. Not until about noon the next day was the break found and repaired, for it had been spliced with rawhide.

Immediately after getting his telegram through on Monday afternoon, Davis began preparing his Scouts to take the field with the regular Army troops who would come from Fort Apache. He ordered the Scouts to assemble at his tent to be issued additional cartridges for their weapons. On the reservation he never allowed them more than four or five each, for the Indians used cartridges as currency with a value of twenty-five cents each; Davis knew how tempting it would be for the Scouts to sell them or gamble them away, so he kept their number small except when in pursuit of hostiles. He kept a thousand rounds in his tent for this purpose. As he entered the tent to secure cartridges to issue, Perico, a half-brother of Geronimo, and two other Indians slipped out of the ranks of the Scouts and fled. Later Davis learned that the three had remained behind at Geronimo's order to kill him and Chatto. However, the loyalty of the other Scouts to Davis and the Army had decided them against it.

During the interim between Sunday afternoon, when the renegades fled, and Monday afternoon, when Davis was organizing his Scouts, Geronimo and Mangus had caused word to be spread among all the Chiricahua and Warm Springs chiefs and warriors that the assassinations would take place and that all other Chiricahua and Warm Springs Apaches had agreed to flee with Geronimo. Chihuahua, Nana, and Nachez thus were frightened into joining Geronimo, along with their followers, bringing the total number of renegades to forty-two warriors and approximately ninety women and children.[8] Over four hundred Chiricahua and Warm Springs Apaches remained peacefully at San Carlos, refusing to join in the flight to the mountain hideouts. The newspapers paid no attention to this fact, however, preferring to stress that hostiles were on the warpath and that more soldiers were needed. The final Geronimo campaign had started.

# FOUR

# IN PURSUIT,

# MAY 1885-DECEMBER 1885

It is laid down in our army tactics (Upton's 'Cavalry Tactics, p. 477), that twenty-five miles a day is the maximum that cavalry can stand. Bear this in mind, and also that here is an enemy with a thousand miles of hilly and sandy country to run over, and each brave provided with from three to five ponies trained like dogs. They carry almost nothing but arms and ammunition; they can live on the cactus; they can go more than forty-eight hours without water; they know every water-hole and every foot of ground in this vast extent of country; they have incredible powers of endurance; they run in small bands, scattering at the first indications of pursuit. What can the United States soldier, mounted on his heavy American horse, with the necessary forage, rations, and camp equipment, do as against this supple, untiring foe? Nothing, absolutely nothing. It is no exaggeration to say that these fiends can travel, week in and week out, at the rate of seventy miles a day, and this over the most barren and desolate country imaginable. One week of such work will kill the average soldier and his horse; the Apache thrives on it.

John G. Bourke, *On the Border With Crook*,
(New York: Charles Scribner's Sons, 1891)

THE FLIGHT OF GERONIMO and his renegades from San Carlos caused near-panic across southern Arizona and New Mexico. "Apaches on Warpath," headlined newspapers, while editorial writers criticized the soldiers for bungling. But while civilians criticized, the Army acted rapidly to get the renegades back to

57

the reservation. Davis with his Scouts was joined by Lieutenant Gatewood, who brought a dozen White Mountain Scouts from Fort Apache, and by Captain Allen Smith with two companies of the Fourth Cavalry. There was little hope of overtaking the hostiles, but the officers did hope to discover what Geronimo intended. During the night of May 18-19, trailing was slow, but increased in speed the following morning. For sixty-five miles, the pursuers rode eastward. Not long after sunrise on Monday morning they came to the edge of a valley estimated to be fifteen to twenty miles wide. On the opposite side of the valley they could see the dust kicked up by the horses of the fleeing renegades. As pursuit was hopeless, except for information, Davis and Smith turned back with their detachments, while Gatewood continued to follow for a short time.

Later it was learned that the Indians had traveled 120 miles from San Carlos without pausing to rest or to eat. During the course of this flight, quarrels had erupted between the chiefs. Geronimo and Mangus had told Nachez and Chihuahua that Davis and Chatto would be killed and that most of the Apaches would flee the reservation with the renegades; neither had happened, and Nachez and Chihuahua were threatening to kill Geronimo and Mangus for the lie. In fact, Chihuahua, his brother Josanie, and another brave actually plotted to kill Geronimo, but he was warned and, taking his personal following of warriors, fled southward into Mexico along with Mangus and his followers. Once in Mexico, Mangus split with Geronimo and led his followers into the Mexican state of Chihuahua, never rejoining Geronimo during the following campaign or participating in subsequent hostilities. The Apache chieftain Chihuahua, meanwhile was indecisive. Finally he determined to hide north of the Gila River near Morenci, Arizona, until Davis had followed Geronimo into Mexico; he planned to return then to the reservation. Davis, however, had followed Chihuahua's tracks, not Geronimo's. When Chihuahua saw the Scouts coming after him, he abandoned hope of going to San Carlos and hit the warpath with

*Mangus, like Geronimo, was a war leader of the Chiricahua Apaches.* Courtesy Arizona Pioneers' Historical Society.

*Unidentified officer on front porch of Officers' Quarters, Fort Bowie.*
Courtesy Arizona Pioneers' Historical Society.

all his strength, eventually uniting with Geronimo both physically and in spirit.

Davis, upon returning to Fort Apache, wired Crook what had
occurred. Crook replied in two telegrams dated May 21. In the
first he advised Davis to pacify the Apaches still on the reservation. In the second he ordered that any Apaches who wished to
join in the pursuit of the hostiles "be encouraged and permitted
to do so." The commanding general of the Army, Philip Sheridan, when notified of the outbreak, had wired Crook to enlist
two hundred additional Scouts and promised all possible support; he also ordered Crook to move his headquarters to a point
on or near the Southern Pacific Railroad so that men and supplies moving to the Territory would come under his immediate
command. Crook immediately complied by moving to Fort
Bowie in southeastern Arizona; Davis's report of the easterly di-

60

rection taken by Geronimo caused him temporarily to move to Fort Bayard, New Mexico (near the town of Deming). Bowie would be his headquarters in the months ahead, however.

A second expedition was readied for the field late in May. This one was commanded by Captain Emmet Crawford, who had been returned to Arizona at Crook's insistence, and included Britton Davis. It was a combined force of ninety-two Scouts and Troop A of the Sixth Cavalry. Lieutenant Gatewood, assisted by First Lieutenant James Parker, also of the Sixth Cavalry, was sent eastward with another one hundred Apache Scouts to patrol the Mogollon and Black mountains for hostiles, after which they were to report to Fort Apache. From Fort Bowie, Captain Wirt Davis and a troop of the Fourth Cavalry left for duty in Mexico, carrying sixty days' rations. Wirt Davis and Crawford were to pursue the Apaches into the Sierra Madre of Sonora and flush out the hostiles. To welcome the renegades, should they try to cross the border into the United States, Crook placed elements of the Tenth Cavalry at every water hole along the border from the Rio Grande westward to the Patagonia Mountains of south-central Arizona. A second line of Tenth Cavalrymen were stationed at strategic points along the Southern Pacific tracks—duty that was not exciting but which was vitally necessary.

By June 2, Crook had his forces deployed, arrangements which he revealed in a telegram to his superior in the Division of the Pacific:

Maj. Van Vliet with five troops of 10th. Cavalry and thirty Apache scouts, is moving north of Bayard toward Datil Range. Capt. Chaffee with one troop 6th. is in vicinity of Cuchillo Negro. Maj. Van Horn with Cavalry from Fort Stanton and Mescalero Scouts is scouting each bank of Rio Grande to prevent Indians crossing. Capt. Madden with two troops 6th. Cav'y is west of Burro Mtns. Capt. Lee with three troops 10th Cav'y is moving across Black Range between Smith and Van Vliet. Maj. Biddle followed trail of ten or fifteen Indians which crossed railroad near Florida Pass beyond Lake Paloma, Mexico [this probably was Geronimo's band].

61

. . . Troops are now moving into positions near all known water holes between railroad and Mexico to intercept Indians going south. Capt. Lawton with three troops 4th. Cav'y and Lt. Roach's scouts is in Guadalupe Canyon near boundary line. Maj. Beaumont with two troops 4th. Cav'y is in Stein's Pass.[1]

Approximately two thousand soldiers and Scouts were in the field, but little action resulted. Lieutenant Gatewood, who completed his assignment in New Mexico without any result, was interviewed in Albuquerque early in June when he came there to catch the train back to Arizona. The reporter for the *Journal* stated: "The lieutenant was as pleasant in address as he was good looking in features. . . ." When asked "What about the Indians?" he replied, "Well, they've all gone south and are probably across the Southern Pacific by this time on their road to Mexico if they haven't been captured, but in order to take every precaution several troops of cavalry have been broken up into squads and are watching all the known water holes. . . . General Crook was at Deming when I left, and Lieutenant Davis and something more than forty Apache scouts, is [sic] on the trail of the savages."

"How many Apaches are on the warpath?" the reporter inquired.

"Just forty-two bucks and about ninety squaws and children," Gatewood responded. "Among the bucks must be included a number of boys who are quite as vicious as their elders, and capable of doing almost as much harm."

Asked to describe Geronimo, Gatewood said, "Old Geronimo is a cunning savage and for the past year or two has shown an agricultural tendency. He has a crop of barley growing now. He looked after it himself until he got tired and then hired another Indian to take charge of it."

"Where have you been scouting, Lieutenant?"

"Down in the Mogollons."

"Did you see any Indians?"

"We saw two bucks far ahead of us at one time, but as soon as

*Lieutenant Charles B. Gatewood with the Apache Scouts at Fort Apache,*
*Arizona. Standing behind Gatewood is Sam Bowman, a civilian scout.*
Courtesy Arizona Pioneers' Historical Society.

they saw us they gave the signals, flushed the others of the gang
and they were off like the wind."

"Do you know of any dead Indians in this raid?"

"I've heard of a few but didn't see any myself."

One other point raised by the reporter was a description of the
renegades. Gatewood responded: "They are wonderfully tough
and muscular, rather short in stature, but all muscles and sinews.
On these raids they ride their horses to death, then steal more or
mount those they have already stolen before and are driving
ahead of them. In this they of course have a great advantage of
the cavalry."[2]

In this account the heavy hand of the journalist is evident, along with Gatewood's guarded attitude. Three weeks later, again in the field in New Mexico with his Scouts, he wrote his wife and openly expressed his feelings:

> Sapillo Creek, 23 miles
> north of Bayard,
> June 30, 1885
>
> My dear wife:
>
> We are still aimlessly wandering around these mountains hunting for Indians that are not, & examining all sorts of rumors that have no shadow of foundation of truth in them.
>
> Some of the settlers are wild with alarm & raise all kinds of stories to induce us to camp near their places, to protect them and buy grain & hay at high prices. Others are quiet & sensible, & laugh at the fears of the timid.
>
> The whole thing has turned out just as I put it up before leaving the post—no truth in any of it. The other day a prospector was fishing near our camp, and having discovered some tracks made by our scouts, lit out for parts unknown. He is probably now spreading dismay through the country.
>
> Another one was going to make it his chief business in life to kill scouts, but he changed his mind when they appeared at his place. Few are friendly toward the troops, unless they can sell things.
>
> Our trip has been without interest. Up one hill and down another would sum up the whole thing.
>
> I sent a report to Gen. Crook to-day setting forth the condition of things, & will have to wait for orders till July 2, which will be the earliest date they can reach me. I think their purport will be to send me back home, & that can't be too quick to suit this chicken. Will write you again the first chance.
>
> Love to Nan and Nuisance [his children].
>
> Your loving hus'd
> Charlie[3]

Gatewood did not find any of the Apaches in New Mexico. On June 8 Chihuahua's band made a daring attack on Lawton's troops of the Fourth Cavalry at Guadalupe Canyon, Arizona.

About noon that day, while Lawton and all officers were scouting, the Indians attacked the non-commissioned officer and seven privates left behind, killing five of them, stealing two horses and five mules along with camp stores; in fact, a newspaper account declared that three wagonloads of government supplies, which included thousands of rounds of ammunition, were either taken by the Indians or destroyed. Chihuahua and his warriors then fled southward into Mexico, where on June 23 Crawford's command, guided by Chatto, found their camp in the Bavispe Mountains northeast of Opunto. However, the Americans failed to surround the village completely before the battle started, and the hostiles made their escape. All Crawford could report was one squaw killed and fifteen women and children captured, along with a number of horses and much of the plunder the Indians had taken at Guadalupe Canyon.

While Crawford continued to search for Apaches in Mexico, Chihuahua fled northward again, eluding the border guards and reaching the Chiricahua Mountains of southeastern Arizona. From there he raided, looted, and killed in Arizona and New Mexico. Outlying ranches suffered particularly, as the Apaches were seeking horses and mules, and several ranchers were killed. The whole region was thrown into a panic: "All is excitement and confusion," wrote Lewis Williams of Bisbee. From Tombstone came word that the "City is wild to-night with rumors of all kinds." National newspapers took up the cry for blood, particularly Crook's. The general never made a direct response to the criticism, although in a letter to the commanding general of the Division of the Pacific on August 13, he stated: "So long as these newspapers confine their opposition to personal abuse of myself and our troops, I have no objection; but when their course is calculated to interfere with and prevent the settlement of this Indian question, I feel it my duty to bring the matter to the attention of proper authority."[4]

Crawford kept up the pursuit of the hostiles in Sonora during the rest of June and all of July, sending pack trains north for more supplies in order to keep in the field. At Opunto his command found the Mexicans as excited as the residents of Arizona. Britton Davis wrote, "When I entered Opunto all the able-bodied men of the town, some thirty-five or forty in number, were lined up in front of the principal *cantina* (saloon) ready to take the warpath. They were armed with every conceivable type of antiquated firearm, aged cap and ball horse pistols, muzzle-loading, single-barrel shotguns; these with a few Sharps rifles that had seen better days made up the major part of the arsenal. . . . One thing, however, was not lacking—abundant provision for Dutch Courage. The *cantina* was doing a land office business." As Davis entered town, the populace reacted strongly, even strangely, at the sight of armed Americans: "If an angel with a flaming sword had suddenly dropped from the skies he would have created no greater sensation. Apparently word had reached them that American troops were in the country, but they had not dreamed that we were so near. In a moment a shout went up: *Soldados Americanos! Soldados Americanos!*" Such villages as Opunto were miserably poor; beans, meat, and mescal were the only food in most of them. The Mexicans were even so poor that they had no extra chili peppers for sale. However, ranchers had abandoned their cattle in the hills out of fear of the Apaches, and the troops did kill some of these "to gain relief occasionally from the eternal bacon."[5]

In their pursuit of the hostiles, Crawford and his men climbed mountain after mountain, just as Gatewood was doing in New Mexico. This was a heartbreaking chore, for no sooner would the command top one range than another could be seen across the valley. Crook on August 18 in a report to the Division of the Pacific took note of the difficulties suffered by the commands of both Crawford and Wirt Davis:

. . . The whole country is of indescribable roughness. The Indians act differently than ever before, are split up in small bands and are constantly on the watch. Their trails are so scattered that it is almost impossible to follow them, particularly over rocks, which often delays the party following the trails several hours, if the trail isn't entirely lost. . . . Owing to the rains which reports show to have been of more than usual severity, the troops have been almost continually drenched to the skin for the last month. . . . Captain Davis's report, states that he swam the Bavispe River eleven times in one day, a stream that is usually easily forded.[6]

Still they kept the trail. On July 28, Wirt Davis's Scouts killed a squaw and a youth; ten days later his command struck a band thought to be led by Geronimo, and killed three braves, a squaw, and a child, capturing fifteen non-combatants. Emmet Crawford, in close pursuit, sent Lieutenant Britton Davis, Al Sieber, Chatto, and Mickey Free, along with forty Apache Scouts, to follow Geronimo. The fifty-six-year-old Geronimo led them a long chase, however, crossing the Sierra into Chihuahua before turning north to slip across the boundary line into New Mexico, eluding the soldiers stationed along it, and disappearing in the interior of the Territory. Davis and the Scouts were left far behind. After suffering across the Sierra, Davis and his men finally reached El Paso. Their horses had given out so that much of the trip across Chihuahua was made on foot. Davis described his appearance at that time as anything but that of an officer and gentleman: "Ragged, dirty, a four months' beard, an old pair of black trousers that had been partially repaired with white thread blackened on the coffee pot, rawhide soles to my shoes, and my hair sticking through holes in my campaign hat; who would have accepted my statement that I was a commissioned officer of the United States army?" The Mexican commandant at the border did not, and Davis had to threaten him with violence before he and his men were allowed to cross. They had ridden and walked five hundred miles through the mountains, most of it in driving rain, then crossed the blistering desert in Chihuahua. The command returned to Arizona, where Davis resigned his commission and retired to ranching as an easier livelihood than chasing Apaches.[7] Even Al Sieber, chief of scouts, had all he wanted of such duty; he was badly crippled from his hard years of service, and never again crossed the border in Army service.

Crawford and Wirt Davis with their separate commands, how-ever, continued to scour the Sierra in search of renegades. So close was the pursuit that the hostiles turned north. On Septem-ber 28 approximately twenty warriors crossed the line into Ari-zona, passing through Guadalupe Canyon within a few miles of a camp of two troops of cavalry. Davis and Crawford followed close behind, pursuing the hostiles to the Chiricahua Mountains, a labyrinth where they were safe. Crook issued a warning to the citizens of Clifton, Silver City, and Duncan, in southwestern New Mexico and south-eastern Arizona, to "be on the watch con-stantly until the Indians are run out of the country," and urged that "all horses and mules be corralled and carefully watched in order that if the Indians attempt to re-mount themselves some of them will be killed."[8]

Despite the warning the hostiles killed two Americans, stole fresh horses, and moved west to the Dragoon Mountains. Then, turning south, they by-passed Tombstone and reached the Mule Mountains; there they turned east, just to the north of Bisbee, and rode for the Chiricahuas once more. Their horses were giv-ing out, however, and it seemed that the troops had them cor-nered at last. But at White Tail Canyon, the ranchers in the vicinity were holding their fall roundup. They were warned on the evening of September 30 that Apaches were in the area, yet they went to sleep leaving thirty of their best cow ponies tied around the ranch house. The next morning the ponies were gone, and the Apaches, freshly mounted, were beyond pursuit. They fled south of the border, having killed three Americans and stolen many horses. Captain Charles Viele with two companies of the Tenth Cavalry pursued them all the way to Ascensión, Chi-huahua, before his horses gave out and he had to abandon the chase.

General Crook decided the time had come to give his troops some much needed rest and to prepare them for a more extended campaign than originally expected. He also traveled to Benson,

*Apache Scouts and soldiers chasing the renegades near Willcox, Arizona, in the fall of 1885.* Courtesy Arizona Pioneers' Historical Society (Gatewood Collection).

Arizona, to hold a conference with Governor Luis E. Torres of Sonora about the question of American soldiers crossing the international border. The treaty of July 29, 1882, under which Americans had pursued Apaches into Sonora had expired after two years, and no new arrangement had been reached. Torres informed Crook at their meeting "that in case the two governments [Mexico and the United States] failed to form treaty to admit reciprocal crossing of the border, he would not interfere with the operations of our troops." In fact, Torres was so anxious to have Crook's troops in Sonora that he issued a directive to his commanders of prefects to render them all possible aid.[9]

On October 3, Crook met with Governor Frederick A Tritle of Arizona Territory and with Colonel Luther P. Bradley, commander of the Department of New Mexico. This conference convinced him that the campaign needed to be organized differently. Bradley wanted Crawford sent into the Mogollon and Black Range mountains of New Mexico to attempt the capture of Geronimo, who was thought, incorrectly, to be hiding there. Crook, however, decided to "break up their main nest down in Old Mexico first," and that meant another extended campaign into Sonora. He therefore ordered Crawford and Gatewood to Fort Apache, where their Scouts were discharged—their six-month enlistment had almost expired. Wirt Davis was sent to San Carlos with similar instructions. Crawford and Davis were each authorized to enlist another one hundred Scouts from the reservation Indians for the projected campaign.

Just as the soldiers and Scouts needed time to rest and to resupply themselves, so also did the renegades. Thus October and early November passed quietly while Crawford and Davis recruited; their activity caused many would-be recruits to call upon their medicine men for séances, termed "spirit" dances, during which they could consult "with the powers of the other world and learn what success was to be expected."

For the Army re-supply was a problem of purchase. For the renegades, however, re-supplying meant further raids. As the poverty-stricken Mexicans in Sonora had little left to steal, the hostiles had to go north of the border into Arizona and New Mexico to find what they needed. Josanie, a younger brother of Chihuahua and a relatively unknown Apache leader, received no formal commission to execute the raid; in typical Chiricahua fashion, he simply decided to do it and asked for warriors to accompany him. Nine volunteers went with him, crossing into the Florida Mountains of New Mexico early in November and joining forces with sixteen warriors already there. On the way north they had avoided waterholes, which they knew would be closely guarded, and thus escaped detection. In New Mexico Josanie's band soon made their presence known, killing two Navajo Scouts, a White Mountain Apache Scout, two civilians, and wounding a soldier. One hostile broke a leg and was left to care

70

for himself, the only renegade casualty. Fourteen others then returned to the Sierra of Mexico, taking plunder from their raids with them, while Josanie and ten followers disappeared into the mountains to hide until pursuit cooled. For three weeks they remained silent, and gradually tranquility settled over the Territory again. The soldiers believed that all the Apaches had fled south of the border.

Then Josanie moved secretly and, with shrewd calculation, struck at the place least expected—Fort Apache. On November 23 the officer in charge at that post, Lieutenant James Lockett, who had replaced the absent Gatewood, reported to Crook that hostiles had been seen within four miles of the Fort. He stated that he was going "in pursuit." Then the telegraph went dead, and Crook waited anxiously for reports. When news came, it was of disaster on such a scale that the general could hardly believe that only eleven renegades had caused it. On November 24 Josanie's band had killed two civilians, William Waldo and Will Harrison, who had charge of the reservation beef herd. Next they attacked the reservation itself, killing twenty White Mountain Apaches, all they could find except a few women and children, who were forced to accompany the hostiles. Then, stealing Chief Bonito's horses, they fled up Eagle Creek Trail. Lieutenant Charles E. Nordstrom, ten soldiers, and eighteen Scouts, including Chatto, set out in pursuit, and Crawford with his one hundred Scouts hurried to Bowie Station to intercept them should they head south.

Josanie was not moving south, however. Riding good horses, he and his men moved eastward through Aravaipa Canyon. At Solomonville, Arizona, they struck a ranch and stole more horses. Local residents there thought the thieves were merely rustlers and formed a posse to track them down; the posse was ambushed by the Apaches near Ash Fork and two of its members were killed. The rest lost all ardor for catching the rustlers and hurried to town to complain to the Army. Josanie then led his warriors through Ash Canyon toward Duncan. Crook wired Colonel

Bradley in New Mexico to station his troops in such a way as to prevent the renegades from entering the Black Mountains of that Territory.

As days passed without Josanie's capture, newspapers in the East were filled with headlines of his daring raid, and pressure was mounted on the Army to do something. The Tucson Ring lost no opportunity to magnify the raid beyond its true proportions, in hopes that more soldiers would be sent thus increasing demand for their grain, hay, and rations. Finally Lieutenant General Phil Sheridan, commanding general of the Army, was alarmed enough to travel to Fort Bowie, Arizona, to confer with Crook about the situation. The outcome was a decision to pursue a more aggressive policy in Mexico so as to break up the hostiles' camp in the Sierra. But while the press was calling for Crook's resignation and Crook and Sheridan were conferring, Arizonans not so concerned with profits were trying to keep the situation in proper perspective. The Society of Arizona Pioneers, an historical and social organization, went on record condemning the "penny-a-liners" who were attacking Crook: "We all know that though the chains of prejudice be thrown around you, true Justice will finally award you a heartfelt greeting and say, 'well done thou faithful servant.' " This organization favored "nothing short of removal from the Territory, of all Indians be they peaceable or otherwise," and had sent Granville H. Oury to Washington as their spokesman. Oury lobbied in the nation's capital to this end, and was able to meet with President Grover Cleveland during the late summer of 1885. The Society's Board of Directors also appealed to the Army for rifles to protect its "exposed" settlers in southern Arizona; they subsequently received "fifteen Stand of Arms and two thousand Rounds of Amunition [sic]" but subsequently had to return these when R. C. Drum, Adjutant-General of the Army, wrote that "there is no law authorizing the loan of arms and ammunition" to civilians.[10]

Despite Crook's instructions to Colonel Bradley, Josanie managed to enter New Mexico early in December, killing two more settlers near Alma and escaping into the mountains. Troops of the Eighth Cavalry, guided by Navajo Scouts, were hard on the renegades' heels, however. On the evening of December 9, near Papanosas, these troops, commanded by Lieutenant Samuel W. Fountain, made their attack. Josanie and his braves escaped afoot, leaving behind their horses, blankets, and supplies. The next day the fleeing renegades came upon a ranch; there they killed the owner and one cowboy and remounted themselves. That afternoon they ambushed a different command of soldiers, killing five and wounding two others before disappearing again. New Mexicans in the vicinity were so terrified that the sight of a lone Indian of whatever tribe would send them scrambling for the safety of a town or fort. Cowboys refused to work their employers' stock, barricading themselves in their bunkhouses. Army reports complained bitterly that some ranchers actually gave cattle and horses to the Indians in the hope that the renegades would then leave them alone.

The trail of blood continued. As Christmas approached, near Alma, New Mexico, a freighter was killed and his wagon ransacked for supplies, and near Carlisle the renegades stole more horses for remounts. On December 27 the hostiles were reported in the Chiricahua Mountains of southeastern Arizona, but a blinding snowstorm covered their trail. Then, with the soldiers hunting in vain, Josanie and his band reached the safety—and warmth—of Mexico. In the month and a half they had been north of the border, they had traveled 1,200 miles, killed thirty-eight people, stolen 250 horses and mules, destroyed thousands of dollars' worth of property, and escaped into Mexico with the loss of but one warrior, killed not by soldiers or Scouts but by a White Mountain Apache near Fort Apache. Josanie's feat is almost unbelievable, but Crook himself attested to it in his reports —and he had no inclination to exaggerate the figures, for they made him and his command look ridiculous.

# FIVE

# IN PURSUIT,

# DECEMBER 1885-MARCH 1886

Another habit of the Apaches contributed largely to their success in keeping out of reach. . . . It was a mysterious manner of vanishing completely when the soldiers and scouts had just caught up with them or were about to attack their camp. Each day the chief designated an assembly point. . . . Then when the troops would find them or were about to launch an attack the Indians would scatter, keeping their minds firmly fixed on the assembly point far away. The scouts, who were experienced warriors themselves, had a hard time tracking down the hostiles, as they were forced to follow the many diverging trails, most of which disappeared in the rocks anyway.

The hostiles would converge on their predetermined rendezvous but instead of camping there would make an imitation camp. They would build several small camp fires and tie an old worn-out horse to a tree to make it look as though the camp was occupied. Then they would move on for several miles and establish their real camp elsewhere. The scouts knowing that their fellow tribesmen, the hostiles, would assemble at nightfall, would lie in wait all through the night ready to attack at daybreak. The attack would land upon a fake camp. The scouts were of course disgusted and disappointed but presently they would laugh, saying, "Oh, my! We were fooled!" They took it as a great joke on themselves.

Jaşon Betzinez, *I Fought with Geronimo*
(Harrisburg: Stackpole, 1959). Used by permission of the publisher

CAPTAIN EMMET CRAWFORD, in reenlisting Scouts in October and November of 1885, had chosen only White Mountain and friendly Chiricahua Apaches—mountain Indians whom he believed were best suited to the rugged task of trailing Geronimo in the difficult Sierra Madre of Sonora. Also, these two tribes were less civilized than the other Apache bands, and thus better suited to the work of warfare at hand. They, in turn, joined the expedition not only because they hated the renegade Chiricahuas but also because they trusted Crawford. Known to the Apaches as "Tall Chief" because of his height and "Captain Coffee" because he seemed to live on that beverage, he was noted for his concern for the Scouts working with him.

Crawford's unit was designated the Second Battalion of Indian Scouts and consisted of two companies each of fifty men, who were enlisted for six months' service. Army lieutenants Marion P. Maus, Crawford's second in command, and W. E. Shipp commanded each company. Tom Horn served as civilian chief of scouts, taking the place of the aging Al Sieber. Because the Mexican government forbade the establishment in Sonora of a supply base for the American forces and their auxiliaries, Crawford was assigned twenty-five packers and two trains of fifty pack animals each to provide logistical support for his fast-moving column. H. W. Daly served as chief packer.

The First Battalion of Indian Scouts, similar in every detail of organization, was commanded by Captain Wirt Davis. He also had with him a troop of cavalry. Davis's Scouts were recruited at San Carlos and were at Fort Bowie on November 16. Ten days later, Crawford arrived with his unit from Fort Apache. General Crook spoke to the two commands, telling of his plans for a new campaign and assuring the Scouts that it would be to their benefit to fight the hostiles. Chatto also made a speech to them. They now were ready for a hard campaign.

On November 27 Captain Davis was sent eastward into New

*Apache Scouts at San Carlos Reservation prior to taking the trail of the hostiles.* Courtesy Arizona Pioneers' Historical Society (Gatewood Collection).

Mexico to pursue Josanie, and on the twenty-ninth Crawford led his men to the Dragoon Mountains to intercept the same hostiles should they cross into Arizona. Both failed, however. Crook thereupon ordered both Davis and Crawford into Mexico. On December 11 at Agua Prieta, Crawford's battalion jogged across the border looking for "sign." For the Apache Scouts, life in Mexico was extremely hazardous: Apache scalps were paid for in silver, and the price was the same whether it came from Geronimo himself or from a reservation Apache in American government service. Furthermore, Indian slavery was still practiced in northern Mexico, where some *hacendados* believed that Apaches made desirable workers. Those Apache slaves who refused to submit were shipped to Yucután to work on the chicle plantations (chicle is the base for chewing gum). There the slaves died quickly because of the unfamiliar climate and the tropical diseases. In addition, the Scouts had to be wary of the renegades, for Josanie's raid at the Fort Apache reservation showed that the hostiles would gladly kill those Indians friendly to the Americans. Finally, the Scouts had to be prepared to defend themselves from Mexican fear of any Indian. For example, on December 23 two of Crawford's Scouts were fired upon by Mexicans near the village of Huasanas; the Mexicans later justified their actions, after learning that these were American Scouts, by claiming that the Scouts were drunk. Crawford reported bitterly that, drunk or sober, the Scouts had been unarmed.

Crook settled himself at Fort Bowie and waited for Crawford and Davis to do their work. He had picked his men well and had confidence in their ability to bring the hostiles to ask for terms. His superiors in Washington were not so confident, however. On November 30, he received word from the Secretary of War to transfer the District of New Mexico to control by the Department of Arizona, thus giving him almost a thousand additional troops. Crook spent his spare moments hunting and trying to trap fox, but such moments were few. Almost hourly communiques arrived from Washington. The Tucson Ring's newspapers were reporting all manner of atrocities, and these stories were being reprinted in the East: horses stolen, civilians murdered, economic activity at a standstill. On December 29 General Sheridan telegraphed that President Grover Cleveland was disturbed by the news from Arizona and was asking when something positive would be reported. Cleveland was the first Democrat in twenty-four years to be elected chief executive. Naturally he wanted a quick end to the Apache raids during his term. Crook responded to the telegram by going hunting, killing five quail and two deer.

Crawford, meanwhile, was moving up the Arras River. The trail was so difficult that he decided to leave his pack trains behind with a small guard and strike out on foot for the rough country near the forks of the Yaqui River. Geronimo reportedly had established his camp there. Finding a fresh "sign" on January 8, 1886, Crawford pushed his men forty-eight hours without sleep in a desperate attempt to find and attack the hostile village.

This march left the Scouts' clothing literally in shreds. As they approached the enemy camp, the Scouts, fearful that the enemy would learn of their proximity and flee, asked the officers to "take off their shoes and put on moccasins." According to Lieutenant Maus, Crawford's command "toiled over the mountains and down into cañons so dark on this moonless night [January 9-10], that they seemed bottomless. However, an hour before daylight, after an eighteen hour march, within a mile and a half of the hostile camp, tired and foot sore, many bruised from falling during the night's march, the . . . companies [of Scouts] were disposed of as near by as possible, so as to attack the camp on all sides at the same time."[1]

At daybreak on the morning of the tenth, at a site some sixty miles northeast of Nacori, the attack was made. But it was no surprise to the renegades; the braying of the pack burros warned them. Tom Horn, the civilian chief of scouts, later wrote: "Geronimo jumped up on a rock and yelled: 'Look out for the horses!' And a minute afterwards he yelled: 'Let the horses go and break toward the river on foot! There are soldiers and Apache scouts on both sides and above us. Let the women and children break for the river and the men stay behind!'" Finally, in desperation at the hopelessness of his position, Geronimo called, "Scatter and go as you can!" Most of the hostiles made good their escape, but Crawford had captured their horses and camp equipment, along with a few prisoners. According to Tom Horn, this equipment, consisting of old blankets, quilts, clothes, and raw-hide sacks, was burned, setting up a dense smoke, for it was a damp, cloudy, dismal day. Toward the middle of the afternoon, as Crawford and his men were taking a well-earned rest, a squaw came into the camp, an emissary from the renegades. She said that Geronimo and his followers had encamped across the Arros River a few miles away and wished to talk to Crawford about surrender. The captain agreed to meet with Geronimo, Chihuahua, and Nachez the following day. A place for the conference was arranged, and the squaw departed. Everyone in the

American camp visibly relaxed, thinking the Apache wars were about to come to a conclusion.

The conference never took place, however. Shortly before dawn on the morning of January 11—the day the meeting with Geronimo, Nachez, and Chihuahua was to have occurred—Crawford was awakened by his sentries and told that troops were approaching. One of the Scouts, believing that the oncoming party was Captain Wirt Davis and the First Battalion of Apache Scouts, began yelling to them in the Apache tongue. His guess was incorrect. The newcomers were Mexican irregulars, or *nacionales,* some 150 of them, and at the sound of Apache voices they opened fire. They did not know whether the voice was from an Apache Scout or from a hostile Apache—indeed, they probably would have opened fire had they been certain of the identity. Unknown to Crawford, Sonoran officials were growing alarmed at the presence of Apache Scouts in their state.

Governor Luis E. Torres of Sonora had written to Crook earlier to complain of "depredations" committed by Scouts in Crawford's command. Crook's reply, ironically dated January 11, 1886, stated, "You cannot regret more than I do that any trouble, great or small, should arise between our military forces and the Mexican people. I have sent copies of your communication to Capt. Crawford by courier and directed him to make a thorough investigation and report." He concluded by saying that any outrages committed by Apache Scouts would bring the "severest punishment." Crawford never received copies of these communications, but that very morning "severest punishment" was inflicted on him and his Scouts.

There is evidence that the Mexican irregulars would have attacked Crawford and his Scouts even had they been aware of their identity. These irregulars received no pay either from the national or the state government. Their remuneration came from booty taken in raids on Indian camps and from the scalps they collected—two hundred pesos for the hair of a warrior and one hundred for that of squaws and children. The action of the Mexicans subsequent to the opening of fire and statements made at a subsequent investigation conducted by the Mexican government indicate that these irregulars knew they were attacking Apache Scouts, not renegades.

Hearing shots being exchanged and anxious to avoid bloodshed, Crawford climbed atop a prominent rock in plain view of the Mexicans. There, dressed in his Army field uniform and waving a white handkerchief, he shouted in a loud voice, *"Soldados Americanos,"* at the same time signaling his own troops not to return the fire. Tom Horn also shouted in Spanish to the Mexicans the identity of the American force. Lieutenant Marion P. Maus's official report of the events that followed stated:

> A party of them [the Mexicans] then approached and Captain Crawford and I went out about fifty yards from our position in the open and talked to them. . . . I told them in Spanish that we were American soldiers, called attention to our dress and said we would not fire. . . . Captain Crawford then ordered me to go back and ensure no more firing. I started back, when again a volley was fired. . . . When I turned again I saw the Captain lying on the rocks with a wound in his head, and some of his brains upon the rocks. This had all occurred in two minutes. . . . *There can be no mistake; these men knew they were firing at American soldiers at this time.*

The man who reportedly fired the shot that hit Crawford was Mauricio Corredor, and the weapon was the nickel-plated .50 caliber Sharps rifle presented to him six years earlier for killing Victorio.[2]

The shooting of Crawford enraged the Scouts, and they returned the fire. For an hour Apaches and Mexicans blazed away at each other—while Crawford lay bleeding, obviously still alive, in plain view between the two forces. Ed Arhelger, a civilian packer, later declared that Lieutenant Maus was unnerved by the shooting and hid in the rocks.[3] Apache marksmanship soon proved superior to that of the Mexicans, and the latter ceased fire, waved a white flag, and asked for a conference. Four of their

*Captain Emmet Crawford, commander of Apache Scouts.* Courtesy Arizona Pioneers' Historical Society.

number had died, including Mauricio Corredor, and five had been wounded. The Americans had lost Crawford, and four of them had been wounded, including Tom Horn.

After the shooting halted, Lieutenant Maus, who had taken command, and Tom Horn, his arm bandaged, entered the Mexican lines. They discovered that the force consisted mainly of Tarahumara Indians, bitter enemies of the Apaches, seeking scalps for the bounty being paid. They apparently had been deceived by the ease with which Crawford maintained control over his Scouts at the initial outbreak of shooting; normally Apaches in battle got very excited, and nothing could dissuade them from firing recklessly. The Mexicans therefore believed that Crawford's command was small and could be easily overwhelmed. The Mexicans allowed Maus and Horn to leave their lines in safety, but the next day they lured Maus back into their camp on the pretext of further negotiations and refused to release him until he provided them with mules to transport their wounded. Maus immediately complied giving them six mules and some equipment, but still the Mexicans proved reluctant to allow the lieutenant to leave. Only after the Apache Scouts raised their near-one-hundred voices in a chorus of war cries did the Mexicans release him. The next day Maus moved his camp four miles away to ease tensions caused by the proximity to the Mexican camp.[4]

Emmet Crawford did not die of his wound until January 18, seven days after the battle, although he never regained consciousness. He was hastily buried near Nacori, Sonora, wrapped only in a blanket. Stone slabs were placed over the grave to protect the remains from wild animals. Two months later E. C. Bunker, a civilian packer, was commissioned to bring out the body. With an undertaker, he journeyed to the lonely grave near Nacori. As no boards were to be had within miles, he and the undertaker made a frame of poles, lined it with canvas, put in the body, and strapped it to a mule's back for the two-hundred-mile trip to Bowie Station. This rude casket was transferred from one mule's back to another and packed over the tortuous mountain trails to the Southern Pacific station in Arizona.[5] The remains were first reinterred in Nebraska and later in Arlington National Cemetery. On January 11, 1896, Congress appropriated five thousand dollars for the Crawford estate with the comment, "Captain Crawford's untimely death resulted from his courageous and strict pursuit of his duty as a soldier of the United States."[6]

Shortly after Crawford's murder the United States government officially protested to Mexican officials, who in turn ordered the state of Chihuahua to investigate the incident (the Tarahumara Indians involved were from Chihuahua). On February 11, 1886, a district judge in Chihuahua City opened hearings on "the armed collision that took place between an American force of Indian auxiliaries and a volunteer force from Guerrero." By May of that year more than thirty individuals had testified. Finally, in February of 1887, the Mexican government offered to return the mules and equipment which Lieutenant Maus had been forced to give the *nacionales*. No apology was forthcoming.[7] General Crook paid the most fitting tribute of all to Crawford; he maintained that, had Crawford lived, the renegades would all have surrendered in January of 1886, thereby saving almost eight more months of pursuit and death.

Crawford's death did not entirely ruin the prospects of peace in January 1886. Two squaws came to Lieutenant Maus' camp on January 13. They reported that Geronimo and his followers had heard the firing and had moved away; they reported, however, that he still wished to hold a council, to which Maus agreed. During the course of that meeting, Chief Nana, a warrior, and seven others including the wives of Geronimo and Nachez, indicated their willingness to return to Arizona with Maus, which they subsequently did. The twenty-two hostile warriors promised that in "two moons" they would meet General Crook if he would come without soldiers and if the renegades could pick the meeting site. Maus agreed to these stipulations and then set out for the border with his ragged command.

When couriers from Maus reached Crook with reports of all

that had happened since Crawford led them into Mexico, the general immediately sought assurances from the Arizona Attorney General that no civil authorities would attempt the arrest of Nana, who was wanted for murder. Such an arrest, without doubt, would cause all the hostiles to remain in Mexico. More than anything else, the renegades feared being turned over to civilians for trial; they knew that a jury of white Arizonans would vote to hang them with only a semblance of trial. The Attorney General agreed to wait.

On February 10, Crook had further dispatches from Maus, indicating that the lieutenant was within five miles of the border, approaching it at San Bernardino, and stating that the hostiles really intended to surrender. Crook could do nothing but await the passage of "two moons." In the weeks that followed, the general was plagued with telegrams from superior officers and politicians in the East demanding action, but he made few replies. To the commanding general of the Division of the Pacific he reported that he intended to go to the rendezvous alone, as stipulated. "I will have to play a heavy bluff game," he wrote. But he said he intended to have five companies of infantry within call should the need arise.

Geronimo used the breathing spell to sound out Mexican officials on a possible surrender to them. As the chief responsible for the outbreak, he was obliged to seek the best possible terms for his followers. In mid-January he sent two squaws to the Prefect at Bavispe to arrange a council at which peace terms would be discussed. Geronimo and his warriors hid in the mountains to wait. Time passed and the appointed day for the return of the women came—without them. As still more days passed and the squaws did not return, Geronimo feared treachery and moved his camp toward the American border. He had a lingering suspicion and hatred of Mexicans dating from the death of his mother, wife, and children in Chihuahua in 1858, and feared that the Mexican authorities might be torturing the two squaws in an attempt to make them lead soldiers to the Apache camp.

*General Crook with his staff, both civilian and military.* Sitting: *fifth from left, Tom Horn; sixth from left, Lieutenant Marion P. Maus; seventh from left, Captain Cyrus S. Roberts; ninth from left, Charles D. Roberts, son of Captain Roberts; tenth from left (center), General Crook.* Standing: *seventh from left, Mayor Charles M. Strauss of Tucson; tenth from left, Lieutenant William E. Shipp; eleventh from left (behind Crook), Lieutenant Samson L. Faison; twelfth from left, Captain John G. Bourke; fourteenth from left (large white hat, dark shirt, and suspenders), Al Sieber.* Courtesy Arizona Pioneers' Historical Society.

Actually, the Prefect at Bavispe had kept the two women waiting until he could correspond with Governor Torres, who counseled arranging a meeting and then murdering the renegades. The two squaws were then released with promises of a Mexican willingness to discuss surrender on liberal terms; when they left, they were followed. However, they were wise enough to lose the pursuers. Arriving at the abandoned camp, they found the trail of the renegades, followed it, and rejoined Geronimo just south of the American border.[8]

On March 16 Lieutenant Maus, who was encamped near the border, reported to Crook that four Chiricahua hostiles had visited him. The four had said that all the renegades, except Mangus and his followers, were within twenty miles and ready to meet Crook at Cañon de los Embudos, which was a short distance across the border in Mexico. Crook may well have wondered if there was any significance to the name of the site selected for the conference: in English it meant "Canyon of the Tricksters." Nevertheless, he agreed and readied a party. With him went Kayetenay, released from Alcatraz at Crook's insistence; Alchise, a friendly Chiricahua; a Tombstone photographer named C. S. Fly; and Crook's staff, consisting of Captains John G. Bourke and Cyrus S. Roberts. Roberts' thirteen-year-old son also was allowed to attend. On March 22 Tom Moore took a pack train from Fort Bowie and, accompanied by Alchise and Kayetenay, set out for Cañon de los Embudos. The next day Crook and the rest followed, going by way of White's Ranch and Mud Springs. They crossed the border at San Bernardino. Three miles south of the international boundary they watered at Contrabandista Springs, then proceeded down the dry bed of the Rio de San Bernardino to a point opposite the Sierra de Embudos, where they turned east into the canyon.

As they ascended on the morning of March 25, they flushed a drove of wild pigs, and Kayetenay shot one while his horse was in full gallop. Shortly afterward, they were met by guides, who took them to Lieutenant Maus' camp. After lunch the hostiles approached, and the conference began. Present on the American side were Crook, Bourke, Roberts, Maus, and from his command Lieutenants Shipp and S. L. Faison, Dr. Davis, packers Moore and Daly, the photographer Fly and his assistant Chase,[9] Tommy Blair, the pack-train cook, Mayor Strauss of Tombstone, young Charles Roberts, and a ten-year-old boy named Howell, who had tagged along from the San Bernardino Ranch. Representing the Indians were Geronimo, Nachez, Chihuahua, Nana (whom Crook had ordered to be there, along with Alchise and Kayetenay), Josanie, Cayetano, and Noche. Interpreters included Montoya, Concepción, José María, and Antonio Besias—all Apache Indians.

86

*Renegade Apaches with Geronimo at the surrender conference with General Crook. Note the young boys at right who are fully armed.* Courtesy Arizona Pioneers' Historical Society.

Captain Bourke later described the scene:

The whole ravine was romantically beautiful: shading the rippling water were smooth, white-trunked, long, and slender sycamores, dark gnarly ash, round-barked cottonwoods, pliant willows, briery buckthorn, and much of the more tropical vegetation. . . . Twenty-four warriors listened to the conference or loitered within earshot; they were loaded down with metallic ammunition, some of it reloading and some not. Every man and boy in the band wore two cartridge-belts. The youngsters had on brand-new shirts, such as are made and sold in Mexico, of German cotton, and nearly all—young or old—wore new parti-colored blankets, of some manufacture, showing that since the destruction of the village by Crawford, in January, they had refitted themselves either by plunder or purchase.[10]

Crook echoed these sentiments, describing the Apache hostiles as "fierce as so many tigers—knowing what pitiless brutes they are themselves, they mistrust everyone else."

Crook opened the conference with a terse, "What have you to say; I have come all the way down from Bowie?" After agreeing on who was to interpret, Geronimo responded by listing the causes for his leaving the reservation, which included malicious gossip that he was a bad Indian and a rumor that he was to be arrested and hanged. Thereafter, he said, "I want good men to be my agents and interpreters; people who will talk right. . . . Whenever I meet you I talk good to you, and you to me, and peace is soon established; but when you go to the reservation you put agents and interpreters over us who do bad things. . . . In the future I don't want these bad men to be allowed near where we are to live. . . ." Ironically, this was the one thing Crook could not promise; he knew that what Geronimo said was true—the Indian Agents all too often were bad—but they were appointed in Washington by the Department of the Interior, not the War Department.

Geronimo waxed philosophical as he continued his speech to Crook: "I know I have to die sometime, but even if the heavens were to fall on me, I want to do what is right. I think I am a good man, but in the papers all over the world they say I am a bad man; but it is a bad thing to say so about me. I never do wrong without a cause. Every day I am thinking, how am I to talk to you to make you believe what I say; and, I think, too that you are thinking of what you are to say to me. There is one God looking down on us all. We are all children of the one God. God is listening to me. The sun, the darkness, the winds, are all listening to what we say now."

Crook responded by reminding Geronimo that two years before, when he had surrendered in January of 1884, he had promised to live in peace, but had lied. "When a man has lied to me once I want some better proof than his own word before I can believe him again." More talk followed. Finally Crook stated the American side bluntly: "You must make up your own mind whether you will stay out on the warpath or surrender unconditionally. If you stay out, I'll keep after you and kill the last one, if it takes fifty years." This threat was the "heavy bluff game" which Crook had indicated he would play; to track Geronimo

The surrender conference between General Crook and Geronimo at Cañon de los Embudos in 1886, taken by C. S. Fly, a Tombstone photographer. Courtesy Arizona Pioneers' Historical Society.

Identification of those at the surrender conference: 1. Lieutenant William Ewen Shipp; 2. Lieutenant Samson Lane Faison; 3. Nachez; 4. Captain Cyrus Swan Roberts; 5. Cayetano; 6. Geronimo; 7. Concepcion; 8. Nana; 9. Noche; 10. Lieutenant Marion P. Maus; 11. Jose Maria; 12. Antonio Besias; 13. Jose Montoyo; 14. Captain J. G. Bourke; 15. General Crook; 16. Charles D. Roberts; 17. Tommy Blair; 18. Henry W. Daly; 19. Josanie; 20. Chihuahua; 21. Tom Moore; 22. Martin Foster (?); 23. Mayor Charles M. Strauss of Tucson.

down in Sonora might well have taken the fifty years Crook mentioned, and he knew it.

Bourke described Geronimo as "nervous and agitated" during this conversation. ". . . Perspiration in great beads, rolled down his temples and over his hands; and he clutched from time to time at a buckskin thong which he held tightly in one hand," wrote Bourke. The meeting adjourned soon after. Geronimo left stating that he wished to ask some questions the following day. Returning to his tent, Crook called Alchise and Kayetenay to him. Alchise, a son of Cochise, was Crook's staunch friend, and Kayetenay's residence in Alcatraz had changed his viewpoint to pro-American. Crook sent these two men into Geronimo's camp to stir hatreds among the renegades and to split them if possible, all the while influencing them to thoughts of surrender.

No formal session was held the next day, March 26, but informal talks were held. Geronimo did meet with Crook, asking questions and receiving answers, while Alchise and Kayetenay moved through the hostile camp spreading division and encouraging surrender. Apparently they were successful and Geronimo was satisfied with Crook's answers. On the morning of the twenty-seventh Crook received word from Chihuahua that the Chiricahuas were preparing to surrender. He wired General Sheridan that morning, "Today things look more favorable."

The second meeting contained the same individuals as the day before. Chihuahua started off the proceedings with a speech, in which he declared, "I am anxious to behave. I think the sun is looking down upon me and the earth is listening. I am thinking better. It seems to me that I have seen the One who makes the rain and sends the winds; or He must have sent you to this place. I surrender myself to you because I believe in you and you do not deceive us." Afterwards he shook the general's hand. Nachez followed suit, saying, "What Chihuahua says I say. I surrender just the same as he did. . . . I give you my word, I give you my body. I surrender; I have nothing more to say than that. . . . Now that I have surrendered I am glad. I'll not have to hide behind rocks and mountains; I'll go across the open plain. I'll now sleep well, eat contentedly, and be satisfied, and so will my people."

Geronimo alone remained to speak. Finally he agreed with the others. "Two or three words are enough," he began. "I have little to say. I surrender myself to you." He paused to shake hands with Crook, then continued, "We are all comrades, all one family, all one band. What the others say I say also. I give myself up to you. Do with me what you please. I surrender. Once I moved about like the wind. Now I surrender to you and that is all." Again he shook Crook's hand.

The terms of this surrender were reported by Crook in a confidential report sent to General Sheridan that same day, March 27:

> The only propositions they would entertain were these three: that they should be sent east for not exceeding two years, taking with them such of the families as so desired, leaving at [Fort] Apache, Nana, who is seventy years old and superannuated; or that they should all return to the reservation on their old status; or else return to the warpath, with its attendant horrors. As I had to act at once, I have today accepted their surrender upon their first proposition.

Crook had gone to Cañon de los Embudos with orders from Washington to get an unconditional surrender with no promises made them "unless it is necessary to secure their surrender." He accepted this stipulation to mean that, failing to secure an unconditional surrender, he was to make the best terms possible. He had made them—two years imprisonment in the East for the renegades and then a return to their Arizona homeland.

Crook had concluded the second conference by stating that he was returning to Fort Bowie the next day, March 28, as he had much work to do there. Alchise, Kayetenay, Lieutenant Maus, and the Scouts were to stay with the renegades and take them to Fort Bowie also. They were to begin their journey north on March 28. These arrangements concluded, Crook went to Bowie as rapidly as possible.[11] His diary records the journey graphically:

March 28. Left camp early in the morning for San Bernardino. Met Geronimo and Noche and other Chiricahuas coming from the San Bernardino direction quite drunk. We took buck-board at San Bernardino and took lunch at Silver Creek with Capt. Smith. Stopped a moment at Lt. Wheeler's camp at Mud Springs, and stopped for the night at Frank Leslie's ranch.

March 29. Left Leslie's at six A.M. Wind blew a gale all day. Arrived at Fort Bowie at about 3 P.M. Killed a curlew, the largest I ever saw in Sulphur Springs Valley.[12]

Crook might well have had forebodings about the drunken Chiricahuas he saw returning from San Bernardino on March 28, but, if he did, he made no mention of it in his diary.

On the twenty-ninth, as Maus was escorting the hostiles toward the boundary, they encountered Bob Tribollet, a notorious bootlegger and crony of the Tucson Ring. He was at Contrabandista Springs operating a makeshift saloon housed in a tent. His stock consisted of three demijons of whiskey, fifteen gallons in all, which he sold at exorbitant prices to those Indians who wished to buy. Maus realized the potential for trouble gurgling inside the demijohns and sent Lieutenant Shipp to destroy them. But the damage had already been done. While the hostiles were drinking the whiskey, Tribollet and his men had told them that they would be murdered as soon as they crossed the line into the United States. One civilian scout later told Captain Bourke that Tribollet had sold thirty dollars' worth of whiskey in an hour to the Chiricahuas; later Tribollet had boasted that he could have sold one hundred dollars' worth at ten dollars a gallon had Lieutenant Shipp not put him out of business.

That afternoon the renegade Apaches gradually sobered. Nursing hangovers and discussing Tribollet's message that they would be murdered north of the line, the hostiles' dispositions were not improved by the weather. Cold drizzling rain was falling. Under cover of the darkness and the rain, Geronimo, Nachez, nineteen warriors, thirteen squaws, and six children decided to return to their hideout in the Sonoran mountains. Two days later, however, two of the nineteen warriors deserted Geronimo and doubled back north to join Chihuahua's band, proceeding on to Bowie with him. This left Geronimo with a total of thirty-eight persons, including himself, on his southward flight. As Geronimo later recalled his decision,

> We started with all our tribe to go with General Crook back to the United States, but I feared treachery and decided to remain in Mexico. We were not under any guard at this time. The United States troops marched in front and the Indians followed, and when we became suspicious, we turned back. I do not know how far the United States army went after myself, and some warriors turned back before we were missed, and I do not care.[13]

Whether or not the Tucson Ring promoted Tribollet's sale to the renegades is still a matter of conjecture. However, only the Tucson Ring stood to profit from a continuation of hostilities. Tribollet had been involved in selling whiskey to the Indians before; in fact, he had been brought to trial for it, but as Crook declared indignantly to Charles Lummis, "He has been tried before, but bought his way out. . . . Why, that man has a beef contract for our Army!"[14] Later, according to one story, Tribollet planned a stagecoach holdup in Mexico but was arrested by *Rurales* and shot while trying to escape.

On March 30 Crook wired General Sheridan the news of Geronimo's flight, adding that Lieutenant Maus and the Scouts had gone in pursuit. Sheridan on March 31 responded, "Your dispatch of yesterday received. It has occasioned great disappointment. It seems strange that Geronimo and party could have escaped without the knowledge of the scouts." This hint of disloyalty on the part of the Scouts was a direct reflection on Crook's ability and judgment, for the Scouts had been his special brainchild. That same day Crook replied testily, "There can be no question that the scouts were thoroughly loyal, and would have prevented the hostiles leaving had it been possible." More telegrams passed between them, during which Sheridan asked what Crook was doing to protect life and property in Arizona and what was being done to apprehend the hostiles. "You have forty-six companies of infantry and forty companies of cavalry," Sheridan stated, "and ought to be able to do a good deal with such a force."[15]

What Crook did not know during this exchange was that because of the nature of his agreement with the Apache hostiles the commanding general of the Army was deliberately baiting him into resigning. Immediately upon receipt of Crook's message containing this agreement—two years' imprisonment in the East followed by a return to Arizona—General Sheridan had gone to the White House to confer with President Cleveland. Cleveland was especially sensitive to the cries of outrage which the Apache raids had raised in that off-year election of 1886, the presidential election just two years away. The Tucson Ring had exploited the situation so effectively, in fact, that it had overplayed its hand. Cleveland was being pressured to end the Apache problem once and for all. On March 30 Sheridan had wired Crook that the President did not agree to imprisoning the Apaches for a mere two years after which they would return to Arizona; "He instructs you to enter again into negotiations on the terms of their unconditional surrender, only sparing their lives."

Naturally this was impossible, as Crook pointed out in his response: "To inform the Indians that the terms on which they surrendered are disapproved would, in my judgment, not only make it impossible to negotiate with them, but result in their scattering to the mountains, and I can't at present see any way to prevent it." He allowed the seventy-five hostiles in Chihuahua's band, who were still on the way to Fort Bowie, to continue to believe that his arrangements with them had been accepted in Washington. Then came the dispatches from Sheridan on March 31 impugning the loyalty of the Apache Scouts. Finally Sheridan reminded him of the number of troops at his command and included the implied criticism of "Please send me a statement of what you contemplate for the future."

94

This dispatch from Sheridan, dated April 1, 1886, was received at 2:11 that same afternoon. Despite the hour, Crook managed to get his reply on the wire to Washington before the day was done:

> Your dispatch of today received. It has been my aim throughout present operations to afford the greatest amount of protection to life and property interests, and troops have been stationed accordingly. Troops can not protect beyond a radius of one-half mile from their camp. If offensive movements against the Indians are not resumed they may remain quietly in the mountains for an indefinite time without crossing the line, and yet their very presence there will be a constant menace, and require the troops in this department to be at all times in position to repel sudden raids; and so long as any remain out they will form a nucleus for disaffected Indians from the different agencies in Arizona and New Mexico to join. That the operations of the scouts in Mexico have not proved as successful as was hoped is due to the enormous difficulties they have been compelled to encounter, from the nature of the Indians they have been hunting, and the character of the country in which they have operated, and of which persons not thoroughly conversant with both can have no conception.

What Crook, in effect, was saying was that General Sheridan and officials in Washington, including the President, were not sufficiently knowledgeable to instruct him about how to conduct the war. He knew he was not confronting an enemy that fought according to the textbooks at West Point. He was facing small bands that did not stand and fight on a broad front, who did not consider it honorable to fight to the death rather than retreat. The Apache in Arizona was fighting as the Spaniards had against the troops of Napoleon, and the use of European tactics against them would be as useless as those employed by the great French emperor. Crook stated in defense of his reasoning, "I believe that the plan upon which I have conducted operations is the one most likely to prove successful in the end." He was stung hard by Sheridan's implied criticism, however, and wanted to know if he still had the commanding general's confidence. He could not ask such a question directly, and thus resorted to a roundabout method: "It may be, however, that I am too much wedded to my own views in this matter," he concluded his telegram, "and as I have spent nearly eight years of the hardest work of my life in this department, I respectfully request that I may be now relieved from its command." For his request to be denied would be a statement of support by Sheridan and the President; its acceptance would mean the opposite.

The next day, April 2, Crook received orders relieving him of command of the Department of Arizona—the same day that the seventy-five hostiles reached Bowie and the same day that Captain Crawford's body left on the train for Kearney, Nebraska. Sheridan's acceptance of Crook's resignation committed the Army to a military conquest of Geronimo and his hostiles, not a diplomatic settlement as Crook had wanted. To effect his desire for a military pacification, as well as those of Grover Cleveland, who felt the Apaches should be turned over to civil authorities in Arizona for trial, Sheridan sent Brigadier General Nelson Appleton Miles to replace Crook.

On April 5, a week before he departed Arizona, Crook received another slap. He was notified that because Geronimo had run away, the agreement he had negotiated with the Apaches was thereby nullified. On such a flimsy legal basis the government was terminating Crook's promise that the seventy-five hostiles who surrendered would be returned to Arizona in two years. They were to be sent into indefinite exile. However, the order continued, Chihuahua and his followers were not to be informed of this decision until after they were at Fort Marion, Florida. On April 7 they were put aboard the train, thinking they would return two years hence. Crook came to Bowie Station to see them off: fifteen warriors, thirty-three squaws (including the wives of Nachez and Geronimo), and twenty-nine children. Five days later, after officially being relieved, Crook also departed from Bowie Station, leaving Arizona in the hands of a soldier committed to a military solution of the Indian problem.

# SIX

# MILES'S CAMPAIGN
# TO CONQUER

Plan—

1. Harrass & give no rest to hostiles, no hiding place. Necessity of always having pickets and look outs.

Formerly they retired to the fastnesses of the Sierra Madre, rougher the farther you go. A regular haven of rest for them.

By treaty American soldiers allowed to enter Mexican territory.

Different columns of American soldiers followed trails wherever found, so long as it could be followed. Sometimes washed out by rains. No let up.

Animals of one command break down, another take its place and then keep up the pursuit.

Several times surprised in fancied security.

Everywhere they went, Am. soldiers followed to the astonishment of the Mexicans.

2nd part of Plan.

After giving them no rest for months, night and day, the Gen. decided to demand surrender. . . .

They were growing tired of war as waged by us . . . in its relentless and tireless prosecution. No fun in it.

Charles B. Gatewood, about 1896, MSS, Gatewood Collection.

BORN ON AUGUST 8, 1839, at Westminster, Massachusetts, Nelson Appleton Miles ended his schooling at seventeen. He went to work as a clerk in Collomare's Crockery Store in Boston, but attended night school at Comer's Commercial College and read extensively on his own. He was convinced that war was inevitable between North and South, and in 1860 began taking instruction from a French veteran in military drill, studying the tactics and strategy of Napoleon at the same time. When the war did start, Miles waited until after the First Battle of Bull Run to be absolutely certain that it would be of long duration, then used his savings, plus twenty-five hundred dollars which he borrowed from an uncle, to raise a company of one hundred volunteers from the town of Roxbury, a suburb of Boston. His commission as captain of this company was actually signed by the governor, but before delivery it was voided on the pretext that at twenty-two Miles was too young. The commission went to someone with political connections. This incident, according to a sympathetic biographer, "made him feel that, if he were to get anyplace, ability and hard work were not enough. He would need influential friends."[1] He never overcame this cynical maxim; in fact, it became the guiding force of his life.

In September of 1861 he did secure a lieutenancy in the 22nd Massachusetts Volunteers. However, he sensed that little future lay with this regiment, owing to his lack of political connections in Massachusetts, and he secured a transfer and became aide-de-camp to Brevet Major General Oliver Otis Howard. When Howard was wounded in the Richmond Campaign, Miles lost that post. In 1862, through the efforts of a newly made friend, he obtained a lieutenant colonelcy as executive officer of the 61st New York Regiment; at the time he was twenty-three. Subsequently he fought in almost every major battle involving the Army of the Potomac: Antietam, Chancellorsville, the Wilderness, Spottsylvania Court House, Reams Station, and the Richmond campaign of 1864. He was wounded four times, very seriously at the Battle of Chancellorsville. By May of 1864 he had risen to brevet brigadier general and before the war ended he was a major general of volunteers. Although just twenty-six years old with an impressive record on the battlefield, he had not lost his conviction that powerful friends and political connections were necessary to promotion.

The end of the Civil War found Miles unwilling to quit the military life. Its pomp and ceremony appealed to the former crockery clerk; its gaudy uniforms lent grandeur to what had been an ordinary life. He therefore applied for a regular commission, knowing that he would have to be willing to accept a reduction in grade in an army top-heavy with general officers. He hoped he would lose only one star, however, not two. To help his cause he secured letters of recommendation from as many prominent figures in the government as possible, and from almost every leading general in the Army. While awaiting word on his petition, he served as commander at Fort Monroe, Virginia in which the president of the Confederacy, Jefferson Davis, was imprisoned. The task fell to Miles of manacling and fettering ex-president Davis. He almost lost his commission in the Regular Army when the public turned against the Army for the harsh treatment accorded Davis. However, in October 1866 he was awarded a full colonelcy and command of a regiment. Then in 1867 he met and began wooing Mary Hoyt Sherman, niece both of powerful Senator John Sherman of Ohio and of General William Tecumseh Sherman. He married Mary on June 30, 1868, perhaps for love, perhaps for the influence she could generate to aid his career.

As commander of the 40th Infantry Regiment, Miles was involved in the Plains Indian fighting. In 1874-1875 he faced the Kiowas, Comanches, and Cheyennes, then was transferred north for the Sioux Wars that saw the death of George A. Custer at the Little Big Horn. Next came the Nez Percé difficulties. In December of 1877 Miles attained national prominence by marching his troops 160 miles through wintery cold to capture Chief Joseph and his followers in northern Montana—a spectacular feat. The following year he effected the surrender of Elk Horn and his band of renegades near Yellowstone Park. For these successes he was promoted to brigadier general in 1880. He had his coveted star once again—but it only made him anxious to gain another. Six long years passed without an opening, however, and there could be no promotions until death or retirement created a vacancy. Then in March of 1886, just as Crook seemed to be bringing the Geronimo campaign to a successful conclusion, Miles learned that Major General John Pope was retiring and that Major General Winfield Hancock had died. Miles exerted all his influence, plus that of his in-laws, but failed to be appointed to either vacancy; Alfred Terry was chosen, in part because of his success in the Sioux wars, for the one post, and Miles' old commander Oliver Otis Howard received the other. Then came Miles' appointment as commander of the Department of Arizona, making Howard, who had become commanding general of the Division of the Pacific, his immediate superior. Miles was bitterly disappointed at failing to be promoted in the spring of 1886, and he came to Arizona determined to win enough glory on the battlefield to make him next in line for promotion when another vacancy occurred.[2]

His wife did not accompany Miles to Arizona. She waited in Massachusetts while he did the fighting. He arrived at Fort Bowie on April 11, 1886, traveling from Bowie Station in a six-mule ambulance. That afternoon he conferred with the departing Crook about the Apache problem, reviewed the troops, and made a speech to the Apache Scouts, whom he ordered home to Fort Apache for discharge. To his wife he wrote that evening:

I arrived today after a long, hot and very dusty trip. I think this is the most barren region I have ever seen. From what I can see and hear of the troops, they are very much discouraged by being kept in the field so long and by the prospect that the campaign must be continued for some time to come. General Crook leaves tomorrow. He appears to feel very much disappointed but does not say much. He tells me that only two of the Apache warriors have been killed since they broke out. In many respects this is the most difficult task I have ever undertaken, on account of the extensive country, the natural difficulties and the fact that the hostiles are so few in number and so active. Still I can only make the best effort possible.[3]

*General Nelson A. Miles.* Courtesy Arizona Pioneers' Historical Society.

*A dress parade of the troops at Fort Bowie in 1886.* Courtesy Arizona Pioneers' Historical Society.

This letter reflects a growing uneasiness. All Miles' training and experience, both in the Civil War and in the Indian campaigns on the Plains, was with an enemy that fought in large numbers. His glimpse of the barren, mountainous Southwest, as well as his conversation with Crook, told him that he was involved in a guerrilla war that might prove difficult—and embarrassing—despite the fact that he had five thousand men with which to fight only thirty-eight hostiles.

After a rapid tour of the Department, Miles began issuing orders to effect his instructions from the President, which were "vigorous operations looking to the destruction or capture of the hostiles." He allowed Crook's orders to stand that all ranches subject to possible attack and all water holes be guarded. More innovative, he divided the country into "districts of observation"; his General Field Order No. 7, issued at Fort Bowie on April 20, directed all commanders in southern Arizona and New Mexico to erect heliograph stations on prominent mountain peaks, using

*The Commanding Officer's quarters at Fort Bowie, Arizona; both Crook and Miles lived here.* Courtesy Arizona Pioneers' Historical Society.

the bright sunlight and clear air to transmit messages, and thus to communicate news of the hostiles, rapidly. Eventually thirty of these stations were erected, at considerable cost, not only in Arizona and New Mexico but in Sonora as well.[4]

The same general order also directed that "where a troop or squadron commander is near the hostile Indians he will be justified in dismounting one-half of his command and selecting the lightest and best riders to make pursuit by the most vigorous forced marches until the strength of all the animals of his command shall have been exhausted. In this way a command should, under a judicious leader, capture a band of Indians or drive them from one hundred and fifty to two hundred miles in forty-eight hours through a country favorable for cavalry movements; and the horses of the troops will be trained for this purpose." The intent of this message was that lieutenants and captains who lost contact with groups of hostiles would answer to Miles.

On April 27, just seven days after this order was issued, Miles got his first taste of Apache warfare. Geronimo and Nachez struck across the border in the Santa Cruz Valley that morning, killing a number of cowboys and capturing the Peck ranch. Mrs. Peck and one child were killed, while Peck and a thirteen-year-old daughter were captured. Peck went temporarily insane from grief, whereupon he was released by the Apaches, who felt that an insane person was inhabited by devils and that the condition might be communicable; they kept the daughter with them. Captain T. C. Lebo was in the vicinity with Company K of the Tenth Cavalry, a company made up of many veterans of the Victorio campaign of six years earlier. Lebo took up the trail as instructed by Miles. Knowing the general's displeasure should he lose the hostiles, he pursued them hotly for two hundred miles. Then as the horses of both Indians and cavalry were giving out, Lebo brought the hostiles to bay in the Piñito Mountains, thirty miles south of the border.

The captain ordered his troops to dismount and prepare to storm the slope leading to the hostiles' position. The Buffalo Soldiers, as the Negro troopers of the Tenth Cavalry were known, responded by rushing up the slope into a withering enemy fire that killed one private and wounded a Corporal Scott. The troops hid behind rocks and returned the renegades' fire, while Corporal Scott lay bleeding in plain sight between the two lines. Lieutenant Powhattan H. Clarke went to Scott's rescue, braving the deadly bullets of the Indians and bringing the trooper to safety, thereby winning the medal of honor. Gradually the fire from the renegades came to a halt, and the soldiers stormed up the hill to find their quarry had vanished. For four more days they trailed the Apaches; then on May 5 they were relieved just as their rations were exhausted.[5]

As ordered, Lebo had reported his pursuit to General Miles, who had sent Troop B of the Fourth Cavalry, led by Lieutenant H. C. Benson, to take up the pursuit. Benson had been at Fort Bowie until April 30, having just discharged the company of Indian Scouts he had commanded under Major Wirt Davis. Ordered to Fort Huachuca, he was detailed to command Company B of the Fourth Cavalry on May 1 and directed to proceed to Nogales, Arizona, there to pick up the trail of the renegades and stick to it. At Nogales on May 2 he learned of Lebo's fight with the hostiles and the direction of pursuit. Waiting only for the arrival of five Indian trackers, he then led his men into Mexico and on May 5 relieved Lebo.

Geronimo was expecting pursuit and selected the worst possible country over which to travel. "During this day I lost three of my sixteen mules over the side of the mountain, as we were often obliged to slide down slopes composed of rock only, and there was not sufficient footing at the bottom to enable the animals to recover their footing, and they pitched over the cliffs," Benson later recalled. After following the trail for several hours, the Indian trackers became so discouraged that they refused to go farther. Benson sent four of them to the rear, but kept Chimney, who could speak English, with him. An hour later Chimney suddenly dashed away into the underbrush and deserted before Benson could prevent it. This left him without an interpreter, but he was able to convince another of his trackers, through sign language, to take up the trail. That afternoon the fleeing renegades set fire to the country over which they had passed to hide their trail, forcing the soldiers to ride through forest fires. The trackers finally reached water late that night.

Day after weary day of such tracking followed, as Geronimo led the troops deeper into the Sierra of Sonora before he finally lost them. Nevertheless, Benson and his company were to remain in the field for four long months.[6] They were part of a larger unit which Miles had picked especially for such duty. Miles later wrote of this unit, "I looked for a suitable command to take up the pursuit of the Indians south of the Mexican border. At Fort Huachuca I found the commander for such a force, Capt. H. W. Lawton, of the Fourth Cavalry. . . ." Miles was very impressed with Lawton, stating that the captain was "a resolute, brave officer, active and ambitious. He was a giant in stature, and a man of great energy and endurance."[7] Perhaps the general saw in Lawton something of himself, for Lawton was also a non-West Pointer and a great admirer of physical fitness.

Born in 1843 in Toledo, Ohio, Henry Ware Lawton had served with distinction in the Civil War, rising from sergeant to brevet colonel of volunteers. With recommendations from Generals Sherman and Sheridan, he had been commissioned a second lieutenant of the Forty-first Infantry in 1866. Twenty years later he was a captain, having served in numerous Indian campaigns in the West. Lawton probably was chosen by Miles to lead the unit pursuing Geronimo in Mexico because he had expressed his belief that the Apaches could be worn down by constant pursuit and forced to surrender on Army terms. Miles declared of the unit that it was an experiment to "ascertain if the best athletes in our service could not equal in activity and endurance the Apache warriors."

Assigned to Lawton's command was Leonard Wood, a contract surgeon. Wood, born in Winchester, New Hampshire, on October 9, 1860, wanted to enter the Army or Navy and have a military career, but he deferred to the wishes of his father and attended Harvard Medical School, graduating in 1884. Upon completing his studies, he practiced general medicine in Boston for a year and a half; yet, as one biographer stated, "the heart of adventure and the thirst for glory were in him." He took the Army examination for medical surgeons, and on January 5, 1886, was appointed an assistant contract surgeon, which paid one hundred dollars a month, free quarters and rations, and forage for his horse. He was sent to Fort Huachuca, Arizona, arriving just in time to join Lawton's projected expedition. Miles described Wood as "a young athlete," a term signifying great approval. The meeting of Lawton and Wood was depicted by Henry Creelman, Wood's biographer, in colorful terms:

> Captain Lawton met the doctor. The captain had known something of Harvard.
> "What in hell do you want to come out here for?" he asked.

"I'm in the service to be transferred to the line. I hope to be a fighting man," answered the doctor.

Lawton laughed, nodded his head and slapped the doctor approvingly on the shoulder. He was a good judge of fighting men and liked the Yankee's strong, lean figure, the determined cock of his head and the look in his gray eyes.[8]

This expedition, which was to "ascertain if the best athletes in our service could not equal in activity and endurance the Apache warriors," consisted of a company of infantry and a troop of cavalry—"one hundred of the strongest and best soldiers that could be found," wrote Miles. Despite Miles' dislike of the Apache Scouts, Lawton's command was to be guided by twenty Indian Scouts with civilian Tom Horn as their chief. Supplies would be carried by one hundred pack mules under the direction of thirty civilian packers. On May 9 Lawton brought the remainder of this force together with the soldiers commanded by Lieutenant Benson, and Miles' experiment began.

A week later Captain Lawton was much discouraged. For seven days he and his "athletes" were led a merry chase up and down mountains, across valleys and rivers, and through innumerable thickets. That day, however, brought heartening news. Lieutenant R. A. Brown of the Fourth Cavalry arrived at Lawton's camp and informed the captain that he had been tracking the Apaches all day and had succeeded in capturing from them five horses, three saddles, their camp outfit, and a complete Winchester reloading outfit. He had been obliged to leave the trail in order to find water and in the process had found Lawton. The next morning Lieutenant Brown put Lawton on the trail again. That afternoon they met the command of Captain C. A. P. Hatfield, also leading a detachment of Fourth Cavalry. Hatfield reported that on May 15, two days previously, he had come upon the renegades near Santa Cruz, Sonora, and had captured twenty ponies, loaded with plunder. Unfortunately these had been recaptured by the hostiles that afternoon. Hatfield's command had been watering in a narrow canyon three miles from Santa Cruz when the Indians suddenly opened fire on them, somehow having managed to work their way between Hatfield's flankers and his advance guard; during the fight that followed, two soldiers were killed, three wounded, and their horses stampeded. Lawton's command separated from Hatfield's after learning that the hostiles were moving north into Arizona.

Geronimo led his followers into the Dragoon Mountains of southeastern Arizona, apparently hoping to rest. Sorely pressed there by units of the Tenth Cavalry, however, the renegades moved toward Fort Apache, apparently to seek aid from their relatives on the reservation. Captain J. T. Morrison and Troop A of the Tenth Cavalry managed to prevent this, and Geronimo again turned south into Sonora. There he disappeared completely for a time.

Lawton, following Geronimo north, had run short on supplies on May 19. That day—for the only time during the campaign—the packers failed him. He immediately sent Lieutenant Benson to Nogales to ascertain what had happened. Benson found that the officer in command had become intoxicated and had taken his command and the pack train to Nogales, where he found them that evening at eleven o'clock. He preferred charges against the drunken officer (who committed suicide before his trial), then took a portion of the pack train and hurried back to Lawton and the cavalry; in all, he rode ninety miles in nineteen hours.[9] From then until June 5 the unit was relatively inactive, for the trail had been lost. On the sixth, however, they again moved south into Mexico, this time to stay until a conclusion was reached.

Lawton's command was not successful in its mission of wearing the renegades down and forcing them to surrender. Miles later wrote that Lawton did manage to follow the hostiles despite "the Indians trying by every possible device to throw the command off their trail. They frequently abandoned their horses, crossed the rugged mountains, jumping from rock to rock. . . ." Miles made no mention in his reminiscence that within a week

*Apache Scouts and civilian scouts on the trail of the hostiles in 1886.*
Courtesy Arizona Pioneers' Historical Society.

after Lawton's command entered Mexico it was forced to abandon its cavalry horses and dismount. Only the Indian Scouts
commanded by Tom Horn enabled Lawton to remain on the
trail, a fact which Miles reluctantly admitted: "the sharp-eyed
Indian scouts with Lawton would pick up their trail where it was
impossible for the white man to discover any trace of their
movements."[10]

Through June and into July the command tracked the elusive
renegades. The days grew progressively hotter, until it was prac-
tically impossible to move in the daytime. The troops would
start the day's march before four in the morning, travel until
about ten a.m., lie in whatever shade could be found until about
five in the afternoon, then, after a hasty meal, march until nearly
ten in the evening. Rest during the day was impossible because
of the heat, and what sleep was obtained at night was too short.
The soil, where it was not stony, was pulverized dust, which covered men and horses and mingled with sweat to form a crust.
And water for washing was only rarely available during the early

109

summer months. Because of their <u>uncleanliness</u>, owing to conditions in the field, these soldiers became carriers for all types of body <u>vermin</u>. One trooper later described the manner of delousing employed on this march:

> When we happened to rest at a place where shade was available, so that the sun would not blister the bare body, the soldier would strip off his underwear and shirt, go to a nearby ant hill, stir up the pile so as to get the ants excited, and then put his belongings on the ant hill. The ants, especially the large red kind, riled up over the disturbance, would attack the cooties, brood and all, and in a short while the pest had been exterminated.[11]

Another declared: "Our clothes, what we had, were in rags. No one seeing us would have taken us for United States soldiers."

Then in July the weather changed, and the rainy season commenced. Toward evening the showers would fall, drenching the soldiers to the skin and ruining even the few hours of sleep they had been enjoying. They had with them no tents, no shelter, no overcoats, only their saddle blankets. The rain did improve the grass, however, so that the horses began to fare better. Captain Lawton, who was "six feet four inches of brawn and muscle," according to one of the privates in the troop, succumbed to the effects of hardship and exposure and had to be carried in a travois, unable to keep his saddle. "It was not the largest men who stood the marches the best; on the contrary it was the medium sized men," according to a survivor of that expedition.

Still they kept doggedly on the trail. The Indian scouts, as well as the white scouts, were ignorant of the countryside being traversed. The Indians on their little wiry mustang ponies were more inured to hardship and had spare horses to ride; in addition, they knew of hidden water holes, of which the American scouts were ignorant. The hostiles had cut away from the regularly traveled paths, making virgin trails over the sharp mountain ranges. The soldiers, most of whom were suffering from diarrhea, were compelled to follow afoot, for their horses were too jaded to continue. "It was only pure American grit that kept us going at times," wrote a survivor of the terrible ordeal. Shoe soles wore out, and their feet became blistered and swollen, were cut on rocks, and festered from cactus spines.

During this interim General Miles was under great pressure from newspapers. The newspapers of the Territory, as well as in the East, were demanding action and a swift solution, but try as he might he found this impossible. To his wife Mary he complained of the criticism, "If the papers had not so much to say about it, I would like it better."[12] In May and June he had made a tour of the reservations, accompanied by Frederick Remington, at the time a relatively unknown artist, and by the son of Secretary of the Interior L. Q. C. Lamar. This tour made him fear that the hostiles, although reportedly moving deeper into Sonora, might double back and secure aid from their relatives on the reservations. To Commanding General of the Army Sheridan and President Cleveland he stated that he found the young braves on the reservation to be insolent and restless, drinking *tiswin* regularly, and openly complaining of their lot. Why not, he asked, move all Chiricahua and Warm Springs Apaches out of the Territory, perhaps to the Indian Territory (Oklahoma)? "It requires a large force to keep them in check," he explained his reasoning to his wife by letter, "and I am anxious to move them to some other part of the country. I believe this can be done. After much talk I have gotten them to consent to go and look at other lands, and go to Washington to make arrangements about it. . . . About a dozen of the prominent Indians have agreed to go." Sheridan and Cleveland agreed to receive these delegates and discuss removal, and Miles was jubilant; such a removal would mean that the hostiles would "have no assistance or place to go."[13]

Then, early in July, came a report from Mexico that the hostiles were talking to the Prefect at Fronteras about a possible surrender to the Mexican government, a prospect that filled Miles with dread. Such a surrender would rob him of the glory he sought. He therefore abandoned all thought that his "athletes" could win a military victory over the hostiles, and turned to Crook's policy of diplomacy. To seek out the hostiles in Mexico and induce them to agree to a talk with him about surrender, he selected two Chiricahuas from Fort Apache, Martine and Kayitah. He instructed the two to travel to the renegade camp, wherever it might be, and inform them of the impending transfer of all Chiricahuas from Arizona and to request their surrender so that they could join their relatives and friends. Their pass, written at Albuquerque on July 9, stated:

To Officers in Comd U.S. Troops.

This is to certify that the Bearers, Martinez and Ke-ta, two friendly Indians, are under orders to go to the hostile camp of the Apaches and carry a communication of importance. This will be their passport and it is desirable that they be afforded an opportunity to reach their destination and return to Fort Bowie.

Should they meet with any Mexican Officials it is respectfully requested that they be granted a safe journey.

Nelson A. Miles
Brig. General U.S.A.[14]

Naturally an Army officer was needed to accompany the two Indian emissaries, and for this important task Miles turned to the one officer still on active service in the Department best known to the Apaches, Lieutenant Charles B. Gatewood. With Crook gone, Crawford dead, and Britton Davis a civilian, Gatewood was the only man available to Miles who stood a chance of going to the renegade encampment and coming out alive. Miles realized that the hostiles would not meet with an officer unknown to them, and Gatewood had nine years' service in the region, the last three in charge of the Fort Apache agency. Gatewood knew and was known to every member of Geronimo's band, was acquainted with their families and their friends, as well as their enemies, and knew the hardships they had suffered

112

on the reservations. Miles could not send one of the officers he had brought with him into the Department, for only one or two of them had even glimpsed Geronimo. Even Captain Lawton had never met the Apache chief before.

Gatewood was summoned to Miles at Albuquerque in the second week of July, and there he was issued his instructions. Written authority was furnished him to call upon any officer commanding American troops, except those of several small columns then operating in Mexico, for whatever aid might be needed. In his verbal instructions to Gatewood, Miles particularly cautioned the lieutenant not to go near the hostiles with fewer than twenty-five soldiers, for the general feared that the Indians would trap the lieutenant and hold him hostage. Gatewood knew that these orders were impossible to execute; he could never get near Geronimo's camp with that many troops. Nevertheless, he accepted the task and set out.

At Fort Bowie Gatewood organized his party,[15] consisting of himself, Martine and Kayitah, George Wratten as interpreter, Frank Huston as packer, and Tex Whaley as courier. He did not take the stipulated twenty-five-soldier escort for, as he later wrote, "a peace commission would be hampered by a fighting escort in this case, and besides, that number of men deducted from the strength of the garrison [at Fort Bowie] at that time, would spoil the appearance of the battalion at drills and parade."

With their supplies packed and the men mounted on good riding mules, he set out. Three days later, near the Mexican line at Cloverdale, Arizona, he found a detachment consisting of "a company of Infantry, about ten broken down Cavalry horses, and a six-mule team,—and you could have knocked the commanding officer down with a feather when I showed my order and demanded my escort." Actually, he did not want the escort; the commanding officer he mentioned had been one of his instructors at the Military Academy, and he was merely having a little fun, as well as establishing an alibi should Miles ask why he had not taken the escort. The two officers had a pleasant dinner together, after which Gatewood left without the twenty-five soldiers.

Riding southward, Gatewood and his little party soon ran short of rations and were reduced to living on ground corn, thickened into a mush with cane molasses. "I can tell you it wasn't very good eating, but it kept us alive and we got along," declared Wratten, the interpreter. "As the Commissary officer for the party, I wasn't able to do very well by my men at that time. We had no fires—for the Indians might *find us* before we found them."[16] On July 21 they met and joined forces with Lieutenant James Parker, who was leading a troop made up of thirty cavalrymen of the Fourth Regiment and fifteen infantrymen. Gatewood again failed to ask for his twenty-five escorts, commenting that "a deduction of the escort ordered would have put them [Parkers command] 'out of the fight.' "

When Gatewood asked to be put on Geronimo's trail, Parker replied, "the trail is all a myth—I haven't seen any trail since three weeks ago when it was washed out by the rains."

"Well," Gatewood answered, "if that is so I'll go back and report there is no trail."

Parker knew such a comment would put him in an unfavorable light. "No," he said, "if General Miles wants you to be put on a trail, I'll find one and put you on it; if not we'll find Lawton who is surely on a trail."[17]

Gatewood was in poor health at the time and probably would have been happy with an excuse to return to Fort Huachuca. Parker ordered his command south toward Bavispe, Gatewood and his party accompanying them. From Bavispe they continued south to Bacerac, Huachinera, Bacadehuachi, and Nacori, scouting the countryside but finding no trace of the hostiles. Finally, on August 3, they arrived at Lawton's camp on the Arros River, some two hundred and fifty miles south of the border. Gatewood again showed Miles's order, but Lawton was reluctant to allow Gatewood to attach himself to the command. Somewhat sullenly he commented that his orders were to track down Geronimo and kill him or force him to surrender unconditionally; he said he intended to do his job but that Gatewood could come along and try to do his. Parker was delighted to be relieved of the peace mission. Years later he wrote, "I was nearly out of rations; I had no money, no supplies, little transportation and a lot of worthless scouts. Lawton in these respects was well fixed, and I therefore, in the interests of speedy success, thought Lawton should go to the job."

While in camp on the Arros River, Lawton received word that the hostiles were two hundred miles to the north, not far from the border, so he ordered his and Gatewood's commands to move in that direction. With great difficulty their supplies were rafted across the Arros, which was swollen from rains in the mountains; the men and horses had to swim. One day's march north, two couriers arrived to report that the renegades had attacked a Mexican pack train, routed the Mexicans and, after resupplying themselves, were heading for the border. Lawton, on receiving this word, instructed Billy Long, one of his couriers, and Private Lawrence Vinton to report to Lieutenant Benson who was at Oposura with Lawton's supply train. Benson, in turn, was to notify General Miles of what was happening. Lawton was so desirous of getting this information to his superior that he instructed Long and Vinton to ride north as fast as possible and, if one of them should be killed or be unable to continue, to abandon him and continue. They also were instructed to make inquiries all along the way concerning the exact location of the renegades. Should they learn anything concrete, they were to hire Mexican couriers to return to Lawton with such news. Vinton, before leaving, reported to Dr. Wood that he was ill with diarrhea; Wood gave him the few remaining opium tablets in his medical supplies to combat the illness.

On their way north, Long and Vinton met George Woodward, a Californian ranching near the Sonoran village of Guasaguas. He reported that the hostiles had been seen in the nearby mountains

115

and probably would take refuge in the Torres Mountains. Long and Vinton hired one of Woodward's vaqueros to take this message to Lawton, then continued on their errand, reaching Oposura and delivering their dispatches to Lieutenant Benson. The next day they set out on their return trip, Lieutenant Benson accompanying them. Rumors were rife of Indians in the vicinity so they decided to travel at night. During a storm that night, while crossing the mountains, Vinton became separated from the other two and was lost. Wet and chilled to the bone, sick, and exhausted, he crawled under a projecting rock for the remainder of the night, then set out to follow the other two the next morning. A little before sunup at the top of a divide, he suddenly came upon the renegades. However, he escaped unseen. Next he was arrested by Mexican civil officials, who thought him a rustler. Eventually he was able to rejoin Lawton's command near Fronteras and the Torres Mountains.[18]

Lawton had gone to Fronteras, not only because of the report of Long and Vinton, but also because Martine and Kayitah had talked with some Mexicans who informed them that Geronimo was at Fronteras talking surrender with the Mexican government. Upon receipt of this news, Gatewood had detached his command and had hurried ahead, escorted by six of Lawton's soldiers. Departing at two o'clock on the morning of August 19, they made seventy miles that day, encamping near Fronteras that evening. The next day in Fronteras, they learned that two squaws indeed had entered the village and had indicated Geronimo's willingness to consider surrender to the Mexicans, provided the terms were acceptable. Lieutenant Wilber E. Wilder of the American Army had happened to be in the village when the two squaws arrived, and had held a conference with them. He had advised them not to deal with the Mexicans, but to make terms with General Miles instead. Wilder also had wired Miles that Geronimo was seeking surrender terms with the Mexicans, and Miles, in turn, had sent a dispatch containing this information to Captain Lawton. However, Lawton had not received this

116

word by August 20 when Gatewood arrived at Fronteras. In addition, Wilder had persuaded the Mexican officials to release the squaws, convincing the Mexicans that the squaws should be allowed to return to the renegade camp in order to tell Geronimo to bring his band in to surrender. The squaws had been allowed to depart with three horses laden with food, supplies, and mescal

The Prefect of the district actually had no intention of accepting an Apache surrender. Secretly he had been amassing about two hundred soldiers, intending to get the hostiles drunk, then to murder the lot.[19] However, Geronimo understood the Mexican mind and anticipated treachery. Later he told Lieutenant Gatewood that he had never had any intention of surrendering to the Mexicans; he had opened negotiations with them only to give his band time to rest, and he had wanted the squaws to be allowed to return with badly needed food and supplies.

The Prefect at Fronteras was greatly annoyed as more and more American troops arrived, for he anticipated getting the reward for killing the notorious Geronimo. He could not order the Americans out of his district because Governor Torres of Sonora had given his permission for their presence. The Prefect did insist that the Americans should not go east, the direction which the squaws had taken when they left the village, for this would interfere with his plans. While Lieutenant Wilder plied the Prefect with wine and compliments, Gatewood took "an escort of six or eight men which Wilder gave me, Tom Horn and a Mexican as interpreters," and set out in pursuit of the squaws. First they went south for some six miles to give the impression to the Prefect that pursuit was not their intention, then, at dark, they turned eastward into the mountains. Early the next morning they circled northward and found the trail of the squaws who had been in Fronteras and followed it. A runner was then sent to Lawton telling what had happened and asking that he follow as rapidly as possible.

After three days of following the squaws' trail, Gatewood began to find fresh "sign," and he and his men proceeded more cautiously. A piece of flour sacking was tied to a stick and held aloft as a flag of truce as they moved forward, for they were in country "full of likely places for ambush." The lieutenant noted that he was quite willing "to give Kateah and Martine a chance to reap glory several hundred yards ahead." Suddenly they came to the head of a canyon leading into the Bavispe Valley, a canyon so likely to produce an ambush that even Martine and Kayitah halted, not wishing to proceed. Gatewood described what ensued:

> The canyon was uninviting, as one might say, soberly unattractive, and besides there was a pair of faded canvas pants hanging on a bush nearby. A canyon like that with a banner on its head would make anybody halt. In the discussion of the matter, everybody gave his opinion, but nobody knew how to interpret what the pants had to say. My idea was that the two Indians should proceed several hundred yards ahead as usual, then several soldiers with George Wratten with the pack mules, and Frank Huston following, should come next; two more soldiers and myself, and a hundred yards in rear, two more soldiers. I still think that was the best plan, but the two Indians said that they were not greedy, but willing to divide the glory to be had equally among the whole party. Then everybody also volunteered to go ahead with the Indians, and I volunteered, so we all went together. That proved to be a very innocent canyon, and I was sorry after we got through that I had not gone ahead.[20]

A few miles farther on, they reached the Bavispe River. There just at the base of a mountain they made camp in a canebrake that afforded a view of more than half a mile of the surrounding countryside. Gatewood stationed a sentinel atop the peak. In case of trouble the canebrake offered several good hiding places. "This peace commission business was getting decidedly tiresome," he wryly commented on that moment years later. Just for good measure, he also placed the white flag high up on a century plant, for what protection that might offer. He said he knew it would not "make a man bullet proof," but he did want to inform any hostiles who might be observing them that he and his men

118

came in peace. He then ordered his men to sleep. Later he learned that Geronimo indeed had them under scrutiny all the time with his field glasses and was wondering what "fool small party" was dogging his footsteps.

Early the next morning, August 24, Gatewood told the two Scouts, Martine and Kayitah, to go ahead alone, to try to locate Geronimo, and to have a conference with him if possible. At the conference they were to arrange a meeting between Gatewood and the Apache chieftain. The two left, climbing a mountain four miles away on which they felt certain Geronimo would be encamped. "We realized the danger of thus proceeding, but we promised General Miles that we would try our best to bring back Geronimo, and we intended to do it," they later declared. "At two o'clock that afternoon we came near to the place where his camp was pitched. Between his camp and us, Geronimo had his men stationed out among the rocks with their guns guarding the camp against attack. We proceeded as carefully as we could but they saw us coming. We knew that they might shoot at us at any moment. In fact, there was much danger of their doing this. We learned later that they were doubtful about what they should do as we came up. However, Kayitah had a cousin in Geronimo's camp who recognized him and who did not want to see him killed."[21] With permission from Geronimo, the cousin jumped atop a rock and called to ask why the two were approaching. They replied that they were messengers for General Miles and Lieutenant Gatewood and wished to talk peace with Geronimo.

The war leader of the renegade Apaches told the two to come into his camp, and all seated themselves at the campfire for talk —which Apaches loved to do endlessly. "Geronimo told us," Martine later declared, "that while he had in the past broken faith with the American soldiers he was now really willing to surrender and make peace." He then had some mescal (cactus) cooked, and from it he took in his hands enough to make a lump about the size of a man's heart. This he squeezed together, wrapped it

119

up, and told Martine and Kayitah to take it to Gatewood, saying it was a token of his surrender. "When the mescal had been sent, there would be no reason for Gatewood to doubt his earnestness in planning to give up," Martine stated.

Kayitah remained in Geronimo's camp while Martine took the mescal to Gatewood, explained what had passed, and pinpointed the enemy camp. Martine also brought a message from Nachez, who said that Gatewood and his men would be perfectly safe in entering the hostiles' camp if they "behaved themselves." Gatewood and his men knew that Nachez was the real chief of the Chiricahuas and that his word did carry some weight, but they still could not relax. The lieutenant ordered the mescal which Geronimo had sent to be sliced, and he and his men ate it between bread. "We lay on our rifles all night, just to be ready in case of need, for we had not yet had our talk with them, and didn't know just what they would do," packer George Wratten later said. They also were aware that should a fight develop, they would have no help available, for a note arrived from Captain Lawton just at dark:

My Dear Gatewood:

I have just arrived in Brown's camp and have rec'd your notes. My Pack Train got off the trail yesterday, and will not be in until in the night. I have sent Lt. Smith back on fresh horse to bring up your tobacco and some rations and will send them over to you as soon as they arrive. I have ordered them to come forward if it kills the mules. It will be too late for me to go over tonight, and besides I do not wish to interfere with you, but will come over if you wish me. Send a man back to conduct pack mules over, and write me what you want. I *hope* and *trust* your efforts will meet with success.

Yours,
H. W. Lawton, Capt.[22]

Gatewood did not order sentries out for the night, however, and they slept unmolested in the canebrake.

At sunrise on August 25, Gatewood and his small party started up the mountain, still holding aloft their white flag of truce. Within a mile of Geronimo's camp, they were met by an unarmed Chiricahua warrior sent to deliver the same message brought by Martine, *i.e.,* that Geronimo wished to meet to discuss terms of surrender. While Gatewood was speaking with him, three armed hostiles appeared with a further communication, this one from Nachez. The hereditary Chiricahua chief suggested that the site of the meeting be a nearby bend in the Bavispe River where wood, water, grass, and shade were available. Nachez also wanted most of Gatewood's party to return to the site where they had spent the previous night, and suggested that the approaching Lawton might also encamp there and await the results of the conference, as should any other troops which might arrive. To all this Gatewood agreed, giving orders for most of his party to turn back and writing instructions for Lawton, while the Indians exchanged signals, consisting of "smoke and shot," with their comrades waiting at the mountain camp.

As Gatewood turned to the designated site of meeting, his party had been reduced to himself, Martine, Wratten, who would act as interpreter, and two soldiers, Martin Koch, and George Buehler. Arriving at the bend in the river, he halted his men outside the meeting space and told them to wait. Riding on in, he unsaddled and threw his saddle over a log, all his arms attached to it. Thus he stood, alone and unarmed, when within ten minutes the hostiles began drifting in quietly and likewise unsaddling. Somehow in taking seats, Geronimo's brother-in-law located himself on Gatewood's saddle, while the lieutenant found himself sitting on that Indian's saddle. Among the last to arrive was Geronimo. He laid his Winchester down about twenty feet away and came up to shake Gatewood's hand, remarking on the lieutenant's thinness and inquiring about his health. He then signalled the rest of Gatewood's party to ride in and unsaddle, which they did. As Gatewood later described this event, he paused to inquire:

> Gentle reader, turn back, take another look at his [Geronimo's]
> face, imagine him looking me square in the eyes, and watching
> my every movement, twenty-four bucks sitting around fully armed,
> my small party scattered in their various duties incident to a peace
> commissioner's camp; and say if you blame me for feeling chilly
> twitching movements.[23]

George Wratten was even more graphic: "Well—Yes—We did
begin to feel a *little* creepy when we saw we were so badly out-
numbered and surrounded. There were about thirty-five or forty
hostiles [he was counting the squaws as well as the braves]
around us before the pow-wow started, and I began to feel as
though there might just as well have been three or four hundred."

The first formal words to pass between hostiles and Americans
was an Apache request for tobacco and liquor. Gatewood truthfully replied that he had but little tobacco and no whiskey. The
tobacco was passed, and soon almost everyone in the camp, Indian and soldier, was puffing away at cigarettes rolled Apache-
fashion in corn husks. The next thoughts were of lunch. As
neither side had brought food, some Apache warriors and George
Wratten went out in search of game. Geronimo then announced
that his party was ready to hear General Miles' message.

Gatewood said it briefly: "Surrender, and you will be sent to
join the rest of your people in Florida, there to await the decision of the President as to your final disposition. Accept these
terms or fight it out to the bitter end." While the translation
was taking place, the hostile warriors listened attentively. Several
old squaws commented to each other loudly. Apache custom dictated that these matriarchs had the freedom of the conference
camp; while they could not participate directly, they could listen
to what was being said and make their feelings known, seemingly
only to each other but usually in voices that everyone could hear.
When the import of Miles's message became clear to the Apaches,
there was "a silence of several weeks," as Gatewood described it.

122

Actually it lasted only a moment or two, after which Geronimo passed a hand across his eyes and extended his arms forward. Both hands trembled badly, and he asked again if Gatewood had something to drink. "We have been on a three day's drunk," he said, "on the mescal the Mexicans sent us by the squaws who went to Fronteras. The Mexicans expected to play their usual trick of getting us drunk and killing us, but we have had the fun; and now I feel a little shaky. You need not fear giving me a drink of whiskey, for our spree passed off without a single fight, as you can see by looking at the men sitting in this circle, all of whom you know. Now, in Fronteras, there is plenty of wine and mescal, and the Mexicans and Americans are having a good time. We thought perhaps you had brought some with you." It was obvious to Gatewood that despite his drinking Geronimo had kept remarkably well informed about the activities of both Mexican and American pursuers.

The lieutenant replied that he and his men had left Fronteras in such a hurry that they had neglected to provide themselves with "desirable drinkables." Since there was nothing to drink, Geronimo said they should go ahead with their business. He stated that he and his followers would leave the warpath only on condition that they be allowed to return to their Arizona reservation, occupy the farms they had held when they left, and be furnished with the usual rations and farming implements with guaranteed exemption from punishment for what they had done since leaving. By the latter, he meant no civil trial by civilians. If Gatewood was authorized to accede to those terms, he concluded, the war would be over.

"I explained that the Big Chief, General Miles, whom they had never met, had ordered me to say just so much and no more, and that they knew it would make matters worse if I exceeded my instructions," Gatewood later wrote. He continued that this would be the renegades' last chance to surrender, for if the war continued they all would be either hunted to the death, or, if they surrendered thereafter or were captured, the terms would not be so liberal. Both Geronimo and Gatewood were speaking in emphatic terms, each stating his absolute wishes, not what he could accept as a compromise.

An hour or more of discussion followed, mostly filled by Geronimo in an impassioned speech. In Apache fashion he detailed the history of his tribe, their troubles, and the frauds and thieving of reservation agents. Gatewood personally could agree with most of what Geronimo said, but he also knew that the Army could do nothing about these matters, which were in the hands of the Department of the Interior. And for purposes of bargaining, he could not state his agreement. So he sat silent through the tirade, then quietly reiterated Miles' demands. The Apaches thereupon withdrew to one side of the clearing for a private conference that lasted another hour. By the time this caucus ended, it was noon and time for food and coffee. After lunch the talk resumed. Geronimo said that for the Chiricahuas to surrender the whole Southwest "to a race of intruders" was too much for Miles to demand, that he and his followers had decided they would return to their lands at San Carlos or they would fight to the death. "Take us to the reservation or fight," was his ultimatum. He delivered it while looking Gatewood directly in the eyes. He meant what he said.

"I couldn't take him to the reservation, and I couldn't fight, neither could I run nor yet feel comfortable," Gatewood declared. They had reached an impasse out of which there seemed no honorable way. Gatewood and his men grew visibly nervous, wondering what their fate would be. Nachez apparently noticed this, for he said that, whether the war continued or was ended, the lieutenant and his party would be safe so long as they did not start hostilities, that they had come as friends and would be allowed to depart in peace. Knowing Nachez's influence to be sufficient to guarantee his words, Gatewood and his men breathed easier.

At this point in the conversation, Gatewood had only one last card to play, and he chose that moment to lay it on the table.

He informed the hostiles that to agree only to a return to San Carlos would be a mistake, for all Chiricahua and Warm Springs Apaches, all four to five hundred of them, were to be removed to Florida to join the seventy-seven who had already surrendered under Chihuahua. Included among those already in Florida were Nachez' mother and his daughter, as well as Geronimo's family. No Chiricahuas or Warm Springs Indians would be left in Arizona, so that to return to the reservation would be only to live among their traditional enemies, the White Mountain, Aravaipa, and other Apache subgroups.

The hostiles were stunned by this information, for they knew nothing of it. Again they withdrew to caucus, consuming still another hour. Afterwards Geronimo announced that they had decided to stay on the warpath but that they wished to discuss it further during the night. Gatewood protested at a conference lasting all day and all night too, but he had no choice but to agree. A warrior was sent to find a beef to kill to furnish meat for the projected Apache night talk, but he returned after a while to say that no beef was to be had. More smoking and conversation followed into the evening hours.

Geronimo suddenly shifted the course of the conversation as darkness fell. What kind of man was General Miles, he wanted to know. He said he knew General Crook well and might surrender to him, but knew nothing of Miles. He asked Miles' age, size, color of eyes and hair, and whether his voice was harsh or agreeable to the ear. Did he talk much or little, and did he mean more or less than he said? "Does he look you in the eyes or down at the ground when he talks? Has he many friends among his people and do they generally believe what he says? Do the soldiers and officers like him? Has he had experience with other Indians? Is he cruel or kind-hearted? Would he keep his promises?" Gatewood answered each of these questions truthfully to the best of his knowledge, pleading ignorance on some points. The Indians listened intently to each of his answers. Then Geronimo said, "He must be a good man since the Great Father sent him from Washington, and he sent you all this distance to us." Apparently he had made up his mind, but gave no indication of what it was.

Gatewood suggested that his party would return to its original camp some four miles downstream, where Lawton had arrived during the day and was waiting. He further suggested that during the night Geronimo and his followers continue their discussion and have their medicine man "take a few glances into the future." To this the hostiles agreed, but before parting Geronimo had a final question for the lieutenant.

"We want your advice. Consider yourself one of us and not a white man. Remember all that has been said today, and as an Apache, what would you advise us to do under the circumstances?"

Gatewood did not hesitate: to have done so would have been fatal to his mission. "I would trust General Miles and take him at his word," he replied.

As his reply was translated, the hostiles looked very solemn. Every one of them knew Gatewood, and they trusted him as a man who had never knowingly lied to them. Finally Geronimo broke the silence to say that the next morning he would let Gatewood know what they had decided. Before the Americans departed, however, Geronimo bespoke an Apache desire for the lieutenant to ride to the nearest American post and communicate with Miles to see if the general's terms might be modified to what the Apaches wanted, a return to the reservation and no punishment. He said that he would send warriors along to protect Gatewood, to warn him of any danger from Mexicans or anyone else. To this proposal Gatewood replied that it would be a useless journey, that Miles had already fully considered the matter and had made up his mind. His message was final, and nothing Gatewood might say or do would change it. With that, the lieutenant shook hands all around with the Indians, and he and his men set out for Lawton's camp.

Not far from the bend in the Bavispe River where the conference had been held, Gatewood was overtaken by Chappo, Geronimo's son. The lad said nothing as he reined his horse alongside that of the lieutenant, and Gatewood rode patiently, waiting for Chappo to speak. After about a mile, when the Indian still had not spoken, Gatewood asked him where he was going. "With you," Chappo replied, "I'm going to sleep close to you tonight, and tomorrow I'll return to our camp. I have my father's permission to do so." Gatewood could not allow the request, for the Apache Scouts at Lawton's camp bitterly hated Geronimo and probably would murder the lad as he slept. "The risk of getting a knife stuck in him during the night was too great to take," Gatewood stated later. "It is easy to understand that injury to him in our camp would never do." In short, the boy's death would have made a continuation of the war inevitable. This he explained to Chappo, who reluctantly agreed to return to his father. Gatewood extracted a promise from him that he would explain the reasons for disapproval to his father, for he did not want to insult either Chappo or Geronimo. Later Gatewood learned that sending the boy back for the reason stated had impressed the wily Apache leader.

Gatewood and his men arrived in Lawton's camp long after dark, explained what had happened, and then proceeded to get much-needed rest. That rest was interrupted early the next morning, August 26, by the cries of the Scouts on picket, who set up a call for "Bse-chee Day-son," Gatewood's Apache name meaning "Big Nose." The hostiles were approaching and asking for the lieutenant. With his interpreters, Gatewood went out to meet "our handsome friend and several of his bucks a few hundred yards from camp." When the hostiles saw him approaching, they dismounted, unsaddled their horses, and put their weapons across their saddles—all except Geronimo, who kept a large pistol under his coat beside his left hip.

Gatewood and the Apaches seated themselves under an ancient mesquite tree and again held a conference, while the American camp waited silently. They made no overt moves, knowing that such would only precipitate a crisis. First the Apaches wanted Gatewood to repeat his entire description of General Miles, which he did. In the process the renegades apparently were satisfied with the lieutenant's answers, for immediately afterward Geronimo stated that he, his warriors, and his squaws and children were willing to meet the general at some point in the United States to talk and to surrender to him in person—provided that Gatewood and the American soldiers would accompany them to the border to protect them from Mexicans and other Americans they might encounter. Geronimo wanted his warriors to be allowed to keep their arms until they had formally surrendered; furthermore, he wanted individuals of each party to have the freedom of the other's camp, and he wished Gatewood to march with the Apaches and sleep with them when possible. To all this Gatewood agreed, then led Geronimo into the American camp to introduce him to Lawton and Leonard Wood, who had never met the Apache chief. Lawton likewise approved the agreement just reached, whereupon all the hostiles entered the American camp. All, soldiers and Indians, visibly relaxed. The Apache wars were over, provided Miles honored his promise to meet Geronimo.

Gatewood took time later that morning to write a letter to his wife wherein he gave details of his past hours:

Aug. 26, '86

My Dear Wife,

I am now in camp on the Bavispe River about 30 miles south of San Bernardino. Well, I've had a talk with Geronimo in person. It took all day yesterday & made me very tired. He and I are grown to be great friends. He laid his arms down and gave me a hearty shake of the hand. My escort was present & so was his. [There were] about 20 bucks all around, but my escort stayed at one side under arms. So you see I ran no risk.

This morning Ger. came to this camp—Capt. L's—. I went out to meet him & he walked right into camp leaving his gun & horse outside. He told me he would go with me any where as I never harmed him, but always helped him along when he was at [Fort]

128

Apache. He wanted to meet Capt. L., so they had a hugging match before the whole command.[24]

Yesterday I delivered Gen. Miles' message to them, but they did not want to go to Florida. They would agree to go back to the White Mtns., the same as before. He begged me to see Gen. M. in person & lay the case before him. They are tired of fighting & want to be united with their families once more. They were all cheerful, feeling sure that since Gen. M. sent me all the way from [Fort] Stanton to meet them he must have a good heart & they believed that I would do my best in talking to them to get their families together. Every one of them showed great pleasure at meeting me & they would remind me every few minutes of my promise to talk to Gen. Miles.

They cracked a lot of jokes and smoked lots of tobacco & were in a jolly good humor generally, except Natchez. He was very blue. All he had to say was that he wanted to meet his children. I really felt sorry for him, for I know how it is to yearn after one's family. It makes me homesicker than usual to look at him. I want to see my wife and little ones too. . . . My mission will be ended when Geronimo & Miles meet and I shall be done with Mexico. If the war continues, I may not get home as soon as I like, but my gadding about down here will end. I do so much want to be with you. But I feel rather light hearted today. If there is no bad break made, the hostiles will surrender & the war will end. I get so happy that I have to sit on myself to keep me down thro' fear of disappointment.

Geronimo dislikes [Captain Wirt] Davis, Chatto & Mickey Free. He said to me, "You can come to our camp any where. You are no more responsible for this war than I. I know you. If Gen. Miles won't make peace, you come & tell us. Never fear harm. If I want to talk, I will come to your camp any where and feel safe. I will go with you now alone to Capt. L's camp if you desire it. That's the way I feel toward you."

He sent a man ahead this morning to tell me to meet him just outside [our camp]. I did so. He laid down his gun, took me by the hand & said, "I'll go with you." He is now loafing around the camp having his talk with Capt. L. They really want to surrender, but they want their families with [them]. Can any one blame a man for wanting to see his wife and children. Wouldn't I prance around lively if they moved you off to Florida? Ger. wants to go to Washington to talk to the Great Father. I will write you again

129

*Lieutenant Gatewood and his wife, about 1881.* Courtesy National Archives.

the soonest possible. The courier leaves directly & I have yet a full report to make to Gen. M.

Hoping to embrace my whole family soon, I am still your loving Hub.[25]

That Gatewood was not lying to his wife, trying to assume more importance in the surrender and thus gain stature in her eyes, is corroborated by statements of George Wratten, who served as interpreter for much of the peace talks. Wratten later wrote, "Would you believe me?—old Geronimo told Gatewood, 'I am your friend, and I'll go with you anywhere.' He always had great faith in Lieutenant Gatewood, for he had never deceived him. He was the only man who could safely have gotten within gunshot of the old savage, and General Miles knew that when he sent him out."

But before Gatewood could embrace his wife, and before Nachez and the Apaches could see their families, they all had to get safely out of Mexico, and Miles had to meet with them to formalize the surrender. These two steps did not prove simple.

# SEVEN

## GERONIMO'S

## FINAL SURRENDER

These people [the Apaches] were anxious to give themselves up, but, of course, upon the best possible terms. They recognized the fact that there was no longer any inaccessible stronghold for them to rest in. Hitherto they could always find a place, especially in the Sierra Madre mountains, where they could be safe from pursuit, but when they found, as in the last campaign, that there was no place safe for them, no place even in the immense stretch of mountains beyond the regions penetrated by no others than themselves, or across the low country stretching to the Pacific coast [of Mexico], they knew it was only a question of time as to their annihilation. The prospect of surrender under the circumstances was welcome. Pursued so that they had no rest, they looked with favor on a chance to lay down their arms with a hope of having their lives spared.

The only thing that an Apache respects is force, and as the word Apache indicates that he regards himself as *the* man, another who gets the better of him commands his profoundest respect. This is why he tortures a cowardly enemy but never a brave one.

It was characteristic that the surrender should take place under the circumstances. They could have no rest and they feared no treachery; hence delivered themselves to a foe they knew superior to themselves.

Charles B. Gatewood, "Report," Albuquerque, N. M.,
October 15, 1886, to General Miles, Gatewood Collection.

As THE REMAINDER OF THE HOSTILES, including women and children, had come into Lawton's camp that morning of August 26, the captain wanted to start immediately for the border. As senior officer in the camp, he had the responsibility for getting Geronimo safely to a peace conference with General Miles. Understandably he was nervous that Geronimo might bolt into the mountains as he had done earlier with Crook—and Lawton did not want such a blemish on his record. Geronimo was agreeable to moving, and that afternoon and the next day passed peacefully, the Indians, accompanied by Gatewood and George Wratten, moving in advance of the soldiers. "We weren't accompanied home by any of the Army, but went along by ourselves, out of sight most of the time of any troops," Wratten recalled later. With pride he stated, "We hadn't gone out with any of the Army, and we didn't need any of them. We knew better than to try to catch Geronimo, or take him in, with any of the soldiers around!"

The night of August 27-28 was spent near the San Bernardino River, still in Sonora. The Indians set out the next morning quietly enough. Before Lawton and his troops could begin their march, however, a Mexican force of approximately two hundred infantrymen suddenly came up from the direction of Fronteras. Geronimo learned of their approach and would have made a dash for the mountains had Gatewood not reassured him that no harm would befall him. He pointed out that Lawton and his force would wait to parlay with the Mexicans, while Geronimo and his Apaches would continue toward the border. This Geronimo consented to do, moving along rapidly at "an eight or ten mile gait." Flankers and a small rear guard were thrown out, the rear guard consisting principally of Nachez and his own warriors. After about an hour, with no pursuit in sight, the hostiles halted, not wishing to get too far separated from their escort of American soldiers; also, should fighting occur between the Mexicans and Lawton's men, they wanted to participate on the Ameri-

133

can side. Geronimo was anxious for one last battle against his ancient Mexican enemies.

While the Indians had been moving north, Lawton had made contact with the Mexicans, but peacefully. As the Mexicans approached, Lieutenant Abiel L. Smith, Packer Tom Horn, and Surgeon Leonard Wood had mounted their mules and had ridden up to the Mexican column. They found it commanded by the Prefect of Arizpe. Lieutenant Smith delivered Lawton's message, which was to "pull out, and keep out of the way." This the Prefect refused, stating that he had come to attack the renegades. Even when informed that the Apache hostiles had surrendered to the Americans and were being taken north of the line, he still angrily insisted on a battle. Lawton replied sharply that any attack on the Apaches would bring an American attack on the Mexicans. This the Prefect did not wish. However, he did want to make absolutely certain that the Apaches intended to surrender, and he wanted this assurance from Geronimo himself. Finally Lawton agreed to arrange a conference between the Prefect and the Apache war chief, each side to bring ten armed men as escorts. The Mexicans thereupon encamped, and Lawton sent Leonard Wood to Gatewood with instructions to persuade Geronimo to meet with the Prefect. The Apache leader steadfastly refused until Lawton himself came to the Indian camp and promised protection during the interview. Geronimo then assented, the site for the interview to be near the Indian camp.

The Prefect with his ten men, all heavily armed, arrived first and was received by the Americans "with due formality and hospitality." Then Geronimo, at the head of his ten warriors, approached cautiously through the bushes. He was dragging a Winchester rifle by the muzzle with his left hand and had his six-shooter handy on the front of his left hip. Both sides obviously expected treachery, for such had been the history of their meetings for centuries. As the Indians advanced toward the tree under which the Mexicans were standing, one of the Mexicans nervously moved his revolver in his belt. Within seconds every

Indian weapon was cocked and pointed at the Mexicans. The Apaches doubtless would have fired had not Lawton's men moved between them and their targets. With American persuasion, hammers were lowered, and tempers cooled. Gatewood later described the interview that followed:

> As he [Geronimo] approached, I introduced him to the Prefect, whose name I have forgotten, and [I] stepped back a little in rear of the latter. After shaking hands, the Mexican shoved his revolver around to his front, and Geronimo drew his half way out of the holster, the whites of his eyes turning red and a most fiendish expression on his face. The former put his hands behind him, and the latter dropped his right hand by his side. Thus serious trouble was averted. The Prefect asked why he had not surrendered at Fronteras. Geronimo replied that he did not want to be murdered. Prefect: "Are you going to surrender to the Americans?". Geronimo: "I am, because I can trust them. Whatever happens, they will not murder me or my people." Prefect: "Then I shall go along, and see that you *do* surrender." Geronimo: "No. You are going south and I am going north. I'll have nothing to do with you or any of your people." And so it was.[1]

Lieutenant Walsh later recalled, "I was standing to one side a few feet from the Indians and what impressed me was the scowls on the Indians' faces and the hatred they showed towards the Mexicans. . . . The Mexicans were decidedly nervous and I have no doubt were very glad when the interview was over. They would have stood no chance [in a fight against the Indians]."[2]

Lawton's report to Miles that day commented that the Indians "do not trust the Mexicans and are afraid they will try and play them false some way. Any statement that they authorized or wish to make terms with the Mexicans, the Indians say are false. . . . Geronimo also told me that he moved away from Fronteras because he feared treachery on the part of the Mexicans." This information proved valuable to Miles, for within hours after its receipt came a telegram from Governor Torres of Sonora stating that the Prefect of Arizpe had reported the Apaches wished to surrender to him but was prevented by American troops from doing so.[3] Miles responded by quoting Lawton's message to the governor.

At least, Miles sent part of the message. In a second section of that same telegraph to Miles, Lawton had reported that his command would be at San Bernardino, Arizona, "with Geronimo, Natchez and their followers, in all 38, tomorrow, the 29th inst." He concluded, "He [Geronimo] came up to this country to surrender and I feel sure he will do so. I hope Genl Miles will not delay and will send instructions soon. So many complications arise that I sometimes fear the result." Each incident was wearing on Lawton's nerves; he was more and more afraid that somehow, for some reason, Geronimo might flee into the Sierra again.

The next morning, August 29, the Indians resumed their march toward the border. With Gatewood and the Apaches were Lieutenant Thomas J. Clay and Surgeon Leonard Wood. Lieutenant Clay had just joined Lawton's command. He had volunteered for service with Lawton and had been sent south with supplies; interestingly, his orders were, after delivering the supplies, "to enlist 20 Teremari Indians in North Sinaloa and scout through the Yaqui Cañon, and try to locate Geronimo and his hostiles." Miles indeed was turning to General Crook's methods of containing the Apaches. "While en route on this mission," Clay recalled, "I met a courier who told me that Lawton had turned north in pursuit of the Indians. I then cut across country and joined Lawton's command at Cachuta Ranch. As there was then no necessity for my going to the Yaqui country [Geronimo having surrendered to Gatewood], Lawton appointed me Adjutant of his command, which position I held during the balance of the campaign."[4]

About two o'clock on the afternoon of August 29, the Apaches halted to allow Lawton and his troops to catch up somewhat, but hour after hour passed with no sign of the soldiers—or of the rations with them. The Indians were not nearly as alarmed about the failure of the soldiers to arrive as were the three Americans; calmly the Indians made camp and the squaws began preparing the evening meal. Gatewood wandered through the camp watching the cooking. Among the three of them, he, Clay, and Wood had only one can of condensed milk. Stopping at the fire of Perrico, brother-in-law of Geronimo, Gatewood presented that warrior's squaw with the can, bowed as he did so, and struck up a conversation. Over an open fire the squaw was roasting chunks of venison from a buck killed that morning. She also had flour, sugar, and coffee. To hungry men such as Gatewood, Clay, and Wood, the squaw was preparing "a toothsome repast." Seeing the American's hungry faces, Perrico, with grace and dignity, invited them to eat with him. They needed no second invitation; Gatewood recalled, "The squaw made everything clean, the edibles were well cooked, and it pleased her to see us eat so heartily."

That evening, before dark, Geronimo became entranced with Surgeon Wood's rifle, a Hotchkiss, a model he had never seen. He asked if he might look at the weapon's mechanism. "I must confess I felt a little nervous, for I thought it might be a device to get hold of one of our weapons," Wood confided to his diary. In such a situation he could not openly object, however, and even showed Geronimo how the weapon worked. The Apache chieftain then asked for some ammunition, stating that he wished to fire at a target. Loading the weapon, he aimed and shot, missing the target but almost hitting one of his warriors. This near-fatal accident he regarded as hilarious, rolling on the ground, laughing loudly, and saying repeatedly, "good gun."[5]

On August 30, Lawton, the soldiers, and the pack train joined the hostiles, and the day was spent waiting for word from General Miles. On the thirty-first all moved to Guadalupe Canyon and again encamped to await some message from Miles. Lawton was gone most of the day to a point where he could communicate with headquarters, and the Indians grew restless in his absence. Several months before they had fought a skirmish in

137

Guadalupe Canyon and had killed several troops: they feared that the soldiers, remembering the battle, might turn on them seeking revenge for their dead comrades. In fact, the officer left in command by Lawton expressed his willingness to have a battle with the Indians on the spot and to end all question of their surrender by annihilating them. The hostiles grew so restless that at one point they mounted their ponies and started out of the canyon, although there was no other water around for six or eight miles. The squaws and children were in the lead, the warriors following. Gatewood, seeing Geronimo among those heading up the trail, mounted and set out at a gallop to catch up. The soldiers likewise mounted and followed, but at a more leisurely pace.

When Gatewood reached Geronimo's side, the Apache war chief asked the lieutenant what he would do in case the soldiers started firing. Gatewood replied that, if possible, he would ride toward the troops and endeavor to halt the shooting; otherwise, he said, he would go with the Apaches. Nachez, who had joined the conversation, said, "You must go with us, for fear some of our men might believe you treacherous and try to kill you." Gatewood cautioned the chiefs, as he had done previously, to keep a good lookout but to trust the soldiers and General Miles. He also said to keep a sharp watch for other American soldiers in the vicinity; he reminded them that Mexican troops had gotten close to them on other occasions when their lookouts had relaxed their vigilance. The Apaches finally agreed with all he said, made camp, and were again united with Lawton's command. Yet even then they feared everyone except Gatewood, and proposed that he flee with them into the mountains near Fort Bowie where they would wait while the lieutenant went to communicate with General Miles and arranged their surrender to him. Gatewood wrote, "I knew the General was not at Fort Bowie, and by the time I could go there and communicate with him, I feared they might be attacked and run out of the country and leaving me 'holding the bag.' So I advised strongly against such a proceeding." He knew, as did Lawton, that any officer who allowed the hostiles to flee, or who could be considered responsible for it, would ruin his career in the Army.

During that day while Lawton was gone, Gatewood learned that some of the young officers had conceived a plot to lure Geronimo into their camp on a pretext and murder him. Fearing Geronimo and the Apaches might hear of this plot, Gatewood that evening proposed to Lawton that he, Gatewood, take his baggage and join some other command. He said that his orders from Miles had been to see that Martine and Kayitah made contact with Geronimo and deliver a message to him, that all this had been accomplished, and that he therefore was no longer under orders to stay with Lawton's command. Lawton responded by saying it was necessary for Gatewood to remain, that they both would be in "trouble" if the Indians fled into the mountains again, and that he would use force, if necessary, to keep Gatewood with him. Gatewood stayed.

During the period August 29 to September 3 many telegrams passed over the wires or by way of heliograph between Lawton and General Miles about the projected formal surrender of Geronimo. On August 29, Miles wired, "If the command [Indians] moves to San Bernardino, it should go with your command or place hostages in your hands that they will act in good faith, otherwise they might not be there." Miles' adjutant, Captain William A. Thompson, added, "General says you can tell those Indians the safest thing they can do is to surrender as prisoners of war. Some of them can remain in your camp as a guarantee. You are fully authorized to receive their surrender. General says not to allow any of your officers or men to put themselves in the hands of the Indians, but the more hostages they put in your hands the better. By command of Gen'l Miles."

The desk soldiers of Miles' staff did not understand the situation in the field, just as the general himself did not. On August 30 Lawton tried to correct their misconceptions in a telegram sent to Miles from San Bernardino, Arizona:

Sir:

Indians are camped 15 miles below here waiting to hear from the General. I have no idea hostiles will surrender to me or anyone but the General, and then only upon a distinct understanding as to what is to be done with them. To deliver up their arms and surrender unconditionally, they, it appears, believe means that some of them will be killed. They prefer to die with arms in their hands and fighting.

It is a difficult task to make them fight when they do not wish, and more so to surprise and surround them when they are watching your every movement.

My infantry have not yet joined me, though I have sent for them twice. I have only 26 cavalry, on horses nearly broken down, and after my forced march from the Arros River and subsequent hard marches, my pack train is becoming much worn out. I have sent a courier to the commanding officer of troops at Cajon Bonito asking him to co-operate in case the hostiles break as I believe they will.

I earnestly wish the General would himself come and conduct affairs in person. If they do not surrender I feel they will raid again in the States, and it will be again as terrible as they can make it, as they will be desperate.[6]

General Miles, however, had no intention of getting near the hostiles until he was absolutely certain they were going to surrender. Just as it would be the ruination of a junior officer's career to be responsible for Geronimo's escape at that point, so also it had been the cause of Crook's disgrace months earlier, and Miles wanted glory from the Geronimo campaign, not a reprimand. On the thirty-first he responded to Lawton's telegram: "Whenever you have an opportunity to secure the person of Geronimo and Natchez do so by any means, and don't fail to hold them beyond the possibility of escape." A little later that day he added additional instructions for such a dishonorable deed: "If you think best when you receive this you can send for them saying you have a message from me and from the President, and when it is read to them you can tell them to lay down their arms and remain in your camp, or you can do whatever you think best. If you have any guarantee or hostages that they will remain, I will go down, but if they are going to put their camp in the hills it might result as other talks have and be only a means of allowing the camp to get several days start on the troops." Yet a third message was sent from Miles to Lawton on August 31, this one even stronger in its hint that dishonorable means would be countenanced if it ended the Geronimo menace: "If the Indians give you any guarantee or hostages that they will surrender to me, I will go down, or you can use *any* other means you think available. You will be justified in using *any* measures. If they surrender they will not be killed but rightly treated. I am ready to start but not unless I am sure it will do good."

Geronimo gave the necessary assurances, sending his brother Perrico (also spelled Porique) with the interpreter George Wratten to Fort Bowie as a hostage for Miles. Perrico was instructed to tell Miles that the hostiles indeed wished to surrender, hoping thereby to be allowed to return to Arizona within a reasonable length of time. Miles was not at Bowie at the time, but when notified that Geronimo had delivered a hostage still expressed doubts about his sincerity. On September 1 he wired Lawton for reassurance: "If you feel sure the Indians will surrender to me I will start tonight." Miles was torn by conflicting desires. If indeed there was to be a surrender, he wanted it to be to himself personally so that he could reap the glory from it; but if the Indians were going to flee into the mountains, he wanted to be nowhere near, thus escaping the fate of Crook. And in the latter instance, he would need a scapegoat—a fact which made Captain Lawton doubly nervous. Lawton's reply on September 2, sent from Skeleton Canyon, showed his growing concern, as well as his understanding of what Miles meant by *"any* measures":

Gen'l Miles:

The Indians were very restless and uneasy in their last camp, made so by the movement of troops which they have observed, and from the flood of couriers coming to my camp which they could not understand. They are unusually alert and watchful, and to surprise them is simply impossible. I could by treachery perhaps kill one or two of them, but it would only make everything much worse than before.

Today in a talk with Gatewood they proposed to move to the vicinity of Fort Bowie, and there await you. They want to see you and say they will do just what *you* tell them. I feel sure, and such is the opinion of the interpreters and of Gatewood, that they are sincere and anxious of surrender, but wish to do it only to the highest authority.

We moved today to this point [Skeleton Canyon], and I feel now that you should see them at once, and secure them as I believe you will, or give me some *positive* and definite order what to do. The responsibility at the present time is too great for me to assume. They are suspicious and timid, and the gathering of troops has made them suspicious of me. Today they said they did not like to give up their guns when soldiers were all around, but when you came if you said so they would lay them down, and I believe they will. They have kept every promise so far.

I am aware now that I assumed a great responsibility when I allowed them to come to my camp and promised them safety until they could see you, and have regretted a thousand times that Lt. Gatewood ever found my command, but I sincerely believed and do yet they wished to surrender, and that I was furthering your plans. I have followed them four months and know how hard it is to surprise them, and believe that they should not now be driven out again.

At the most a little diplomacy will bring them *all* in our hands as prisoners. I think Lt. Gatewood will be in to confer with you, but send this at once as I think you should know of the change of camp as soon as possible. I would be glad to have an officer directly from yourself come out and take command.

This telegram seems to have been directed more toward a future board of inquiry than to General Miles. Both men were posturing themselves as favorably as possible should something disastrous occur, such as a break for the mountains by Geronimo.

What Miles had suggested as plainly as was possible was that Lawton lure Geronimo into the American camp and there murder him in cold blood. Lawton's answer shows that he understood Miles's intent, but knew that the Apaches were almost impossible to surprise and that some would escape to exact a bloody revenge. He explained that if only Miles would come to Skeleton Canyon in person, all the hostiles would surrender and the war would be over. In the meantime, he wanted definite orders, not the fuzzy phrase "do whatever you think best." Or, failing that, he wanted an officer of greater rank sent to assume the command—and the responsibility.

Lawton's message was received at Fort Bowie, sent at a gallop to the nearest heliograph station, and relayed to Miles, who was moving toward the hostile camp by wagon. Captain Thompson's reply to Lawton was that the general would reach San Bernardino that evening, September 2. Miles indeed was moving toward Skeleton Canyon, but very slowly and with many precautions to posture himself in the most favorable light possible under the risky circumstances. Governor Luis E. Torres of Sonora on August 31 had wired his knowledge, given at last by the Prefect of Arizpe, of what was going on: "Express just received from Arizpe brings news of surrender of Geronimo and his party to your troops. I anxiously wait to have these news confirmed by you." To Torres, Miles replied that same day: "Indians have been talking about surrendering and have been near our troops at the junction of the San Bernardino and Bavispe Rivers, but I do not think they intend to surrender and believe it would be well to take every precaution against their raiding or returning to the Sierra Madre mountain country."

On September 2 he informed the commanding general of the Division of the Pacific, Oliver O. Howard, "I go down to-day to the Mexican Boundary to see the hostiles, but do not anticipate any favorable result. They are still in the mountains and not within the control of our forces. Still there is a possibility that some good will result." Even to his wife he took the same tone, while putting himself in the best possible light, in a telegram also on September 2: "I go down this morning to see the hostiles under Geronimo. They have said they wanted to see me. I have very little faith in their sincerity and do not anticipate any good

143

results. But still there is one chance they may come in, and I feel like exhausting every effort to get them in without any more loss of life, if possible."[7]

Military precautions were also being taken. As Miles was moving toward the meeting with Geronimo, his adjutant, Captain Thompson, wired the commanding officers at Forts Grant and Thomas: "Hostiles now 25 miles north of line, and this move ordered in case they may break for [Fort] Apache. Squads should look for them from the south." Other officers in the field were nervous, aware of punishments to men and sad consequences for careers should some hitch develop in the surrender proceedings. Major E. B. Beaumont of the Fourth Cavalry, who was camped at Silver Creek, Arizona, wired General Miles on September 3: "Lawton did not inform me which way he would march, as he should have done. . . . I have to trail him as if he were a hostile." Everyone, from commanding general of the Department to lowest officer, wanted his position on record just in case of trouble.

On September 3 the wires were humming with messages, and the heliographs were flashing more of them through the clear, bright Arizona air. Thompson, who was waiting at Fort Bowie and coordinating these communications, telegraphed the general: "Lawton's camp last night at Skeleton Cañon about 18 miles from you. . . . You could meet him by going to John Grey's Ranch about ten miles from you and have your courier find out where he is camped. He may go to Skull Cañon, which is about 8 miles north of Skeleton. Lawton says the hostiles will surrender to you but if he does not see you today he is afraid they will leave. All the officers feel sure they will surrender to you at your terms."

Miles was proceeding at a snail's pace, apparently in no hurry to have the confrontation with the hostiles. He later wrote, "I must confess that I went with some forebodings, though I still had hope that the promises of Geronimo would be fulfilled." He had taken both saddle horses and wagon and a heliograph op-

144

erator who, when in the vicinity of a station, would send and receive messages. On the night of September 2 Miles camped in Rucker Canyon and late on the afternoon of September 3 reached Skeleton Canyon where Lawton was waiting. Geronimo lost no time in presenting himself for an introduction; of that meeting Miles later wrote:

> Soon after my reaching Lawton's command, Geronimo rode into our camp and dismounted. He was one of the brightest, most resolute, determined looking men that I have ever encountered. He had the clearest, sharpest, dark eye I think I have ever seen, unless it was that of General Sherman when he was at the prime of life and just at the close of the great war. Every movement indicated power, energy and determination. In everything he did he had a purpose.[8]

Through an interpreter Geronimo wanted to know what terms the general would give him. The talk was interpreted from English into Spanish and from Spanish into Apache and then the reverse. An American named Nelson did the translating of English into Spanish, and an Apache, Jose María Yaskes, interpreted Spanish into the gutteral Apache language. Miles responded to Geronimo's question by drawing a line upon the ground and saying, "This represents the ocean." He then placed a rock beside the line. "This represents the place where Chihuahua is [Florida] with his band." He then placed another stone a short distance from the first and said, "This represents you, Geronimo." He picked up a third stone and put it near the second one. "This represents the Indians at Camp Apache. The President wants to take you and put you with Chihuahua." He thereupon picked up the stone representing Geronimo and his band and put it beside the one representing Chihuahua in Florida. Finally he picked up the one representing the Indians at Fort Apache and likewise put it beside those representing Geronimo and Chihuahua and commented, "That is what the President wants to do, get all of you together [in Florida]."[9]

145

*Fort Bowie, Arizona, in 1886. Note its strategic position in Apache Pass.*
Courtesy Arizona Pioneers' Historical Society.

Miles indicated in this conversation that the stay in the East
would be of indefinite duration, but that at the end of it the
Apaches would be returned to Arizona. He concluded, "Tell
them I have no more to say. I would like to talk generally with
him [Geronimo], but we do not understand each other's tongue."
Geronimo thereupon turned to Gatewood, smiled, and said in
Apache, "Good, you told the truth." Then he shook hands with
Miles and said that no matter what the others did he was surrendering. Until they left for Fort Bowie the next day, Geronimo
rarely let Miles out of his sight, as if fearing the general would
forget their agreement. Geronimo knew enough about civil law
in Arizona to have no desire to be turned over to the sheriff of
Cochise or Pima County for civil trial. Florida was much prefer-

146

able to the type of justice the Arizona pioneers would mete out to him.

The one difficulty that evening of September 3 was that Nachez had not appeared for a conference with Miles. The surrender would not be complete until the hereditary chief of the Chiricahua Apaches also submitted to American jurisdiction. Nachez had moved several miles away into the mountains to mourn his brother, who had gone back into Mexico to fetch a favorite horse and had not returned; Nachez assumed his brother had been killed by the Mexicans and was lamenting his death. According to Gatewood's account of the surrender and Geronimo's autobiography, he and Geronimo went to talk with Nachez, who had with him twelve to fifteen warriors and their families. They explained to Nachez that Miles had arrived and that his presence was required. Lieutenant Thomas J. Clay reported that the conversation was brief. Gatewood said, "Nachez, you promised me that when we got to the line you would talk with General Miles about surrendering." Nachez thought a moment, then replied, "That's so," and immediately went with Gatewood to meet Miles. Gatewood said that Nachez did not wish to meet Miles because of his grief, but thought it would show disrespect to the general to delay further. He therefore gathered his band, brought them in, and formally surrendered. All hostiles gave up their arms, and preparations were made for the trip to Fort Bowie.

On the morning of September 5, Miles placed Geronimo, Nachez, and three other Apache leaders in his wagon and set out for Bowie at a rapid pace, escorted by a small contingent of troops commanded by Lieutenants Wilder and Clay. To the driver of the wagon, Bill Gadd, Miles reportedly said, "Don't let the sun go down on you," meaning that he wished to reach the post before dark. They departed at ten o'clock that morning. It was sixty-five miles to the fort, a most difficult trip by horse. Wilder rode ahead of the command as it neared Bowie, returning with a bottle of whiskey. Miles asked what it was for. "Clay must be very tired of riding behind the ambulance, and I thought I would get him a drink," Wilder replied. Miles retorted, "No, wait till Clay gets the Indians in the guard house and he can take all he wants to drink."[10]

Just before they reached Bowie, Geronimo looked toward the Chiricahua Mountains and commented, "This is the fourth time I have surrendered." Miles's quick reply was, "And I think it is the last time. . . ." At the fort, which they reached before night-fall, and while Lieutenant Clay was busy with his drinks, Miles drafted several telegrams. First he answered General O. O. Howard, commanding general of the Division of the Pacific, who on September 4 had telegraphed: "The surrender of Geronimo and his Apaches is reported in the evening papers. Report the same officially. If true great credit is due yourself and officers and men for indomitable perseverance in an almost hopeless task." Miles responded affirmatively. Then to Governors Conrad M. Zulick of Arizona, E. A. Ross of New Mexico, and Luis Torres of Sonora went identical messages: "The hostile Apaches surrendered as prisoners of war on the 4th. I arrived here last night with Geronimo and Nachez and three others. Capt. Lawton brings the remainder. Am moving all from Fort Apache and the sending of those and the hostiles 2000 miles east will I hope give permanent peace to the people living in Mexico, Arizona and New Mexico. Your hearty co-operation has contributed much help in the solution of this difficult problem."

To his wife Mary, then at Nonquit, Massachusetts, he wired jubilantly, "The last of the hostile Apaches surrendered yesterday at Skeleton Canyon, named so by the number of skeletons found there, the result of massacre many years ago. I left there this morning and after a ride of sixty-five miles arrived at this place bringing Geronimo, Natchez, the hereditary chief of the Apaches and three others. The remainder under charge of Lawton will be here in three days." The next morning, September 6, he telegraphed L. Q. C. Lamar, Jr., in the Department of the Interior, "The Indians surrendered as prisoners of war on Sept. 4th.

*General Miles and his staff, Bowie Station, September 8, 1886, watching the Apaches depart for imprisonment in Florida. From left to right: Surgeon Leonard Wood, Lieutenant Ames, Lieutenant Wilder, Captain Lawton, General Miles, Captain Thompson, Major Kimball, Lieutenant Dapray, and Lieutenant Clay.* Courtesy National Archives.

I returned here last night bringing Geronimo, Natchez heredi-tary Chief and three others. Lawton will bring in the remainder to-morrow, about 40 in all. Indians are perfectly submissive and will do whatever I say. I intend to ship them to Florida in a few days, unless otherwise ordered. . . ."[11]

Lawton indeed had set out for Fort Bowie on the morning of September 5 as ordered, but he reached his destination with fewer prisoners than anticipated. The order of march began with Lawton, his troops, and the Scouts in the lead, followed by the pack train and, at the rear, the renegade Apaches. No guard de-tail followed. Some seven miles short of Fort Bowie three war-riors and three squaws fled into the Chiricahua Mountains. De-spite immediate pursuit, they eluded the Americans and reached

Mexico. Lawton's arrival at Fort Bowie with the remaining prisoners meant that, for all practical purposes, the Indian wars were over. The six escapees, along with Mangus and his followers, were yet free, but they were being hunted. Two more months were consumed in this chase. The six refugees from Geronimo's band were taken by Colonel Emilio Kosterlitzky and the Sonoran *Rurales* (a militia-police force); in that fight all of the refugees except one squaw were killed. Mangus finally surrendered in October to Captain Charles L. Cooper of the Tenth Cavalry after being caught on the open flats near the Black Mountains of New Mexico; this was the only engagement fought between American troops and Apache renegades during which the Indians actually surrendered.[12]

Miles might well congratulate himself—and he was quick to do so. On September 7 he wrote to his wife from Fort Bowie: "If you had been here you would have seen me riding in over the mountains with Geronimo and Natchez as you saw me ride over the hills and down to the Yellowstone with Chief Joseph. It was a brilliant ending to a difficult problem."[13]

The next day, September 8, the Apache renegades were put aboard the train at Bowie Station. Miles had a final meeting with Geronimo and Nachez at which he said to them, "From now on we want to begin a new life." He held up one of his hands with the palm open and horizontal. Marking lines across it with a finger of the other hand, he said, "This represents the past; it is all covered with hollows and ridges." Then he rubbed his other palm over it and said, "That represents the wiping out of the past, which will be considered smooth and forgotten."[14] Going with the hostiles on the train were Captain Lawton, Lieutenants Clay and A. L. Smith, Surgeon Wood, and twenty men of the Fourth Cavalry, along with Packer George Wratten who would serve as interpreter. Field Order No. 89, issued by General Miles, directed this detachment of troops to "take charge of the surrendered Chiricahua Indian prisoners of war, and proceed with them to Fort Marion, Fla."

*Nachez (left) and Geronimo at Fort Bowie, Arizona after their surrender. Geronimo was wearing an alpaca coat which he had purchased for fifty cents and a twelve-dollar pair of boots, both acquired at Fort Bowie after his arrival there. At right are members of the Fourth Cavalry band.* Courtesy Division of Manuscripts, University of Oklahoma Library.

Just as the train was pulling away from the station, the Fourth Cavalry band began playing "Auld Lang Syne":

> Should auld acquaintance be forgot,
> And never brought to mind?[15]

The Indians could not understand why the soldiers guarding them found the tune so humorous. Nor perhaps could Martine and Kayitah, whom Miles had ordered aboard the same train to share the renegades' confinement in Florida. The process of forgetting the past, its promises, already had begun, not only to the loyal Scouts but to Geronimo and his people as well.

# EIGHT

# THE BETRAYAL OF
# THE APACHES

. . . The Government decided to make an end to the ever recurring outbreaks, and round up all of the trouble makers and their
kith and kin, and transport them to the far distant Florida. This
was the only practical solution of the question, for as long as
the blood-thirsty Apaches were on their familiar grounds, which
offered them an easy opportunity to escape and hide in inaccessible mountains, after committing an outrage, so long would they
continue their bloody work.

Colonel William Stover, "The Last of Geronimo and his Band,"
Washington, *National Tribune,* July 24, 1924.

IN MAY AND JUNE OF 1886, not long after taking command of the
Department of Arizona, Miles had made a tour of the various
reservations in the Territory. Most especially he had wanted to
see the Chiricahua and Warm Springs Apaches who had not fled
the reservation with Geronimo and Nachez. From Fort Apache
on July 3 he had telegraphed his observations to General Howard, commander of the Division of the Pacific: "There are the
strongest military reasons why these Indians should be located
outside Arizona, and it should be done peaceably if possible.
There are several places east of New Mexico where they could
be located, and I respectfully request authority to send a few of
the tribe to Washington, under charge of two officers, and to
locate such land as the Government may be willing to grant

them. Mr. [L. Q. C.] Lamar, who is here from Interior Department, concurs with me as to *advisability* of the measure."[1] Removal eastward was Miles's solution to the vexing problem of the recurring Apache flights from the reservations, and his proposal was forwarded through Army chains of command.

The key phrase in Miles's telegram to his commanding general was "it should be done peaceably if possible." For a large military force suddenly to appear at San Carlos and Fort Apache and to begin rounding up the Indians for a forced march to the nearest railhead would certainly cause the greatest outbreak in the history of Arizona Territory. The Apaches feared treachery leading to mass hangings in reprisal for their many raids in the Territory. Miles knew of this fear, and on July 5 he telegraphed the Adjutant-General in Washington, "Request that my telegram of . . . [July 3] regarding Apaches and Warm Springs Indians be considered strictly confidential. Ten principal men have agreed to go, and I believe it will result in much good." He wanted tribal representatives to journey to Washington, where they would be given "red carpet" treatment and would then agree to the tribe's removal eastward. He also was most desirous that the two officers accompanying these ten Apaches to Washington be men who would present him in a most favorable light.

The Chiricahua and Warm Springs Apaches he wanted to remove from Arizona numbered 434 men, women, and children and were located near Fort Apache. They technically were prisoners of war on their reservation, although many of them had served as Apache Scouts for the Army and had never been disarmed or dismounted. Their leaders included Loco, Chatto, and Kayetenay—all of whom had led raids in the past, but who had helped to fight renegades as well. They were farming near Fort Apache, cutting and selling hay and wood to the Army as well as increasing their herds of cows, sheep, and horses. According to some authorities, they were trying to "take the white man's road," as so many Agents had exhorted them to do. Yet, for this, they were hated by the Tucson Ring for the competition they provided in the fight for lucrative contracts to supply grain and hay to the troops. And they were intensely feared by most civilians of the Territory, who saw the reservations as resting places for the Indians between raids. Miles, in his conversation with these Chiricahua and Warm Springs Apaches, indicated that the government would grant them farms and provide them with money, agricultural implements, and rations if they would only agree to move eastward. He was so persuasive in his oratory that Chatto agreed to lead a delegation of ten to Washington. Captain J. H. Dorst was assigned to escort them, and Mickey Free, Concepción, and Sam Bowman went along as interpreters.

While promising a beautiful future to these Apaches, Miles was writing persuasive letters to Washington urging their removal. On July 7 from Fort Apache, he sent a long letter through channels containing his thoughts on the subject:

There are now at Fort Apache 198 Warm Springs Indians that were several years ago forcibly removed from New Mexico and 236 Chiricahua Apaches. These two bands have for years affiliated under the leadership of Mangus Colorado, Cochise, Victorio, Chatto, Geronimo, and others, and the Apache tribe has raided the settlements of New Mexico, Arizona, and Old Mexico for hundreds of years. Certain promises have been made them and very great privileges have been granted them. The 440 men, women, and children now living on the military reservation of Fort Apache are nominally prisoners of war, yet they have never been disarmed or dismounted and are in better fighting condition to-day than ever before, and yet without arms they would, in their present position, be in danger of being raided by any hostile Indians. To hold this tribe under restraint and close military surveillance has required a strong force of troops. They were located in the heart of the most remote, mountainous, and inaccessible region of the United States; remote from the fact of its being 100 miles south of the Atlantic and Pacific Railway and 130 miles north of the Southern Pacific.

Raiding parties from this tribe at Apache, and from Geronimo's camp in Old Mexico, have for years committed the most serious depredations in the belt of country (200 miles wide) between Fort

Apache and the Mexican boundary. The hostile element under Geronimo and Natchez will be worn down, and in time destroyed or captured by the troops, yet this result could not produce a lasting peace, so long as the Apache tribe remains in the rugged and almost inaccessible mountains of Arizona. Their boys of to-day will become the Geronimos of a few years hence. They are the remnant of a once powerful and warlike tribe that has contended against civilization for three hundred years. All their traditions perpetuate the spirit of war. By their conflicts with the Spanish or Mexican forces and those of the United States they have become greatly reduced in numbers but the feeling of animosity toward the white race has only been intensified.

Miles admitted that he did not think it advisable to keep the Apaches permanently in Florida, for "They are a mountain race, accustomed to high altitudes, and would in a short time, most likely, die, if kept in the lowlands of Florida." To convince officials in Washington to consent to this removal, he used the most convincing argument possible—money: "It now costs the Government at least $40,000 per annum to feed these Indians, and it takes hundreds of thousands of dollars annually (over and above the ordinary expense in time of peace) to keep the troops in the field actively campaigning against hostiles and to protect settlements scattered over a vast area of country."

His recommendations were cogently stated: the Apaches should be removed at least one thousand miles away from the mountains of Arizona; each family should receive one hundred dollars worth of farming utensils and two hundred dollars worth of domestic animals the first year, along with three hundred dollars worth of stock the second year; additionally, the head men of the tribe would be given five thousand dollars worth of domestic animals for the general benefit of the tribe. The site of removal, according to Miles, should be the Indian Territory (Oklahoma).

Miles's proposal received a positive reception in Washington, and on July 10 Lieutenant General Sheridan wired him, "Send ten of the Apache and Warm Springs Indians to Washington under charge of one good officer from your department who knows them, and upon arrival report them to the Secretary of the Interior." On July 13, Field Orders No. 74, Department of Arizona, directed Captain J. H. Dorst of the Fourth Cavalry to this duty, stipulating "Upon completion of this duty he will return with the party of Indians in charge of Fort Apache, Arizona. . . ."

The announcement of this delegation's departure brought an immediate change of heart in Tucson, for the removal of 440 Apaches would deprive the Tucson Ring of many profitable contracts. Their newspapers spoke hotly in opposition to the move. Another source of opposition was George Crook. Captain John Gregory Bourke, ex-aide to Crook and still a close friend and warm supporter of Crook's views, was in Washington when the delegation arrived. He attached himself unofficially to it and used his considerable influence with the Apaches to convince them that their interests would not be served by moving. Miles was stung by this tactic, writing to Mary: "Captain Burke [sic] made himself very offensive. . . . I think he has furnished the press with very unfavorable reports, has frightened the Indians and in fact has done much mischief." Captain Bourke responded that he was only trying to be helpful.[2]

In Washington the Apaches met the Secretary of the Interior and the Secretary of War. They also were presented at the White House where they had a brief conversation with President Cleveland. Chatto was given a large, silver peace medal and Secretary William C. Endicott of the War Department gave him a certificate. Chatto was highly pleased with these gifts. He believed they signalled good things for him and his people: that they would not be removed from Arizona but would be given good Agents and an actual means of making an honorable living at Fort Apache. But just as Miles had lied to Geronimo at the surrender, so Cleveland and Sheridan lied to Chatto. While the delegation was yet in Washington, Sheridan telegraphed Miles: "The President wishes me to ask what you think of the proposition to

*Chatto in 1886*. Courtesy Arizona Pioneers' Historical Society.

forcibly arrest all on the reservation and send them to Fort
Marion, Florida, where they can be joined by the party now
here."

Miles was taken aback by this question. In his original proposal and in sending the delegation to Washington, he had
thought the Apaches would be removed to the Indian Territory.
On August 1, by wire, he answered Sheridan that there would be
both advantages and disadvantages to such a move and that he
would send a letter containing his views. For the present, he suggested that Captain Dorst take the delegates to Carlisle, Pennsylvania, and keep them at the famous Indian school there until the
government should reach a final decision. His letter of August 2
listed the advantages of the move: it would please many Arizonans; it would relieve a large number of troops for duty elsewhere and it would permanently end the Apache menace. The
disadvantages, as he saw them, were more numerous: the Apaches
would consider such a move "an act of bad faith," especially
since the delegates had gone to Washington at official govern-
mental invitation; it would make other Southwestern tribes hesitate to send delegates to Washington; it would, he felt, "necessi-
tate a war of extermination" against Geronimo's band, for if the
peaceful Indians were to be banished the warriors "would expect
their fate to be much worse"; finally, the removal of the Apaches
eastward would please Arizonans, but would anger the citizens of
the region wherein they would be located.

To Mary he wrote, "I do not approve of the suggestion of
sending all the Apaches to Florida, especially as a part are now
in Washington by authority of the government. I think they will
yet adopt my plan of putting them on some reservation agreeable to them east of New Mexico and sending all the others
there."[3]

Miles's recommendations were given serious consideration,
which required several days. Captain Dorst was directed to take
the delegation to Carlisle. Arriving there on August 4, he stated,
"Can find means to keep the Indians interested for four or five

days, if necessary, and they will be more contented than they were in Washington." On the ninth of August, Dorst was directed to stay at Carlisle with the delegates until further notice, but owing to a failure of the telegraph Dorst did not receive these orders before beginning his journey westward to Fort Apache. Furious telegrams passed back and forth in a search for Dorst and his charges. Orders had already gone out from Washington for all Chiricahua and Warm Springs Apaches in Arizona to be moved to Florida. Dorst finally was located at Emporia, Kansas, and diverted to Fort Leavenworth, Kansas. There on August 14 he made a report on the "frame of mind" of Chatto and the others at the request of President Cleveland:

> After leaving Carlisle the Indians appeared convinced they were to remain undisturbed at Fort Apache. Chatto had not received written assurance he requested, but the present of a medal from Secretary Interior, the possession of an unimportant certificate from Captain Bourke and Secretary of War, and the fact he had not been told he would have to move seemed to satisfy him. The detention here causes much uneasiness because only surmises can be offered in explanation. I have tried to quiet their fears, but Chatto has just told me they believe their families will be moved here to meet them. Interpreter Bowman says that if some reasonable explanation is given and they are allowed to proceed home at once, no trouble due to present circumstances need be apprehended. His opinion is entitled to consideration, but since their suspicion is aroused, I hesitate to say they can be so completely removed that the recollection of them will cause no lurking uneasiness. Whether they return or stay here, I would like to have something to tell them coming from high authority.

R. C. Drum, the Adjutant-General of the Army, responded on August 16 to Dorst's evaluation with directions to the captain, still at Fort Leavenworth: "Your telegram received and confirmed apprehensions here. The removal of the Indians from Fort Apache is now so probable that you must arrange to get along with those with you until removal is effected."

Miles had an interview with Captain Dorst, and on August 20

further clarified his position in a telegram to Drum: the delegates to Washington should be told that their choice was simple; they could be "either *treaty Indians* or . . . they must be regarded as prisoners of war and must abide by what disposition the Government deems best for the welfare of all concerned." What he wanted the Indians told was either to sign whatever treaty was tendered them, which would entail removal, or become prisoners of war and be removed. He concluded, "Colonel Wade, commanding Fort Apache, who is now here, informs me that he can move those at Fort Apache without difficulty, and arrangements have already been considered."

Four days later the Secretary of War, W. C. Endicott, endorsed this proposal from Miles with the comment about removal to Fort Marion, Florida: "The only hesitation the President had in regard to this course arose from his desire to be assured by General Miles that all of this dangerous band could be secured and successfully conveyed away; for if a few should escape and take to the war-path the results would be altogether too serious." General Sheridan likewise endorsed the proposal, and all was in readiness for the removal. However, Adjutant-General Drum thought to inquire of the commanding officer at Fort Marion if the Indians could be quartered there; the reply was brief: "Can accommodate seventy-five men, women, and children in addition to those now here. Fort Marion is a small place; all must live in tents. Have tentage by taking battery tents. Need no particular preparation, but will have to expend $200 for additional tent floor, privies, and lavatories. Would recommend no more Indians be sent here." A prison costing only two hundred dollars to prepare was too appealing to the President and his advisors for them to pay any attention to the commanding officer's recommendation that no more Indians be sent to that fort. On August 27 the President's order went out:

> I do not think the Apache Indians should be treated otherwise than as prisoners of war. As it is quite certain they will not agree with the Government as to their location, which I am now satis-

160

*A distant view of Fort Apache, Arizona, taken in 1884.* Courtesy Arizona Pioneers' Historical Society.

fied should be <u>Fort Marion</u>, and since we are informed that their <u>removal</u> can now be successfully accomplished, I think it should be done <u>at once,</u> and that the state of feeling reported as existing among them at Fort Leavenworth justifies us in preventing the return of any of them to the reservation.

The chiefs at Fort Leavenworth, led by Chatto, had already started for Arizona once again. Frantic telegrams for their recall again reached Captain Dorst at Emporia, Kansas, on August 28, and for a second time these chiefs were imprisoned at Fort Leavenworth.

During the last two weeks in August, anticipating the removal of the Chiricahua and Warm Springs Indians at Fort Apache, General Miles had gradually increased the number of soldiers at that post, sending to it two troops from Fort Thomas and one each from San Carlos and Alma, New Mexico. The commander at Fort Apache, Lieutenant Colonel James F. Wade of the Tenth Cavalry, called a conference with all the warriors on September 5 at which he informed them that the entire tribe was to journey to Washington for a conference with the "Great Father." No weapons would be allowed at this conference and so all were to turn in their arms. After the warriors were thus peacefully disarmed, the women and children were instructed to pack. The nearest railroad depot was Holbrook, Arizona, one hundred miles to the north. On the morning of September 7, while Miles was at Fort Bowie congratulating himself on the termination of the Geronimo campaign, Colonel Wade ordered the 434 Chiricahua and Warm Springs Apaches at Fort Apache to begin their march. The caravan stretched some two miles as it moved north, for it contained some wagons, 1,200 Indian horses, and an estimated 3,000 dogs. At the front and rear of the column marched infantry companies, while cavalry units covered the two flanks in single file. In the lead went Apache Scouts "with their carbines always ready for instant action." The Scouts were guarding against attack by other tribes hostile to the two groups being moved, as well as any escape. Behind this column came the commissary, beef on the hoof. Each evening a camp was made. Lieutenant William Stover, who accompanied this march, later wrote:

> After arrival in camp the scouts would kill the number of steers required, by shooting them, and then the squaws would rip open the carcass, drag out the entrails, and, grabbing all one could hold, squat down behind some bush or rock and begin to weave the intestines into a braid, which operation at the same time removed the smelly contents. After this, the tidbit was ready for the evening meal. To see those savages fighting for raw meat, covered with gore from the struggle, and then draw to one side with the spoil, was a sight worse than to watch a pack of hungry coyotes fighting over a decaying carcass.[4]

The lieutenant did not comment on what he and his men would have done had they been in the same position as the Apaches. His views about the cleanliness of the Apaches and his willingness to eat with them stand in sharp contrast to those of Lieutenant Gatewood. Gatewood knew the Apaches far better than Stover.

During the night, the soldiers kept an especially close watch over the Apaches to see that none escaped and to protect the Apaches from a band of cowboys who were following the caravan closely, watching for a chance to even up old scores against the Indians. The Apaches were aware of the pursuers and stayed close to the camp. The days thus passed, the caravan wending its way northward at a slow pace. Lieutenant Stover commented on the drought, "Clouds of dust rose high to heaven and the movement could be seen for 20 miles." Five nights and six days were consumed in making the one hundred miles to Holbrook, the caravan arriving late on the afternoon of September 12. Eighteen "tourist cars" were waiting on the siding of the Atlantic and Pacific Railroad. The cavalry formed a large semi-circle around one side of these cars, while the infantry guarded the far side of the train. During their final night in Arizona, the Apaches were allowed a last feast. Steers were killed, fires were started, and meat was soon cooking. Lieutenant Stover described that evening:

> What a sight! I was standing on the railroad track on elevated ground, and, overlooking the great camp in the [Little Colorado] river bottom, saw a spectacle that perhaps no man will see again. Several hundred fires were glowing among the low brush, and around each fire was a group of Indians, dancing and singing in celebration of their coming journey to see the "Great Father" in Washington. Drums were sounding incessantly, and the frenzied, monotonous chant of the Indians pervading the night air, and the mournful howling of the thousands of dogs over all (they seemed to scent a catastrophe), made a curious and wonderful impression, never to be forgotten. All night this powwow lasted, and many of the inhabitants of the little frontier town of Holbrook spent all night watching the spectacle.

Early the next morning of September 13, at a signal from Colonel Wade, the soldiers began to close in toward the train, forcing the Apaches aboard the cars. Very few of the Indians had ever been on a train and thus hesitated to climb on. To forestall trouble, the soldiers began picking up squaws and children bodily and putting them aboard despite their loud screams. The warriors gradually followed their families, and the loading passed without incident. All the windows in the cars occupied by the Apaches had been securely fastened to prevent escapes, despite the September heat; this measure proved necessary, for when the train started forward with a jerk, all the Indians stood up and began yelling. Gradually this excitement died down, and all resumed their seats to look out in wonder at the passing scenery. All their camp belongings—and dogs—were left behind, and as the train started, "the thousands of deserted dogs tried frantically to keep abreast of the moving cars, every one howling with all his might. They were so thick that there wasn't room enough for all of them to run, and half of them would be on the ground and the other half scrambling over them. What a sight." Gradually the dogs thinned out as the train gathered speed, but a few of them kept up for almost twenty miles. Lieutenant Stover later inquired of a resident of Holbrook what had become of the dogs. "We just had to turn out and shoot them," he replied, "and, believe me, it kept us busy. The cowpunchers helped us and they had great sport with the dogs, shooting them from the saddle." The Indians' horses did not prove so troublesome; the Tenth Cavalry drove them to Fort Union, where they were sold at public auction.

On the moving train, the first and last cars were occupied by the escorting soldiers, and between each car, on the platforms, was an escort of four soldiers. Stops were made only at lonely water towers along the route, not in the towns. Rations would be placed in six piles, and six braves, designated "captains," would be called out to carry food inside to those in their groups. Because of the locked doors and windows, the unwashed nature of the Indians, the September heat of the Southwest, and the lack of cooking and sanitary facilities, the odor inside the cars grew extremely offensive. Lieutenant Stover later recalled:

> At the first halt, after the Indians had been let out, the division superintendent of the road, who was on the train, wanted to go

164

inside one of the cars, but he did not get further inside than the door. "Whew!" he exclaimed, "That's awful! I guess all we can do with this equipment is to burn it when we get to our destination." That night I had to go to the rear car on the train, and as there were no stops, I was compelled to make my way thru the whole train. Heavens! When I think of that trip, even at this time, I get seasick. Something had to be done to clean up the cars, but ordinary methods would have been inadequate, so when the train stopped for the morning feed, the superintendent had each car washed out with a hose and a powerful stream of water. Of course it was not a pleasure to have to go into one of the cars after this cleaning, but it was the only way to make it possible for any human being, other than an Indian, to enter them at all.

The train went by way of Albuquerque toward St. Louis. As it slowly made its way eastward, stopping on sidings for all other trains, the Indians grew more and more suspicious that they were not on their way to Washington to see the "Great Father." The soldiers made every effort to pacify them with promises that they would be well treated, yet they were filled with misgivings and "in a constant state of alarm." When the train entered a long tunnel, the Apaches were convinced that they were being taken into the earth and uttered shrieks of terror. When the train came out the far end of the tunnel, most of them were found under their seats. East of St. Louis, a squaw gave birth to a child. At the next stop, a warrior managed to hide outside the train and was not missed when it started again, as the head count seemed correct aboard the train. It took the escapee a year to make his way undetected back to Arizona, where he made occasional raids at San Carlos.[5]

From St. Louis the train proceeded to Atlanta, and then to Fort Marion, Florida, arriving there on September 20. That same day Chatto and the chiefs who had journeyed to Washington also arrived at Fort Marion; orders had gone to Fort Leavenworth on September 12 for this move. Chatto threw away his peace medal, asking bitterly why it was given to him. In vain he and the others protested their removal, pointing to their years of government service as Apache Scouts. Their reward was confinement as prisoners of war.

At the same time that the Fort Apache Indians were being moved slowly eastward by train, Geronimo, Nachez, and their followers likewise were being removed by train to Florida. In fact, the renegades who surrendered to Miles at Skeleton Canyon started eastward on September 8, five days before their peaceful relatives departed from Holbrook. But Geronimo and his hostiles arrived much later, owing to delays at San Antonio—they were lucky to arrive at all instead of being turned over to civil authorities in Arizona. Just before the train departed Bowie Station, Arizona, on September 8, Captain William A. Thompson, Miles' adjutant, reportedly patted his pocket and said to Surgeon Leonard Wood, "I've got something here which would stop this movement, but I am not going to let the old man [Miles] see it until you are gone."[6] General Miles left Bowie within an hour after the departure of the Indians, arriving in Albuquerque on September 14 where he held a conference with Colonel Wade as the Indians from Fort Apache passed through town going east. In Albuquerque, word reached Miles that the President, as well as General Sheridan, were not happy that he had sent Geronimo and his followers east to Florida. In fact, correspondence began to arrive which indicated a far different solution had been intended by his superiors.[7]

On September 7, General Howard had wired Washington from his headquarters at the Division of the Pacific: "General Miles has returned to Fort Bowie with Natchez, the son of Cochise, Geronimo, and his brother, with three other Apaches, all as prisoners of war; surrender unconditional. . . . After congratulating General Miles and his command upon the successful issue, I have instructed him that the Apaches and Warm Springs Indians [at Fort Apache] must be sent on straight to Fort Marion, Fla., as the President, through the War Department, directed. What shall be done with Geronimo and the hostiles now prisoners of war?" Miles obviously misunderstood—intentionally or unintentionally—the order to mean that *all* Chiricahua and Warm Springs Apaches, which would include Geronimo and his followers, were to be sent to Florida. Or else, as a sympathetic biographer has claimed, he wanted to remove Geronimo and the renegades from Arizona for fear of civilian lynching parties until the President should determine their final disposition.[8]

Upon receipt of General Howard's telegram, to the effect that the surrender had been unconditional, President Cleveland had instructed the War Department: "All the hostiles should be very safely kept as prisoners until they can be tried for their crimes or otherwise disposed of, and those to be sent to Florida should be started immediately." This order, dated September 7, was sent down through channels to Howard and then to Miles. That same day, September 7, General of the Army Sheridan wired Miles, "As the disposition of Geronimo and his hostile band is yet to be decided by the President, and as they are prisoners without conditions, you are hereby directed to hold them in close confinement at Fort Bowie until the decision of the President is communicated to you." Acknowledgment of receipt of this order was requested. Apparently this telegram was not delivered until the eighth of September, and it was the one to which Captain Thompson, Miles' adjutant, referred when he patted his pocket and said to Surgeon Leonard Wood that he had something "which would stop this movement" of Geronimo eastward.

On September 8, despite the fact that he had already ordered the hostiles aboard the train, Miles telegraphed his superiors in Washington, "There is no accommodation here for holding these Indians, and should one escape in these mountains he would cause trouble and the labor of the troops be lost. Everything is arranged for moving them, and I earnestly request permission to move them out of this mountainous country, at least as far as Fort Bliss, Tex., or to Fort Union, N. Mex., or Fort Marion, Fla., for safety." Miles's request was forwarded to President Cleveland, who was vacationing at Bloomingdale, New York, by the Adjutant-General of the Army, R. C. Drum, who was acting as Secretary of War in Endicott's absence. Cleveland responded immediately: "I think Geronimo and the rest of the hostiles should be immediately sent to the nearest fort or prison where they can be securely confined. The most important thing now is to guard against all chances of escape."

The President and his advisors in Washington, believing that Geronimo had surrendered unconditionally, had determined to turn the hostiles over to civil officials in Arizona. Their decision was motivated by political considerations, and would have been popular in the Southwest. But Miles knew he had made certain promises to Geronimo, and on September 9 at Rincon, New Mexico, where he received the President's message of September 7, the one suppressed by his adjutant, he tried to clear up the confusion. While the train carrying him to Albuquerque was halted at that tiny station, he sent a wire to General Howard at the Division of the Pacific: "There is an erroneous impression regarding Indian prisoners of war. They surrendered with the understanding that they would be sent out of the country." Howard realized that the issue of the Indians' future had become political, not military, and that a blunder had been made; he immediately forwarded Miles's telegram, adding his own comment to it: "To-day I got the order of the President, sent direct to General Miles from the War Department, to send Indian prisoners to nearest fort or military prison. Meanwhile General Miles has sent Geronimo and his band to San Antonio, Tex., *en route* to Fort Marion, Fla., which is certainly not a compliance with the President's orders to send them to nearest fort or military prison."

General Drum, as acting Secretary of War, also realized the mistake and telegraphed Brigadier General D. S. Stanley, commanding the Department of Texas, at San Antonio to "take charge of these Indians and securely confine them at San Antonio barracks and hold them until further orders." Stanley complied on September 10 when the train bearing Geronimo and the hostiles arrived. While the Apache renegades waited in San Antonio, the telegraph wires and the mail were loaded with messages determining their fate.

On September 13 the President requested Miles to make a full report on the terms of surrender he had made with the Apaches. Meanwhile, the congressional delegates from New Mexico and Arizona were pressuring the President to turn Geronimo and the hostiles over to civil authorities for trial by jury, just as were the newspapers in the two territories. Cleveland thus faced a dilemma: should he comply with these requests, which were politically expedient for the first Democrat elected to the Presidency in twenty-four years and facing re-election in two years, or should be honor General Miles' promises to the Indians, whatever these might be? If the surrender indeed had been unconditional, then he could do both easily. Anxiously he and other officials in Washington waited for Miles to make the special report requested. Officials in Arizona likewise waited, at the same time moving to secure the person of Geronimo for trial should he be returned to the Territory; warrants for his arrest on several charges of murder were issued, as well as for other prominent hostiles in the group.

Miles, however, was unavailable for immediate comment. He was on his way to Albuquerque by train. The only telegram he sent after the stop at Rincon, New Mexico, was an order to Lieutenant Clay to forward to him the "spurs or rifle of Geronimo." He was more interested in souvenirs than in complying with the President's request. At Albuquerque, after learning that the hostiles had been halted at San Antonio and were being confined there, he requested that Lawton, Wood, and the troops of the Fourth Cavalry that had been escorting the renegades be returned to Albuquerque. Finally on September 24, from Whipple Barracks, Arizona, the general belatedly made the full report that had been requested. In it he recapitulated the events surrounding the pursuit of Geronimo through the summer months, his sending of Martine and Kayitah under Lieutenant Gatewood to the meeting at which Gatewood had persuaded Geronimo to surrender (and, in detailing this, Miles gave Lawton more credit than he did Gatewood), and he told of the move north, including the meeting with Mexicans. On the crucial point of surrender terms, Miles's report stated that he had told them:

> . . . should they throw down their arms and place themselves entirely at our mercy we should certainly not kill them, but that they must surrender absolutely as prisoners of war to the Federal authorities and rely upon the Government to treat them fairly and justly. I informed them that I was moving all Chiricahua and Warm Springs Indians from Arizona, and they would all be removed from this country at once, and for all time. Geronimo replied that he would do whatever I said, obey any order, and bring in his camp early next morning, which he did.

This report, in its ambiguity, conflicted with what Miles was privately writing his wife about the Indians, "They placed themselves entirely at our mercy, and we were in honor bound not to give them up to a mob or the mockery of a justice where they could never have received an impartial trial. After one of the most vigorous campaigns they surrendered like brave men to brave men, and placed themselves at the mercy of the government." Five days later he wrote her that "all such statements . . . that I was ordered to accept only unconditional surrender are able-bodied lies."[9]

Miles's report of September 24 apparently caused consternation in Washington, pointing ambiguously to the promise of removal. On September 25 General Drum, as acting Secretary of War, wired Miles: "It would appear . . . that Geronimo, instead of being captured, surrendered, and that the surrender, instead of being unconditional, was, contrary to expectations here, accompanied with conditions and promises. That the President may clearly understand the present status of Geronimo and his band, he desires you to report by telegraph direct the exact promises, if any, made to them at the time of surrender." Miles's response, made the same day, was a request to come in person to Washington in order that the President "may fully understand every fact and circumstance which led to that gratifying result, and some other important matter of which I believe you should be apprised." Miles had powerful friends in Washington, including his uncles-in-law, Senator John Sherman of Ohio and retired General William T. Sherman; with their aid he would be able to put himself in a more favorable light than he could by telegraph. His request to come to Washington was denied, however, on the grounds that he should "continue with your command," and again the order was repeated for him to report the promises made at the time of surrender.

On September 29, somewhat huffily, Miles responded by referring to his report of the twenty-fourth, adding only that the Indians were told to surrender "entirely at our mercy." He concluded, "I desire the fact may not be overlooked that at that time I was removing 400 other Apaches over 100 miles through a mountainous country; the escape of a portion of either band would have endangered the security of the others. As prisoners of war, they are now entirely under the control of the President, and the universal wish of the people of these Territories is that none may ever be returned for any purpose." This last thrust had political overtones which gave President Cleveland pause; while the politicians in the two territories of Arizona and New Mexico might wish the hostiles placed on trial, the citizens there might not welcome the return of them even for trial.

Failing to obtain the information he wanted from Miles, and apparently despairing of getting it from him, Cleveland decided to ask the Indians themselves what terms they had made. On September 29 General Stanley was ordered to "ascertain, as fully and clearly as practicable, the exact understanding of Geronimo and Natchez as to the conditions of the surrender and the immediate circumstances which led to it." Stanley replied the following day, September 30:

> In obedience to your instructions, I examined Geronimo and Natchez to-day, separately, and this without raising their suspicions; Captain Lancaster, commanding the post, being present. Both

171

*Nachez (left) and Geronimo (right), with some of their followers, while at Fort Sam Houston at San Antonio, Texas.* Courtesy Division of Manuscripts, University of Oklahoma Library.

chiefs said they never thought of surrender until Lieutenant Gatewood, Interpreter George Wratton, and the two scouts [Martine and Kayitah] came to them and said the Great Father wanted them to surrender . . . and that when Geronimo met Miles at Skeleton Cañon, the latter said, "Lay down your arms and come with me to Fort Bowie, and in five days you will see your families, now in Florida with Chihuahua, and no harm will be done you;" that when Natchez came Miles said the same thing to him and his young men; that Geronimo and Natchez went with Miles to Fort Bowie; that the latter said, "We are all brothers; don't fear any one, no one will harm you; you will meet all the Chiricahuas; leave your horses here, maybe they will be sent to you; you will have a separate reservation with your tribe; with horses and wagons, and no one will hurt you;" that Miles talked very friendly to us, and that we believed him as we would God; that we did not surrender sooner because we did not think we would be allowed to do so; that Miles again said that we would see our families in five days,

172

and no harm would befall us. These families are now anxious to go to Florida. George Wratton confirms this report of Miles's talk to Geronimo and Natchez at Fort Bowie. Lieutenant Clay and Dr. Wood, when at San Antonio, stated to me that to their knowledge promises were made to these Indians that their lives should be spared.

Stanley wired on October 1 that a sentence inadvertently had been omitted from his dispatch the day before, a statement by Geronimo that "at Fort Bowie, General Miles did thus, said everything you have done up to this time will be wiped out like that and forgotten, and you will begin a new life."

With Miles's report in hand, as well as the statement taken by Stanley from Geronimo and Nachez, the President considered the fate of the renegades. On October 19 he reached a decision, manifested in an order from Secretary of War Endicott to General Sheridan:

By direction of the President it is ordered that the hostile adult [male] Indians, fifteen in number, recently captured in Mexico and now at San Antonio, Texas, . . . be sent under proper guard to Fort Pickens, Florida, there to be kept in close custody until further orders. These Indians have been guilty of the worst crimes known to the law, committed under circumstances of great atrocity, and the public safety requires that they should be removed far from the scene of their depredations and guarded with the strictest vigilance.

The remainder of the band captured at the same time, consisting of eleven women, six children, and two enlisted scouts [Martine and Kayitah], you are to send to Fort Marion, Florida, and place with the other Apache Indians recently conveyed to and now under custody at that post [Chihuahua's band].

Just how Martine and Kayitah could have been considered "captured" was never explained by anyone.

The renegades departed from San Antonio by special train at four o'clock on the afternoon of October 22. Three days later they were at Fort Pickens where Major General J. M. Schofield reported perhaps one of the greatest lies ever written: "Geronimo says they are well satisfied." Stanley reported on the twenty-seventh that when he had <u>informed</u> the <u>renegades</u> that they were to be sent to Fort <u>Pickens</u>, while their <u>families</u> were to <u>go</u> to Fort <u>Marion</u>, "They <u>regarded</u> the <u>separation</u> of themselves from their <u>families</u> as a <u>violation</u> of the <u>terms</u> of their surrender, by which they had been <u>guaranteed</u>, in the most positive manner conceivable to their minds, that they should be <u>united</u> with their <u>families</u> at Fort <u>Marion</u>." In fact, it was this desire to see his family that most influenced Nachez; Lieutenant Gatewood repeatedly had referred to the hereditary chief's loneliness and desire to see his family as they marched north out of Mexico.

On October 19, the same day that the President ordered Geronimo and the renegades sent to Florida, Miles wired General Howard that Captain Cooper and troops from the Tenth Cavalry had captured the final hostiles: "Mangus and his whole party, consisting of Mangus, 2 men, 3 squaws, and 5 children; also 29 mules and 5 ponies, all of which were brought in." Mangus explained his much reduced band by stating that a portion of his followers had been captured by Mexicans and never heard from again; indeed they had been caught on October 3, and were immediately executed by Tarahumara Indian irregulars hunting scalps for bounties.[10]

By the time this report reached Washington, the fate of the Apaches had been determined, and orders to move Mangus and his followers to Florida were forthcoming on October 26. That day Adjutant-General Drum advised Howard by telegram: "The Lieutenant-General commanding the Army [Sheridan] directs that you cause Mangus and the two other adult male Indians, recently captured in Arizona, to be sent to Fort Pickens, Florida, for confinement; and the three squaws and five children of the same party to Fort Marion, Florida." Lieutenant Clay, Tenth Cavalry, was placed in charge of this detail, which left Fort Apache on October 30 for Holbrook. There they boarded the Atlantic and Pacific Railroad for the journey east.

174

The trip was not without excitement for Lieutenant Clay. At Albuquerque on November 2 he reported the death of one of the braves from natural causes. The body was left at Fort Union for burial. Two days later, November 4, Clay reported from Coolidge, Kansas, that Mangus had tried to escape the night before. Somehow he slipped his handcuffs off over his hands (Miles claimed in his *Personal Recollections,* "It is impossible to handcuff an Indian securely, as his hands are smaller than his wrists");[11] then, even though under guard by a wide-awake sentinel, he smashed through the plate-glass window of the train, which was moving at thirty-five miles an hour. The train was stopped, and Clay rushed outside to find that Mangus had been stunned by his fall and thus was unable to make good his escape. A doctor examined him at Coolidge and found him only slightly injured. On November 6 the gates of Fort Pickens closed behind him and his remaining warrior, marking a final close to the long and bloody Geronimo campaign of 1885-86. However, for the victors there was popular adulation which promised promotion, medals, and even political gain. Thus the fight for credit for the surrender of Geronimo, who had become the focal point of all popular attention during the conflict, would be as hard fought and even more lengthy than the campaign itself.

# NINE

# THE FIGHT

# FOR GLORY

Miles give anyone credit? Hell, NO. He was never known to do
that at any stage of his career.

Dad Golden to E. A. Brininstool,
April 3, 1928, Letter No. 342, Gatewood Collection.

ON THE SAME DAY THE TRAIN LEFT Bowie Station carrying Geronimo and the Apache renegades eastward to San Antonio, and
eventually to Florida, Nelson A. Miles issued Field Order No. 90.
Paragraph seven stated, "1st Lt. C. B. Gatewood, 6th Cavalry,
having reported at these Headquarters upon the completion of
the duty to which he was assigned in connection with the Chiricahua and Warm Springs Indians, will rejoin his station at Fort
Stanton, N. M., via Albuquerque, N. M." Ironically, that statement was followed by the standard entry, "The travel as directed
is necessary for the public service."[1]

Gatewood's transfer to his duty station at Fort Stanton was intended to remove him from the public spotlight, for no sooner
had Geronimo departed Arizona than the fight began to secure
whatever glory—and promotion might be had therefrom. Gatewood was not safely hidden at Fort Stanton. Too many people
knew of his part in the recent campaign, and newspapermen
might reach him there. Miles therefore changed his mind about
sending the young lieutenant back to his regiment. On October

10, Gatewood was named aide-de-camp to Miles, which meant he was always close enough for the general to keep him under close surveillance. The only positive recognition which Miles extended Gatewood for his exploit came in the form of an invitation to accompany a delegation of Arizona Indians to Washington. Captain John A. Dapray was instructed by Miles to tender this invitation to Gatewood. "I shall never forget the expression on . . . [Gatewood's] face when I made known to him General Miles's wish in that respect," Dapray later recalled. "He looked positively alarmed, saying, 'These clothes on my back (pointing to his blue flannel shirt, which he was wearing without a blouse) are all the clothes I have with me. I can't go to Washington very well and I hope the General will let me off." Dapray explained that the invitation was meant as a "bit of rest," whereupon Gatewood replied, "Well, tell the General if it is that only, I will appreciate it much more if he will let me go into the Post for a few days to see my wife and child."

Even as Miles's aide-de-camp, Gatewood kept receiving letters from Army friends and from civilians in the region congratulating him on his splendid and courageous achievement in securing Geronimo's surrender. Miles grew so jealous that he began enacting a petty revenge. Gatewood's wife later detailed one such incident:

A fete was given in Tucson, the guest of honor being Lieut. Gatewood. In the arrangements, so much was said of him that Gen. Miles got enraged at playing second fiddle, and at the last minute, after we had accepted invitations of all sorts & had clothes made for the occasion, he ordered Lt. Gatewood to stay behind and look after the office during his absence—a clerk's work & unnecessary. Some papers came to the office to be signed (Los Angeles) certifying that the servants in the Miles . . . household were "packers," receiving packers wages from the government. Lt. Gatewood refused to sign the papers, for which Gen. Miles did not forgive him, and sought on several occasions to court martial him, but failed to find a reason which would not show up some of his own practices. It was common gossip at Hdqrs that Amos Kimball [the servant indicated above] had made much money at Govt expense with Miles' connivance, notably on a contract for stores for the Army, and that Miles had an old man of the mountain [a blackmailer] on his back and had to take him everywhere he went. Such a storm of comment and inquiry met him when Lt. Gatewood—the man for whom the Tucson fete was arranged—did not appear that he found himself cornered, and made the mistake of publishing in a S[an] F[rancisco] paper, that he "was sick of this adulation of Lt. Gatewood, who only did his duty." No soldier ever received a higher compliment, & once more Miles was made to feel that he had made a slip.

Wishing to transfer from Miles's direct command, a transfer from his own regiment, Gatewood applied in December 1886 for a position in the Quartermaster or Commissary Department. Miles agreed to the request, sending it forward with his endorsement and recommendation. In fact, he came close in this endorsement to giving Gatewood some measure of credit for his exploit in the Geronimo campaign: "His zeal and courage," wrote Miles, "are of the highest order, and recently in the campaign against Geronimo he bore a very conspicuous part, especially at the close, when his good judgment and heroism aided much in bringing about satisfactory results." Two years later, in 1888, Gatewood again applied for a transfer to the Commissary Department, as well as promotion to captain; this time he sought political endorsement and secured it from the lieutenant governor of California and a state senator and two National Democratic Committeemen from the same state. The influence of these men was too slight to help, however, and he continued as Miles's aide-de-camp. Finally on September 14, 1890, he was allowed to rejoin his regiment, the Geronimo campaign now forgotten by the public. From Fort Wingate, New Mexico, the regiment was transferred to the Dakotas to participate in the Sioux War (the ghost dance episode).

He was in the field against the Sioux from December 1890 to January 1891, when his health broke and he took sick leave for a year. He still had not been promoted beyond first lieutenant or had any recognition for his earlier services, despite his wife's use of family connections. She had written Senator A. P. Gorman of Maryland, a friend of her father, who responded, "I fear that I cannot have any great influence with the powers that be, but will take pleasure in doing what I can. . . . I think he deserves it."

In the fall of 1891 Gatewood's health recovered sufficiently to permit him to return to duty with his regiment, which was then stationed at Fort McKinney, Wyoming. There he and the regiment were involved in a smoldering feud that came to be known as the Johnson County War.[2] Wyoming was then undergoing a struggle between the big ranchers, most of whom did not own title to the ranges they were occupying, and the farmers, who were homesteading the land. In this bitter struggle, the cattle barons had sufficient strength to annihilate the farmers, so the "nesters," as they were derisively called, allied themselves with a horde of cattle thieves then in the Territory. Both hated the ranchers enough to join forces. The ranchers first tried legal remedies to rid themselves of the rustlers, but failed because the farmers held political power through strength of numbers: their elected sheriffs would not arrest them. The big ranchers thereupon took matters into their own hands. They formed an association, hired "detectives," who more often than not were professional killers, and meted out "hemp justice" to end the rustling and to remove the nesters.

The use of imported "detectives" stirred the controversy and further cemented the relationships between farmers and thieves. However, that relationship almost dissolved in fear when word spread early in 1892 that the cattlemen's association had drawn up a list of one hundred names of persons alleged to be cattle thieves and who were to be killed on sight by their "detectives." The top two names on this list were Nate Champion and Tom Waggoner. The detectives caught Waggoner and lynched him, then prepared to catch Champion. The expedition for this purpose was readied on April 5, 1892, the same day that thirty gunmen arrived from Texas to fight for the cattlemen. That day the

179

gunmen, the ranchers, their managers, and their cowboys left Cheyenne by train, arriving at Casper the next day.

At sunrise on April 7 the cattlemen's expedition saddled up, loaded their wagons with supplies, and departed to the north to round up Champion and all settlers in the vicinity. According to rumor some people were to be hanged and others deported. Forty miles from Casper, the expedition learned that Champion and a small gang were camped on the North Fork of the Powder River. It halted while scouts checked this report. On the afternoon of the eighth the scouts returned with hard information that Champion and his partner, Nick Ray, were in a cabin at Nolan's K. C. Ranch. During the night of April 8-9, the expedition surrounded the cabin, and the next morning Champion and Ray were killed. A settler and his son who happened to be passing saw what happened and fled to spread the alarm to all homesteaders in the vicinity. The cattlemen's expedition, after killing Champion and Ray, decided to ride for the town of Buffalo, some sixty miles away. Twenty-two miles from the town, however, they learned that two hundred armed and angry farmers, led by Arapahoe Brown, a renowned Indian fighter and mountain man, had departed from Buffalo to do battle with them. The expedition thereupon detoured to the T. A. Ranch, located on the bank of Crazy Woman's Fork twelve miles from Buffalo. There the two parties confronted each other on the morning of April 10.

Brown deployed his force in a semi-circle along the crest of a ridge overlooking the ranch buildings, while the cattlemen forted up inside. For two days the opposing forces fired ineffectively at each other. Early on the morning of April 13, just as the farmers were preparing to storm the buildings and kill the ranchers, a detachment of the Sixth Cavalry arrived in response to a call for Federal assistance from Acting Governor Amos W. Barber. Colonel J. J. Van Horn, in charge of the troops, induced the cattlemen to surrender, and they were taken to Fort McKinney for detention. The stockade was not large enough to hold all of the cattlemen; the overflow was locked in the band barracks, which was vacated for that purpose.

A few nights later a guard saw two men running away from the band barracks and sounded the alarm. An investigation revealed a huge bomb hidden under the band barracks. It was made from a hot-water boiler filled with gun powder and rifle bullets, with a firing mechanism made from an old gun. About two hundred yards of wire led from it to the nearby stables. When those who had planted the bomb—and it was widely assumed the deed had been done by the nesters—tried to explode it, the wire had broken. The guard was redoubled around the barracks until Easter Sunday morning, April 17, when the prisoners were moved out on their way to Cheyenne and a civil trial. The troops then relaxed, only to be awakened on the morning of May 18 by cries of "fire." Later three cowboys of the Red Sash Ranch crew would be arrested for the crime. Their motive was that the troops were hindering the cattlemen's efforts to wipe out the farmers and rustlers. The cowboys had thrown kerosene on the Post Trader's store and set it afire, hoping that the high winds would blow the flames onto four connecting wooden barracks. The water system at the post proved inadequate, and the troops formed a bucket brigade. Still the fire grew.

Lieutenant Gatewood, the post ordnance officer, was called to blow up the second barracks and save the final two from destruction. As one side of the second barracks ignited, Gatewood and two helpers entered it to lay two sixty-pound bags of rifle powder inside, placing iron bunks atop them to increase the explosive force. There was no fuse; the fire would ignite the powder. Just as Gatewood, the last man out, was leaving the barracks the powder exploded, and one of the iron bunks hit his upraised left arm, smashing it. He was badly burned also. That arm never healed properly, and he took sick leave on November 19, 1892, retiring to Maryland to live. Then in 1896 he began having severe stomach pains and went to Fortress Monroe for treatment. There he died at 11:45 p.m. on May 20, 1896, of stomach cancer.

At the time, he was awaiting medical retirement—and promotion for he was senior lieutenant in the Sixth Cavalry and eighth ranking lieutenant in the entire Army. The day after his death his body was moved by steamer to Washington. From there it went by caisson to Arlington National Cemetery for interment with full military honors.

On May 23, 1896, Colonel D. S. Gordon, colonel commanding, Sixth Cavalry, issued General Order No. 19, which stated:

It is with extreme sorrow and regret that the colonel command-ing the regiment announced the death of 1st Lieut. Charles B. Gatewood at Fort Monroe May 20. Too much cannot be said in honor of this brave officer and it is lamentable that he should have died with only the rank of a lieutenant, after his brilliant services to his Government. That no material advantages reverted to him is regretted by every officer of his regiment, who extend to his bereaved family their most profound, earnest and sincere sympa-thy. . . . As a mark of respect to his memory, the officers of the regiment will wear the usual badge of mourning for the period of 30 days.

Years later, his son Charles B. Gatewood, Jr., would state the same sentiment, but with brevity and bitterness: "His reward, for services that have often been described as unusual, was like that of many another soldier who has given his all that his country might grow and prosper: for himself a free plot of ground in Arlington Cemetery, and to his widow a tawdry seventeen dollars a month."

A belated movement to get Gatewood the Medal of Honor as recognition for his services in the Geronimo Campaign, made in 1895 when it was widely assumed his health was such that he would not live, was denied on the basis that he had never come under actual fire. Curiously, the commanding general of the Army, Nelson A. Miles, had endorsed the recommendation, which was submitted by Captain A. P. Blocksom of the Sixth Cavalry: Miles signed it, even though it carried the statement: "for gallantry in going alone at the risk of his life into the hostile

Apache camp of Geronimo in Sonora. . . ." This was contrary to what Miles was then writing in his *Personal Recollections,* published in 1897. Gatewood would certainly have been justified in feeling bitter when he saw others, whose contributions were smaller, receiving promotion and medals. His son, Charles B. Gatewood, Jr., later commented: "My father was deeply and terribly hurt, more in his sense of the fitness of things than in any sense of his own injury. . . . If my father had decided to fight the issue, he would eventually have forced all the honorable opposition into his camp, leaving the culpable ones in a position where they might easily have been exposed and disgraced, but he did not. It would have caused a scandal and worked injury to the Army, and knowing my father as I did, I feel sure that this consideration rather than his own hurt pride or fear of the opposition kept him silent."

There was considerable controversy in the years that followed over who should get the credit for securing Geronimo's final surrender. As indicated by Gatewood's son, the lieutenant never took a personal part in such arguments. Charles D. Rhodes, who graduated from the Military Academy in 1889 and joined the Sixth Cavalry, later wrote of his intimate association with Gatewood: ". . . nothing could drag out of this modest, unassuming, and even diffident officer, anything which might glorify in the least his part in the ending of the interminable Apache raids. . . . My regiment was a unit in feeling that all credit for Geronimo's surrender belonged to Gatewood, and there was considerable quiet criticism that no sentimental recognition was accorded Gatewood for the outstanding act of courage and good judgment, which only field-soldiers could truly appreciate."

One aspect of the Gatewood legend that grew among his comrades and admirers was his "lack of fear." Despite Gatewood's own comments to the contrary, showing his healthy respect of Apache strength and occasional fears for his safety, others wrote that he was "never afraid." J. A. Cole, in 1886 a second lieutenant with the Sixth Cavalry, later stated, "Genial, careless, devil-may-care, not in a reckless way, but just naturally so, he was the man with the steel spine when that kind was needed. . . ." George Wratten can be excused for the statement, "No! We weren't *afraid!*" which he made in describing the journey into Geronimo's camp; he said this as an old man almost two decades after the event. However, on one point almost all who knew Gatewood was unanimous; he was modest. Cole stated, ". . . he was modest to and past a fault." The meek may inherit the earth, but they rarely get credit during their lives for what positive good they achieve.

Another loser in the Geronimo campaign was George Crook, forced to request reassignment because not all the Apaches surrendered in March of 1886 and because of political pressures in the East. Upon departing Arizona, he was assigned to command of the Department of the Platte. It was a very quiet region in 1886, and Crook had time for meetings of the Loyal Legion and the gatherings of the veterans' organization, the Army of West Virginia. He also found time to continue his fight about the treatment of the surrendered Apaches and to attempt the embarrassment of his foe, Nelson A. Miles. In Omaha in 1886 he published a pamphlet entitled *Resumé of Operations against Apache Indians, 1882-1886,* wherein he defended his position that diplomacy rather than force was the proper method for ending the Apache wars. He presented the Apaches as dignified human beings in this work, just as he had in 1885 in statements subsequently published in Philadelphia under the title *Letter from George Crook on Giving the Ballot to Indians.*

When Chatto went to Washington in July of 1886 at the head of a delegation of Apache chiefs, Crook had his aide, Captain John G. Bourke, go to Washington and accompany them. Bourke found several opportunities to raise embarrassing questions about Miles's conduct of the campaign in Arizona. Then in February of 1887 Crook was in Boston giving a series of speeches sponsored by the Boston Indian Citizenship Committee. In one of these speeches, he said: "The Indian is a human being. One question today on whose settlement depends the honor of the United States is, 'How can we preserve him?' My answer is, 'First, take the government of the Indians out of politics; second, let the laws of the Indians be the same as those of the whites; third, give the Indian the ballot.' But we must not try to drive the Indians too fast in effecting these changes. We must not try to force him to take civilization immediately in its complete form, but under just laws, guaranteeing to Indians equal civil laws, the Indian question, a source of such dishonor to our country and of shame to true patriots, will soon be a thing of the past." These certainly were radical views to most Western Americans in the 1880s.

In March of 1888 Major General Alfred H. Terry retired from the Army, creating a vacancy for promotion. Miles and Crook were the two candidates, opponents in philosophy of Indian fighting and bitter personal enemies. Miles desperately wanted the second star and fought hard for it although Crook was the ranking brigadier and normally would have had it without question. Crook made no active campaign to get the promotion; others did it for him without his having to request help. Former President Rutherford B. Hayes wrote a lengthy letter supporting the senior brigadier, stating, "His appointment will be especially gratifying to all who take an interest in just and humane treatment of the Indian. His attitude to Mr. Cleveland's administration is not in his way, and he is the most distinguished soldier named for the place." On April 6, 1888, Crook was notified that he had been promoted, and in May he became commander of the Division of the Missouri with headquarters at Chicago. His informality soon changed the atmosphere of the office; a feature story in the *Chicago Herald* declared: "There is precious little red tape around Crook's headquarters. . . . The doors are all wide open, and the visitor simply walks in. He doesn't see anybody in uniform. Everybody, from General Crook down, is in citizen's dress."

In Chicago Crook found his health failing rapidly. However,

he wanted one last fight with Miles, this one about the treatment of the imprisoned Apaches. When the Chiricahuas had surrendered to Crook in March 1886, seventy-seven of them had been sent to Fort Marion, Florida. Then in September of that year, Miles had sent Geronimo and his warriors to Florida with the understanding that they were to be reunited with their families; instead, the seventeen men were detained at Fort Pickens as prisoners of war, a violation of their terms of surrender. Then in September of the same year all the Chiricahua and Warm Springs Apaches had been sent to Fort Marion, including many of Crook's former Scouts. Thanks largely to the efforts of Herbert Welsh, head of the Indian Rights Association (a benevolent society dedicated to helping the Redman), the families of the warriors at Fort Pickens were allowed to join them there in April of 1887; all the other Apaches in Florida were transferred to Mount Vernon Barracks, near Mobile, Alabama. In May of 1888, Geronimo, Nachez, Mangus, and the warriors at Fort Pickens, along with their families, were sent to Mount Vernon Barracks. These years in the East were especially hard on the Apaches, accustomed as they were to the aridity of the Southwest; by 1890 almost twenty-five per cent—120—had died, of whom thirty were children. They suffered from malaria and other diseases alien to their desert homeland, as well as psychological factors which demoralized them. Remembering his promises to them, Crook was eager to help the Apaches, especially his former Scouts, whom he felt had been unjustly removed from Arizona.

In the fall of 1889 he accompanied a delegation of Sioux to Washington, and he made use of the occasion to fight for the voiceless Apaches. With the help of retired General O. O. Howard, he secured a report detailing the miserable condition of the Apaches in Florida. With this report he gained permission from the Secretary of War to look for a suitable reservation for the Apaches, one removed from the inhospitable climate of Florida. In December of 1889 he was at Bryson, North Carolina, but found it far too different from Arizona. From there he went on

to Mount Vernon Barracks in Alabama for a talk with the Chiricahuas. Chatto, Chihuahua, Kayitah, even Geronimo, came forward to greet their aging opponent. George Wratten was still
with the Apaches, and served as Crook's interpreter. Crook's report of this interview was cited by President Harrison in asking
for Congressional passage of an act removing the Apaches to
Fort Sill, Oklahoma.[3] Since the passage of such an act would be
interpreted as a reprimand to Miles for sending them to Florida,
and through him, to Grover Cleveland, the bill was hard fought
by Democrats and friends of Miles. In attempting to get the bill
defeated, Miles claimed that the Apache Scouts had been disloyal
and that they had supplied the renegades with arms and ammunition. Crook responded gleefully:

> This [Miles's statement] is all false. These stories are being circu-
> lated for a purpose. Chatto was not only faithful, but it was due
> entirely to the efforts of his Indian scouts that the hostiles under
> Nachez and Geronimo surrendered to me in March, 1886. It is
> true that General Miles did discharge the Apache scouts and after
> operating against thirty-three Indians for over five months without
> killing or capturing a single one of them, he sent Lt. Gatewood
> and two of Chatto's scouts, who succeeded in securing the sur-
> render of the renegades upon the promise that they should not be
> harmed, and should be sent to join their families in Florida.

The Senate finally requested all documents relating to the campaign of 1885-86, with an eye to moving the Indians to a better
climate, and the Geronimo campaign seemed about to be fought
once more. But while the bill for their removal was making
favorable progress, Crook suddenly died of a heart attack on the
morning of March 21, 1890. His death ended all hope of Congressional passage of the bill, and the Apaches remained at Mount
Vernon Barracks until August 6, 1894, when they were removed
to Fort Sill. Crook was interred at Arlington National Cemetery
with full military honors. Red Cloud, the great Sioux chief,
spoke not only for his people but for most Indians as well when
he said of Crook, "He, at least, never lied to us."[4] The Indians

could say as much about few other white men who fought them
—or, for that matter, about few who controlled their destinies in
the Indian Office.

Although Gatewood and Crook never profited from the Geronimo campaign, nor even sought profit from it, Nelson Appleton
Miles did seek and gain recognition and advancement. The newspapers of Arizona, immediately after Geronimo's surrender, were
filled with his praises, and they encouraged the citizens of the
Territory to donate to a subscription fund, the proceeds of
which would be used to purchase a presentation sword for Miles.
The fund was far undersubscribed; Miles did not want to lose
the opportunity for public recognition, which was certain to be
reported in Eastern newspapers, and quietly supplied the money
needed to buy an extravagant blade. The sword came from Tiffany's of New York. With the exception of the Damascus blade,
the grip, and a fifty-six-carat India star sapphire, it was entirely
of gold. Engraved on it were scenes from the Apache wars. The
presentation was made in Tucson on November 8, 1887. The
festivities started with a street parade and ended with a banquet
hosted by the Society of Arizona Pioneers. Miles used the occasion to call for irrigation projects to open the Territory to more
farming.

At almost all subsequent public occasions and appearances,
Miles assumed personal credit for persuading Geronimo to surrender at Skeleton Canyon. Since he had not gone personally into
Mexico, he could not claim he had tracked Geronimo down; but
he could, and did, claim that his strategy of hot pursuit had so
tired the Apache chief and his followers that they wanted to
give up. He wrote in his first autobiographical effort, *Personal
Recollections and Observations,* published in 1897, that Geronimo did not intend to surrender at Skeleton Canyon until Miles
persuaded him. He wrote:

> I had a conversation with Geronimo in which I induced him to
> talk quite freely, and then tried to explain to him the uselessness
> of contending against the military authority of the white race,

owing to our many superior advantages. I told him that we had the use of steam, and could move troops with great rapidity from one part of the country to another; that we also had the telegraph and the heliostat, both superior to any of their methods of communication. He wanted to know what that was, and I said I would explain it to him.

We were then near a pool of water with no cover overhead. The operator had placed his heliostat on an extemporized tripod made by placing three sticks together. I said to Geronimo:

"We can watch your movements and send messages over the tops of these mountains in a small part of one day, and over a distance which it would take a man mounted on a swift pony twenty days to travel."

Geronimo's face assumed an air of curiosity and incredulity, and he said:

"How is that?"

I told him I would show him, and, taking him down to the heliostat, asked the operator to open communication with the nearest station which was about fifteen miles away in an air line. He immediately turned his instrument upon that point and flashed a signal of attention. As quick as thought the sunlight was flashed back.

As I have previously had occasion to remark, when an Indian sees something that he cannot comprehend, he attributes it to some superior power beyond his knowledge and control, and immediately feels that he is in the presence of a spirit. As those stalwart warriors in Montana in using the telephone for the first time had given it the name of the "whispering spirit," so this type of the wild southern savage attributed the power he saw to something more than a mere human being. He told me that he had observed these flashes upon the mountain heights, and believing them to be spirits, had avoided them by going around those points of the mountains, never realizing that it was a subtle power used by his enemies, and that those enemies were themselves located upon these lofty points of observation and communication. I explained to him that it, the instrument, was not only harmless, but of great use, and said to him:

"From here to that point is a distance of nearly a day's march. From that point we can communicate all over this country. I can send a message back to Fort Bowie, sixty-five miles away, or to Fort Apache, nearly three hundred miles from here, and get an answer before the sun goes down in the West."

He comprehended its power and immediately put my statement to the test by saying:

"If you can talk with Fort Bowie, do this: I sent my brother to you there as a guarantee of my good faith; now tell me if my brother is all right." I said to the operator:

"Open communication with Fort Bowie and ask the officer in command, Major Beaumont, or Captain Thompson, my Adjutant-General, if Geronimo's brother is at Fort Bowie.

"Now," I said to Geronimo, "you must wait, for that inquiry with the reply will have to be repeated six times."

In a short time the answer came back that Geronimo's brother was there, was well, and waiting for him to come. This struck the savage with awe, and evidently made a strong impression upon him. I noticed that he said something to one of the warriors close by him, at which the warrior quickly turned upon his heel, walked back a short distance to where his pony was lariated, jumped on his back, and rode rapidly back in the direction of the mountains whence Geronimo had come. This excited my curiosity, and I asked the interpreter, who was standing near by, what Geronimo had said to the young warrior. The interpreter replied: "He told him to go and tell Natchez that there was a power here which he could not understand; and to come in, and come quick.[5]

Lies so abound in this passage that it can rightfully be called little more than a product of Miles's imagination. The most ridiculous part is to the effect that the heliograph (or heliostat as he called it) led to the final surrender both of Geronimo and Nachez. Not a single battle resulted from its use, not a single shot was fired because of it, and Geronimo definitely understood both its function and its working long before the surrender occurred at Skeleton Canyon. In truth, the heliograph was an expensive toy whose only benefit was in reporting the movement of troops. Nor was Miles the originator of the idea, even among the Indians. As early as August of 1885, according to C. A. P. Hatfield, an Army officer who participated in these campaigns, the Apaches had taken a "position on a conspicuous, lofty mountain, called Sierra Azul, in Sonora about seventy-five miles southeast of Fort Huachuca, and kept up a brisk signalling to parties in Arizona. The signalling was done by torch at night and could be plainly seen."[6]

Soon after the Tucson banquet, at which he was presented the sword he helped to buy, Miles was honored in San Francisco. Immediately after this event, the newspapers owned by George Hearst began mentioning Miles's name for the presidency in 1888. Miles offered no public rebuttal to this move; in fact, he rather fancied the idea. The movement failed ingloriously, the Republican nomination—and election—going to Benjamin Harrison. Thereby he lost his second star. When recommended for the vacancy created by Terry's retirement in 1888, opposition newspapers declared editorially that Miles had been promoted to brigadier solely on the strength of the influence of his wife's relatives, Senator John Sherman and General William T. Sherman. The promotion went to Miles's bitter opponent and critic, George Crook, instead, much to Miles's chagrin. However, Miles was given command of the Department of the Pacific, a post which normally was held by a two-star general, which was some consolation.

Then in March of 1890 Crook died, and Miles pulled every string at his command to be promoted to fill the vacancy. First he secured recommendations from Leland Stanford and George Hearst, both of whom had powerful connections in Washington. Next Miles wired Senator John Sherman to ask his support, and he requested an interview with President Harrison. To Mary, his wife, he confided just before meeting Harrison, "My future rests on that interview." The next day, April 6, 1890, he sent the details to her: "At first I found the mind of the President prejudiced by some one although he received me cordially. I soon disarmed his prejudice and removed from his mind some irronous [sic] ideas that he had formed. I think in half an hour we were on good terms and at the end of an hour I am satisfied he had made up his mind to appoint me." His sense for his own destiny never failed him, and this time his confidence was not misplaced: he had, indeed, convinced Harrison. The nomination was announced that same day. Again he wrote Mary, "The top round of the ladder gives me more pleasure I think than any of the others, and I know how delighted you will be. . . ." He pompously signed that letter to his wife, "Nelson A. Miles, Major General, U.S.A."[7] The promotion brought with it command of the Division of the Missouri, and thus he was confronted with the final Sioux Wars of 1890-91.

As commander of the Division of the Missouri, he also had to oversee the breaking of the railroad strike in Chicago in 1894. This cost him popularity with the mass of voters—and thus helped deprive him of the nomination for the presidency in 1896, which he coveted even more than his second star. He did become commanding general of the Army in September of 1895, however. Two years later he went to Europe as an observer of the war between Greece and Turkey and as the United States military representative at the Diamond Jubilee of Queen Victoria. He enjoyed the trip to England, where he was lionized as the conqueror of Sitting Bull and Geronimo.

It was the nation's misfortune that Miles was still in command of the Army during the Spanish-American War. When that conflict came, the Army had no plans for it, and, as had happened in previous wars, there was no reserve of weapons or trained men. During the war, planning was so haphazard that more soldiers died from eating beef preserved with formaldehyde than from Spanish bullets. In fact, the situation was so chaotic that volunteers invaded Cuba, while Miles stormed ashore in Puerto Rico with the regulars. Again his political hopes were dashed. Instead of winning the glory that would have brought him the presidency, his campaign in Puerto Rico captured few headlines; the Spaniards surrendered with little fight. When Miles landed at New York City after the war was over, he was greeted with no parade, and he had to share honors at a formal dinner with the hero of the war, Theodore Roosevelt. Neither man appreciated that fact, for both loved the spotlight too well to wish to share it. They were cut from the same cloth.

Miles finally received the coveted third star in 1901. At the time he was promoted, he had a photograph taken with his hand on the sword presented him by "grateful" Arizonans. Roosevelt, when he saw the picture, referred to Miles as a "strutting peacock." Unfortunately for Miles, Roosevelt became President in 1901, a position which he used to make Miles uncomfortable whenever possible. In the summer of 1903 Roosevelt attempted to retire Miles prematurely by issuing an executive order that all Civil War veterans still on active duty had to prove their physical fitness by riding ninety miles cross-country on horseback within seventy-two hours. In July Miles made the ride from Fort Sill to Fort Reno, Oklahoma, in nine and one-half hours, a feat which he had well publicized in the newspapers. However, on August 8, 1903, he reached the minimum retirement age, sixty-four, and Roosevelt removed him immediately and as humiliatingly as possible. There was no message of congratulations to Miles either from the President or the Secretary of War, Elihu Root, nor was there a parade. Roosevelt was so anxious to be rid of Miles, in fact, that Samuel B. M. Young was sworn in as a lieutenant general two hours before Miles retired at eleven a.m., although the law stipulated that the Army could have only one three-star general at a time. Miles departed his office without cheers or shouting—just a handshake from a Senate messenger who had been in Miles's command at Fortress Monroe at the end of the Civil War and had guarded Jefferson Davis. Miles lived until May of 1925, dying in Washington. Fittingly he was at the circus. No epitaph was carved on his tomb at Arlington National Cemetery.

Of those who served in the Geronimo campaign under Miles's direction, only two—and both of them non-West Pointers—were rewarded: Henry Ware Lawton and Leonard Wood. Miles commended them for pursuing Geronimo until the Indian begged for peace, for thereby he was commending his own policy of a military solution to the Indian problem. The general also rewarded Lawton in a tangible way; by 1889 he had promoted the captain two grades to the rank of lieutenant colonel. Lawton remained a lieutenant colonel until the Spanish-American War. During that conflict he commanded the Second Division of the Fifth Army Corps, which invaded Cuba, and was promoted to colonel in the regular Army and brigadier general of volunteers. After the fall of Santiago he was appointed commander of the district and promoted to brevet major general. In December of 1898 he was ordered to the Philippines as second in command to Major General E. S. Otis, and there led the First Division of the Eighth Army Corps. On December 19, 1899, he was killed in an attack upon intrenched Filipinos at San Mateo, Luzon; ironically the insurgents were being led by a Filipino called Geronimo. The rumor persisted in Army ranks for years that Lawton was shot by one of his own men.

Lawton's report of the capture of Geronimo was made on September 9, 1886, while he was en route to San Antonio with the Apache prisoners. Gatewood's widow claimed it later was rewritten at Miles's insistence to make it seem that military coercion, not Gatewood's diplomacy, had forced Geronimo's surrender. In the report Lawton stated: "On the evening of the 24th I came up with Lieutenant Gatewood and found him in communication with the hostiles; but on his return from their camp he reported that they declined to make an unconditional surrender, and wished him to bear certain messages to General Miles." That much of the report technically was correct. The rest, however, was fabricated to correlate with the public position taken by General Miles: "I persuaded Gatewood to remain with me, believing that the hostiles would yet come to terms, and in this I was not disappointed. The following morning Geronimo came into camp, and intimated his desire to make peace, but wished to see and talk with General Miles. I made an agreement with him that he should come down from the mountains, camp near my command, and await a reply to his request to see and talk with General Miles. . . ."

In bestowing praise on himself, Lawton observed, "During this latter portion of the campaign the command marched and scouted 1,645 miles, making a total of 3,041 miles marched and scouted during the whole campaign. The command taking the field May 5, continued almost constantly on the trail of the hostiles, until their surrender more than four months later, with scarcely a day's rest or intermission. It was purely a command of soldiers, there being attached to it barely one small detachment of trailers. It was the persistent and untiring labor of the command which proved to the hostiles their insecurity in a country which had heretofore afforded them protection, and seemingly rendered pursuit impossible. This command, which fairly run [sic] down the hostiles and forced them to seek terms, has clearly demonstrated that our soldiers can operate in any country the Indians may choose for refuge, and not only cope with them on their own ground, but exhaust and subdue them."[8]

Lawton's report was fanciful in its estimate of the ability of the soldiers to pursue the Indians. It also was filled with errors of omission in that it did not point out that the "barely one small detachment of trailers" were the Indian Scouts that Miles wanted disbanded, and they were the ones who kept the soldiers on the trail of the hostiles. Nor had the command "fairly run down the hostiles and forced them to seek terms." He was truthful in saying his troops were in the field for four months and marched 1,645 miles. But they never endangered the Apaches' places of refuge. In fact, when Gatewood joined Lawton's force, the captain admitted having no knowledge whatsoever of the Apaches' location. Also, had Geronimo been inclined to surrender to Lawton because of the unrelenting pursuit, he could easily have found him without Gatewood. When General Stanley interviewed Geronimo and Nachez in San Antonio, both commented that they had no thoughts of surrender until Gatewood came to them. Lawton's report was filled with lies—but it contained what Miles wanted.

Lawton, in his report, recognized the efforts of a few subordinates, praising especially the assistant surgeon with him:

I desire to particularly invite the attention of the department commander to Asst. Surg. Leonard Wood, the only officer who has been with me through the whole campaign. His courage, energy, and loyal support during the whole time; his encouraging example to the command, when work was the hardest and prospects darkest; his thorough confidence and belief in the final success of the expedition, and his untiring efforts to make it so, has placed me under obligations so great that I cannot even express them.

Leonard Wood was courageous and had performed well beyond the call of an assistant surgeon's duties, but he was far from the only officer with Lawton "during the whole time." Lieutenant H. B. Benson, who had taken the field against the hostiles on May 1, 1886, before Lawton had his entire command ready, later wrote, "I was present during the entire time, and as a matter of fact was on the expedition longer than either Captain Lawton or Doctor Wood." He also noted that "Troop B of the 4th Cavalry started on this expedition on May 2d and remained with it until the end, so that besides the three officers—that is, Captain Lawton, Doctor Wood, and Lieut. Benson—there were at least forty enlisted men who were with the command from start to finish." Benson went on to point out other inconsistencies in Lawton's report, concluding:

While it is never necessary to tell a lie, it is not always wise to tell all the truth, consequently many facts connected with this campaign will probably never be known; but this much is certain: First, that Lawton and Wood were not the only men who endured the whole campaign; Second, that water was not scarce nor did the command ever travel where there was no shade nor grass visible; Third, that the command was never without supplies; Fourth, that no company of soldiers ever became exhausted and were ordered back to barracks for this reason; Fifth, that no portion of Captain Lawton's command, except Troop B of the 4th Cavalry, ever had a fight with the Indians during the entire campaign, and at this fight Doctor Wood was not present; that Doctor Wood never saw a hostile Indian from the time he started until Geronimo came into Lawton's camp to talk surrender, and that he never heard a shot fired at any hostile Indians; Seventh, that the nom-

*Rough Riders in 1898; left to right: Colonel Leonard Wood, Lieutenant John C. Greenway, Orderly Charles Sipes, and Lieutenant Colonel Theodore Roosevelt.* Courtesy Arizona Pioneers' Historical Society.

inal command of a few soldiers of infantry—travelling over the country for a few weeks in the wake of a detachment of Indian scouts . . . secured for the person in nominal command [Wood] a reputation—entirely outside the Army—for command and capacity in Indian fighting and also a medal of honor.[9]

Wood did indeed get the medal of honor; it came in 1898, curiously when he was White House surgeon to his good friend, President William McKinley.

At the outbreak of the Spanish-American War, Dr. Wood and another friend, Assistant Secretary of the Navy Theodore Roosevelt, organized the Rough Rider Regiment with Wood as colonel and Roosevelt as lieutenant colonel. Both ranks were brevet. Wood commanded this regiment at Las Guasimas, and led a brigade at the Battle of San Juan Hill. On July 8, 1898, he was commissioned a brigadier general of volunteers, and then on December 7th that same year was promoted to major general of volunteers. In Cuba he governed first the city of Santiago, then the Department of Santiago and early in 1899, upon the resignation of General John R. Brooke, became Governor-General of the entire island. For three years he administered the island, his administration being noted for its honesty and efficiency. While there in 1901 he was commissioned a brigadier general in the regular Army, the appointment being submitted to Congress by Theodore Roosevelt, who had become President after McKinley's death. In 1903 Wood departed Cuba for the Philippines, where he commanded a division of the Army, and that year he advanced to major general in the regular Army. After five years in the Philippines, he returned to the United States, where he commanded the Department of the East in 1908-09. In 1910 he served as a special ambassador to Argentina, then became commanding general of the Army from 1910 to 1914. When the World War began in Europe in 1914, Wood and his friend Roosevelt were leading advocates of preparedness for this nation. Yet when the United States actually entered the conflict in 1917, the Wilson administration refused to give him an overseas command, despite the fact that he was the ranking general in the Army. Angry at this affront, Wood became an active candidate for the presidency, almost winning the nomination of the Republican Party in 1920. With the victory of the Harding ticket, Wood was named governor-general of the Philippines in 1921, where he advocated independence for the islands. He died in Washington on August 7, 1927, shortly after his return from the Philippines.

Among the most ridiculous claims to fame from the Geronimo campaign of 1885-86 was one advanced by Tom Horn, who had served as Chief of Scouts. Horn declared that he alone was responsible for persuading Geronimo to talk with Crook in March of 1886. Then, after Miles assumed command and sent Lawton into the field, Horn asserted that Miles was forced to send for him:

> The General told me . . . that he wanted me to go to Mexico and find Captain Lawton . . . , and act as chief of scouts with him and see what we could do.
>
> I went down and struck Lawton's camp at a place in Sonora, called Sierra Gordo. . . . As we were coming up by Fronteras, as usual, we found a couple of women who had given out, and we put them on pack mules and took them on to Fronteras. There Captain Lawton had a helio dispatch to drop the chase, and for me to come to [Fort] Huachuca. The dispatch had been there for two days.
>
> Before I got ready to start, there came another to wait there, as Lieutenant Gatewood and a couple of Chiricahua bucks [Martine and Kayitah] were coming up to try to open communications with Geronimo. These were two men who had come in with Chief Chihuahua.
>
> The Chiricahuas had been leaving signs for a couple of weeks that they wanted to talk, and these signs had all been reported by me to Captain Lawton, and by Lawton to General Miles.
>
> We stopped close to Fronteras for four days to let Gatewood and his two men get ahead, so they could communicate with Geronimo, but at the end of that time Gatewood came back and reported to Captain Lawton that he could not get his two friendly Indians to approach the Chiricahuas.
>
> Gatewood told Captain Lawton that he could not open communications in that way.

Lawton then, according to Horn, turned to the Chief of Scouts and asked if he could do anything. "I told him frankly that I was the only one who could do anything!" was Horn's reply—at least, that was how he later recalled it.

Horn, however, insisted that he be allowed to go to Geronimo's camp alone. Gatewood responded that, by order of General Miles, Horn could not go alone. A telegram was then sent to Miles, according to Horn, who responded that Gatewood and Horn were to be allowed to "see what we could do." Horn continued:

Then I could not go, because I did not know what I could tell
Geronimo, and Lawton said, "Tell him anything you want to,
but get him to come and talk to Miles." I said that was what I
wanted to do, but could not unless Miles said he wanted to talk to
him. I told Lawton that I could never tell Geronimo but one lie,
for he would find it out, and the next time I went into his camp
he would tell me I had lied to him, and then he would kill me. I
refused to go unless General Miles promised me he would meet
old Geronimo at a date Geronimo and I should fix.

This word was sent to Miles, and he said for me to fix a date
and he would keep it. Ten minutes after I got this dispatch I
mounted my horse to start, and Gatewood said he would take his
chances if I would let him go. I told him he would not be taking
any chances, and to come on.

. . . We did not have to go up to the mountain, as Geronimo
met us down on the Bavispe River, and we had a long talk. I
made arrangements to go with him to the Skeleton Cañon, in the
United States, and meet Miles there in twelve days. That would
give Miles time and to spare, and I was afraid he would not come,
as he was the kind that wanted to make a renegade Indian think
he was a big man, and Geronimo was just about as vain as Miles
was, and thought that he, too, was a big man.

The only courier I had was Gatewood, and I sent him back to
tell Captain Lawton the arrangements I had made with Geronimo,
and for all the troops with him at Fronteras to come to the mouth
of Caballon Creek, and I would meet him there with the renegades. . . . Captain Lawton was very much gratified to see how
well I had done, and said for me to stay with the renegades and he
would do as I said. He told me he had sent a dispatch to Miles to
meet us at the Skeleton Cañon as I had directed.

Horn even claimed that Geronimo refused to surrender at
Skeleton Canyon unless "Talking Boy," as he insisted the Apache
chief called him, served as the interpreter. He said that Miles
refused this demand by Geronimo and that Geronimo thereupon
rode south, away from the projected meeting at Skeleton Canyon.
At John Slaughter's ranch at San Bernardino, Arizona, Horn
claimed to have been awakened to receive a heliograph message
from Miles, stating, "Make any arrangements you want to for me

*Tom Horn.* Courtesy Arizona Pioneers' Historical Society.

to meet Geronimo. I will go where and when you say to meet him." Horn claimed that he then rode south, overtook Geronimo, and in a week had him at Skeleton Canyon. Of the meeting between Geronimo and Miles, he wrote that he served as interpreter, and that Geronimo said of him: "When he comes to my camp do you suppose I ask him if he is telling the truth? No! That I never do. . . . Nothing a man does is wrong if he tells me the truth. . . . You [Miles] sent him word that you would have nothing to do with him, and I sent you word I would not have anything to do with anyone else."[10]

Horn's reminiscence was written as he waited to be hanged in Wyoming in 1902. After the Apache wars ended, he followed a path of violence that took him to the Pleasant Valley War in Arizona in 1887, saw him a deputy sheriff in Yavapai County, Arizona, and later made him a Pinkerton operative and a cattle-detective in Wyoming. During the Spanish-American War, he was employed by the Army as a Packmaster at Tampa, enlisting on April 23, 1898, at one hundred dollars per month; on August 1 he was promoted to Chief Packer at $133 per month, then was discharged on September 6, 1898. He was arrested for murder in Wyoming on January 13, 1902, following a series of brutal sniper slayings. Tried in October of that year in a bitter court fight, which had lingering overtones of the Johnson County War, he was found guilty and sentenced to hang. His last months were spent on his autobiography, entitled *Life of Tom Horn: A Vindication*, although curious errors of omission and commission show that it was written by someone else. On November 18, 1902, he was hanged in Cheyenne while two cowpuncher friends stood at the foot of the gallows and sang "Life's Railway to Heaven."[11]

Of all the participants in the final Geronimo campaign, not even Lieutenant Gatewood—who was robbed of the promotion and the glory—had to suffer as much as the two men who made possible the surrender conference on the banks of the Bavispe River in August of 1886: Martine and Kayitah. The same train which took Geronimo's band to Florida carried these two loyal Scouts to imprisonment as prisoners of war at Fort Marion. Ace Daklugie, son of Juh, nephew of Geronimo, and a child at the time, later said:

> There was just one good thing about being shipped to Florida and being Prisoners of War twenty-seven years, and that was that the scouts were rounded up and shipped along, too. They underwent the same punishment as did the combatants, and probably more. They had to endure the contempt and dislike of their people all that time.[12]

Descendants of the Apache warriors spoke in the 1950s of the lingering hatred of the Scouts and of the feuds that existed seven decades later between the descendants of Scouts and renegades.

In 1926, Martine wrote Charles B. Gatewood, Jr., from the Mescalero Apache reservation in New Mexico seeking monetary compensation. In that letter he stated, "Gen. Miles promised if we [he and Kayitah] would get Geronimo we would get $3000 apiece and the gov't. would take care of us from that time on and we would not have to be prisoners of war any longer, and this ought to be in your father's report or in Gen. Miles report." He declared that "Every body was afraid of Geronimo then, and if the gov't had not promised us we would not have risked our lives. . . ." He asserted that the two went not as Scouts or even as soldiers, but simply as bounty hunters seeking the $3,000 reward. He asked that Gatewood find this information and send it to the pension officer in Washington. Gatewood did help, and on February 19, 1927 Martine wrote to thank him: the two old Scouts had not received the $3,000 apiece, but they were given pensions. "I am getting to be an old man now," he wrote, "but I am getting along all right since I received my pension."[13]

No one, then, on the American side of the conflict received what he wanted. Gatewood's career was not advanced, and he went to a premature grave. Crook wanted peace with justice for the Indians, but died before achieving either. Miles and Leonard

Wood aspired to the presidency, but it eluded both of them. Lawton saw his career improved through promotion for his part in the campaign, but died in the Philippines, reportedly at the hand of one of his own troops. Tom Horn, who did play a vital role in the final capture, lied so much in his autobiography that he was discredited totally. The Apache Scouts who served so loyally went to the same jail that the renegades occupied. And when Nelson A. Miles became commanding general of the Army as a result of the campaign, he bungled the Spanish-American War. Even the Tucson Ring, which had done so much to promote the conflict, saw all the Chiricahua and Warm Springs Apaches transferred to Florida, thereby depriving the Ring of its lucrative contracts.

# TEN

# GERONIMO'S
# TRIUMPH

One could fill volumes from the Indians' point of view of the injustice that has been heaped upon them, as they did not have the advantage of the press to print the story of their wrongs, or the protection of the politic power. If they had been allowed to work out their destiny, in the same way that is accorded the peoples of other nationalities that emigrate to these shores, there would have been but few Indian wars.

Too little consideration and respect has been paid to the Indian's rights, as he is no different from other nationalities that are being blended into the American nation. The great mistake and weakness of the Caucasian race, especially in the United States, is in assuming to place all members of another race in the same category, making no allowance or distinction for the progressive or the non-progressive element. It is an unnatural law, and one that will not survive. The Indians love the country of their birth, and want the protection of the law. The majority are capable of fulfilling the rights and obligations of citizenship, but as long as these privileges that have made labor honorable are denied them, so long there will be an Indian question.

The Apaches often speak of General Crook and the officers that were associated with him, and of their high character. Their memories often linger back to the few who gave them a square deal.

Antonio Apache, 1909, quoted in M. Salzman, Jr.,
"Geronimo: Napoleon of the Indians,"
*The Journal of Arizona History,* VIII (Winter 1967)

*Geronimo in Florida.* Courtesy Arizona Pioneers' Historical Society.

ONLY GERONIMO STOOD ALOOF from the fight for glory in the years immediately after his surrender—there was no glory for him or for the other Apache renegades. As a prisoner of war at Fort Pickens, Florida, "They put me to sawing up large logs. There were several other Apache warriors with me, and all of us had to work every day. For nearly two years we were kept at hard labor in this place and we did not see our families until May, 1887. This treatment was in direct violation of our treaty made at Skeleton Cañon."[1] After the removal to Mount Vernon Barracks, Alabama, Geronimo and his people still suffered from the harsh climate. Both states proved so unhealthy for the Apaches that many of them died. When some of the prisoners, those who had

*Winter camp of Apache prisoners-of-war on arrival at Fort Sill, Oklahoma Territory, October 1894. Wickiups covered with Army tentage.* Courtesy U.S. Army Artillery and Missile Center Museum, Fort Sill.

not committed offenses and were not prisoners of war, were permitted to move to the Mescalero Agency in New Mexico, Geronimo was so pessimistic about his situation that he allowed one of his wives to go with them, taking with her two of their children. This separation was equivalent to a divorce among the Apaches, and that wife subsequently remarried.

The move to Fort Sill, Oklahoma, in 1894 brought a better life for the Apache prisoners of war. Houses were built for them, and they received cattle, hogs, turkeys, and chickens, along with farming instructions. Geronimo declared, "The Indians did not do much good with the hogs, because they did not understand how to care for them, and not many Indians even at the present time [1906] keep hogs. We did better with the turkeys and chickens, but with these we did not have as good luck as white men do. With the cattle we have done very well, indeed, and we like to raise them. We have a few horses also, and have had no bad luck with them."[2]

*After branding Apache calves, Fort Sill Apache cowboys turn the cattle into a large pasture on the east range of the military reservation, east of Cache Creek, where there is plenty of good grass and water.* Courtesy U.S. Army Artillery and Missile Center Museum, Fort Sill.

*Apaches baling hay at Fort Sill for sale to the Post Quartermaster, 1897. 500 tons baled, 344 tons loose.* Courtesy U.S. Army Artillery and Missile Center Museum, Fort Sill.

In captivity Geronimo, along with the other Apache prisoners, faced the philosophical question of restructuring his life. Some of the chiefs, such as Chatto, took to alcoholic beverages and deteriorated. Geronimo chose at first to "take the white man's road." He became a <u>farmer,</u> and he joined the Dutch Reformed Church, even teaching a Sunday School class for a time. He was expelled from the church, however, because "He cannot resist the temptation to bet on a horse race or on his skill as a rifle shot and is always ready to challenge all comers." <u>Photographers</u> frequently came to Fort Sill to take pictures of him holding a watermelon he had grown during the period when he was farming, just as earlier they had journeyed to Florida to pose him in loincloth and moccasins, holding an empty Sharps rifle. These pictures were sold to Easterners eager for a glimpse of the famous Apache warrior.

Geronimo apparently made a conscious decision late in life

*Former Apache warriors served as U.S. Indian scouts at Fort Sill even while technically listed as prisoners-of-war. At center, front, wearing campaign hat with the crossed arrows of the Indian Scouts, is Chief Nachez of the Chiricahua Apaches, youngest son of the great Cochise. Seated, far left, is Perico, one of Geronimo's most trusted warriors and his brother.* Courtesy U.S. Army Artillery and Missile Center Museum, Fort Sill.

not to follow the "white man's road." He did not return to the old ways, however; he became a showman. With special permission from the War Department, he attended the Omaha and Buffalo expositions and the St. Louis World's Fair as an "Attraction." At these events Geronimo gloried in his reputation—and used the opportunity to make money selling souvenir bows and arrows and pictures of himself. He spent a year with a "Wild West" show doing the same thing. On one occasion during these excursions, he spotted Nelson A. Miles in the stands and became so angry he momentarily reverted to his savage self; he jumped into the stands intending to murder Miles. The general afterward laughed about the incident and claimed that the old Apache had merely wanted to shake his hand. More reliable witnesses claimed that Geronimo wanted to kill Miles for lying in their agreement of 1886.[3]

At the special request of Theodore Roosevelt, Geronimo was brought to Washington to ride in the inaugural parade of March, 1905, along with Quanah Parker, Black Bear, Little Plum, Hol-

*Geronimo and family in their watermelon patch at Fort Sill. At left is his 6th wife, Zi-yah, who died at Fort Sill in 1904.* Courtesy U.S. Army Artillery and Missile Center Museum, Fort Sill.

*Geronimo at Fort Sill, about 1900.* Courtesy U.S. Army
Artillery and Missile Center Museum, Fort Sill.

low Horn Bear, and American Horse, chieftains from other
tribes. The next day Geronimo was interviewed at the Indian
Hotel in Washington by Dr. S. M. Huddleson of the Department
of Agriculture. Huddleson wrote afterward that, when he had
asked for Geronimo, the Apache "came forward with the quiet
tread of a cat stalking its prey. He was slender and not so tall as
he seemed the day before in his feathers and ceremonial paint.
He is inclined to stoop: age is getting the old Indian; but when
recalling the past his eyes turn brilliant and fiery, and he stands
as straight as an arrow. At times he is the very picture of savage
dejection, and at other times, the fearless and indomitable warrior of old."[4] Through George Wratten, the interpreter still with
the Apaches, Huddleson was able to ask Geronimo several questions, and Geronimo, in turn, was able to satisfy his own curiosity
on a number of points:

Among other questions, he signalled to know where we lived, and was surprised and disappointed to learn that we lived in only *one* house and on only *one* street. "Ugh!" he said in gruff disgust, and signalled that if *he* were to live in the city, *he* would live in every house in it! He liked Washington, he said, and was sure the "Little Father" (Indian Commissioner) would do the right thing by him and his people.

He also indicated a desire to see the President and ask for a pardon in order that he "might go back to his old home in Arizona, as had once been promised him." He wished to see again the land of his youth and of his ancestors, but "as a free man and not as a prisoner of war."

Wratten told Huddleson, "I had pretty near to make *that* Indian [Geronimo] all over again! He had absolutely no education, no manners and no idea of cleanliness. I taught him as I would a

*Geronimo center foreground, by buffalo. This picture was actually taken at the 101 Ranch in Oklahoma during a national editors' convention in 1905. Fort Sill officials gave permission for Geronimo to appear there. President Theodore Roosevelt was not amused.* Courtesy U.S. Army Artillery and Missile Center Museum, Fort Sill.

wee boy in school. What civilization or education he has he owes to me. He will print his name for you if you ask him. He is very fond of doing that." Geronimo obligingly wrote his name for Huddleson, and then he displayed a number of his possessions of which he seemed proud:

Geronimo possessed a boy's size, small suit-case. It was the pride of his heart and he kept it secluded on a high shelf. He unlocked it, patted it with his slender, small, aristocratic looking fingers (he had a beautifully formed hand), and gingerly drew from the interior of the suit-case his war bonnet of goat skin, gold beads and long eagle feathers. He donned the bonnet for our edification, showed how he had worn it the day previous for the Inaugural, and then muttered, "Good Injun," with a good natured and humorous smile. The bonnet tail was as long as he was tall; he flaunted it in the air, drew himself up to his full height, and made every individual feather in it quiver and flutter as though alive. He showed us his beaded belt, and made us carefully observe the design in blue and white,—some sign of his tribe of which he was very proud. Of course, we did not know its meaning, and we could only judge that it meant a great deal to him. He produced his beaded wallet also to show us the same insignia, and, with a child-like simplicity which he so often assumed, he offered it to us "Because it is Geronimo's"; but we thought it best to decline with thanks.

While on that visit to Washington, Geronimo was taken by Wratten to Arlington National Cemetery to visit the graves of the officers against whom he had fought. He was intrigued by the bronze tablet in bas-relief on Crook's monument depicting the conference at Cañon de los Embudos in March of 1886. At the nearby grave of Lieutenant Gatewood, "We shook hands all around in memory of Lieutenant Gatewood," wrote Huddleson. "Geronimo looked far away towards the setting sun and murmured that he too would soon go on the long trail."

Geronimo died at Fort Sill on February 17, 1909, still a prisoner of war and without ever returning to the desert Southwest, even for a brief visit. He was buried in the Apache cemetery at

*The burial of Geronimo, February 17, 1909.* Courtesy U.S. Army Artillery Museum, Fort Sill.

the post. The ceremony was conducted by Reverend L. L. Legters of the Dutch Reformed Church in a manner "as similar to the Apache system of burial as the clergyman thought proper." During the funeral ceremony Geronimo's widow attempted to kill the chief's favorite sorrel driving horse, as Apache custom held that a warrior would need a horse to ride in the afterworld. She was prevented from sending the horse with its master, however.

Yet for a time it seemed he had outwitted his keepers in death and gained a final triumph. On February 16, 1930, an Associated Press dispatch from Fort Sill reported:

The grave which tourists, army officers and enlisted men have looked upon in the little Apache cemetery here twenty-one years as the resting place of the bones of Geronimo, notorious war chief of the Apaches, is empty, Sergt. Morris Swett, post librarian, has revealed on the anniversary of the old warrior's death. . . . "The

215

*Some of the Apaches who settled on allotments in Oklahoma after leaving Fort Sill following release as prisoners-of-war by Act of Congress, 1913.* Courtesy U.S. Army Artillery and Missile Center Museum, Fort Sill.

remains were removed secretly at night, a short time after the funeral," Sergt. Swett said. "It is probable that no living soul save the remnants of a little band, composed mostly of old women, ever has known where they were taken and reburied. . . . I would not be surprised," Sergt. Swett continued, "to learn that after reburying the body somewhere around here, members of that little group of friends re-exhumed the bones and secretly took them back to New Mexico. . . ." Sergt. Swett said he found the body missing while seeking to raise a fund to provide a monument for Geronimo's grave.[5]

The following year, Sergeant Swett was told by those old women that Geronimo's bones actually had never been moved. The tribe

*Robert Geronimo, last living son of Geronimo, visiting the grave of his father, January 13, 1964.* Courtesy U.S. Army Artillery Museum, Fort Sill.

feared vandalism and desecration of the grave and so had only pretended to have moved the remains. Through questioning several descendants of the old chieftain, Swett convinced himself and the Army that Geronimo's remains indeed are still at Fort Sill.

Yet if Geronimo physically was still a captive, even in death, his memory was not—and that memory was undergoing a remarkable change in the minds of many Americans. As the years passed, he gradually came to symbolize the brave fight of a brave people for independence and ownership of their homeland. Articles began to appear praising him as a great fighter and a superb tactician. For example, Maurice Salzman, a native of Arizona who became a lawyer in Los Angeles, wrote in 1909, the year of Geronimo's death:

> . . . Few men, of whatever extraction or age, ever received and deserved as much of a powerful government's attention. It cost us fully a million of dollars to subdue the Apaches, and when we remember that such men as Crook and Miles, Gatewood and Lawton, Chaffee, Willcox and Bourke, the best Indian fighters that we at that time had, were necessary to accomplish the difficult task of many years' duration, we need not apologize for calling Geronimo the Napoleon of the Indian race. Further than this, had not the various generals and captains in command been able to acquire the service of the Indian scouts, there is no telling how much longer the depredations would have continued.[6]

Salzman quoted General Crook, who said that "Geronimo has the best head on his shoulders of any Indian with whom I have ever come in contact." He concluded with a personal assessment:

> I venture to prophesy that as time passes and all the obtainable material is collected and properly compiled, leaving us at a point sufficiently remote and high from contradictory statements or facts distorted because of lack of sufficient detail; that, when we shall be able to look back upon this Indian war chief with a historical perspective, we will decide that he was one of the greatest "Americans" that ever lived.

*Geronimo during one of his public appearances, "on leave" from Fort Sill. Possibly taken in Washington, D.C., during President Theodore Roosevelt's Inaugural.* Courtesy U.S. Army Artillery and Missile Center Museum, Fort Sill.

In the decades that have passed since his death, Geronimo indeed has grown steadily in stature as a great American. Novels, movies, and television have portrayed him frequently in a sympathetic light. During World War Two, paratroopers of the United States Army began using the cry "Geronimo" when they jumped from an airplane, further popularizing the Apache war chief and enhancing his reputation. Today, Geronimo is far better known than any of his contemporaries, either friend or foe. Crook, Gatewood, Miles, Wood, Lawton—all have been forgotten by the bulk of the people, but not Geronimo.

Defeat compels a man to examine why he lost and, beyond that, to discover what he has left. Geronimo was defeated in battle. His self-examination revealed that he had not lost his dignity, his heroism against overwhelming odds, and his knowledge of that bravery. These brought him to the forefront of his own people; these made him target for defeat; and these enabled him to survive as a great American.

# NOTES

## CHAPTER I

1 Robert M. Utley, "The Bascom Affair: A Reconstruction," *Arizona and the West*, III (Spring 1961), 59-68; and B. Sacks, "New Evidence on the Bascom Affair," *Arizona and the West*, IV (Autumn 1962), 261-278.

2 As an example of their propaganda, see *Memorial and Affidavits Showing Outrages Perpetrated by Apache Indians in the Territory of Arizona for the Years 1869-1870* (San Francisco: Francis & Valentine, 1871).

3 A fictionalized version of Jeffords's life is in Elliott Arnold, *Blood Brother* (New York, 1947); much of his material came from the Jeffords File, Arizona Pioneers' Historical Society, Tucson.

4 "The Capture of Geronimo," *San Dimas* (California) *Press*, April 21, 1927, contains a luncheon address by Clum; see also John P. Clum, "Apache Misrule," *New Mexico Historical Review*, V (April, July 1930), and Clum, "Geronimo," *New Mexico Historical Review*, III (January, April, July 1928). For biographical details, see Woodworth Clum, *Apache Agent* (Boston, 1936).

5 For a general history of the Apaches, there are many good books, including Will C. Barnes, *Apaches and Longhorns* (Los Angeles: Ward Ritchie Press, 1941); Gordon Baldwin, *The Warrior Apaches* (Tucson: Dale S. King, 1966); Grenville Goodwin, *The Social Organization of the Western Apache* (Chicago: University of Chicago Press, 1942); Frank C. Lockwood, *The Apache Indians* (New York, 1938); Morris E. Opler, *An Apache Life-Way* (Chicago: University of Chicago Press, 1941); and Edward H. Spicer, *Cycles of Conquest: The Impact of Spain, Mexico, and the United States on the Indians of the Southwest* (Tucson: University of Arizona Press, 1962).

## CHAPTER II

1 XIV U.S. Stat. 332; XV U.S. Stat. 318; XVI U.S. Stat. 317; XVIII U.S. Stat. 72; see also Russell F. Weigley, *History of the United States Army* (New York, 1967), 267.

2 For details of the life of the common soldier, see the excellent study by Don Rickey, Jr., *Forty Miles a Day on Beans and Hay: The Enlisted Soldier Fighting the Indian Wars* (Norman: University of Oklahoma Press, 1963).

3 E. G. Cattermole, *Famous Frontiersmen, Pioneers and Scouts* (Chicago: M. A. Donohue & Co., 1884), excerpt in Gatewood Collection.

4 For autobiographical details on Crook's life, see Martin F. Schmitt (ed.), *General George Crook: His Autobiography* (Norman: University of Oklahoma Press, 1946).

5 See Bernard C. Nalty and Truman R. Strobridge, "Captain Emmet Crawford: Commander of Apache Scouts, 1882-1886," *Arizona and the West* VI (Spring 1964), 30-40; and Crawford file, Arizona Pioneers' Historical Society, Tucson.

6 Britton Davis, *The Truth About Geronimo* (New Haven: Yale University Press, 1929), 31-32.

7 Biographical file, Gatewood Collection, Arizona Pioneers' Historical Society; see also T. J. Clay to C. B. Gatewood, Jr., August 17, 1925, Letter no. 113, Gatewood Collection.

## CHAPTER III

1 John G. Bourke, *On the Border with Crook* (New York, 1891, and reprints), 438.

2 This newspaper article is quoted in *ibid.*, 438-440.

3 George Crook to Charles B. Gatewood, January 22, 1885, Letter no. 4, Gatewood Collection.

4 Davis, *The Truth About Geronimo*, 144-148.

5 Copies of this telegram are in the Gatewood Collection, and in Dan Thrapp, *The Conquest of Apacheria* (Norman: University of Oklahoma Press, 1967), 313.

6 This conversation is reported in Dan Thrapp, *Al Sieber: Chief of Scouts* (Norman: University of Oklahoma Press, 1964), 294.

7 Quoted in Lockwood, *The Apache Indians,* 280.

8 There is some controversy as to the number who fled. Britton Davis to C. B. Gatewood, Jr., San Diego, April 25, 1926, Letter no. 248, Gatewood Collection, states there were "forty bucks, including all boys old enough to bear arms, and 103 women and children." Most sources, including Gatewood's reminiscence, place the figure at 42 men and 90 women and children.

## CHAPTER IV

1 Crook to Assistant Adjutant-General, Division of the Pacific, June 2, 1885, quoted in Thrapp, *Conquest of Apacheria*, 322-323.

2 Albuquerque *Journal*, June 7, 1885.

3 Gatewood to his wife, July 11, 1005, Fort Bayard, N.M., Letter no. 7, Gatewood Collection.

4 Crook to AAG, Division of the Pacific, August 13, 1885, quoted in Thrapp, *Conquest of Apacheria*, 330.

5 Davis, *The Truth About Geronimo*, 165-169.

6 Crook to AAG, Division of the Pacific, August 18, 1885, quoted in Thrapp, *Conquest of Apacheria*, 331-332.

7 Davis, *The Truth About Geronimo*, 191-193.

8 Quoted in Thrapp, *Conquest of Apacheria*, 332-333.

9 Torres, Decree to all Prefects, October 2, 1885, "Apache Folder, 1856-1886," Archive of Sonora (microfilm copy in Arizona Pioneers' Historical Society, Tucson). The treaty of July 29, 1882, allowing U.S. troops to cross the border in pursuit of hostiles, ended after two years; thus in 1885 Crook had no treaty rights to enter Mexico and had to make his own arrangement with Governor Torres.

10 Minute Book, Arizona Pioneers' Historical Society, June 3, 4, 10, and August 3, 1885; R. C. Drum to Commanding General, Department of Arizona, Washington, October 17, 1885, 5645 AGO 1885, copy in Arizona Pioneers' Historical Society.

## CHAPTER V

1 Maus to C. S. Roberts, April 18, 1886, Maus Collection, Special Collections Division, Library, University of Arizona.

2 For the events related to the killing of Victorio, and Corredor's part in it, see Chapter I.

3 Ed Arhelger to C. B. Gatewood, Jr., Maywood, California, May 5, 1928, Letter no. 661, Gatewood Collection. For Tom Horn's comments related to this campaign, see Tom Horn, *Life of Tom Horn: A Vindication* (Denver: The Louthan Company, 1904), 184-196.

4 Maus's report and other documents are in the Maus Collection, Special Collections Division, Library, University of Arizona, and the Maus File, Arizona Pioneers' Historical Society. See also Nalty and Strobridge, "Captain Emmet Crawford: Commander of Apache Scouts"; "The Killing of Captain Crawford," Prescott *Morning Courier*, March 24, 1886; W. E. Shipp, "Captain Crawford's Last Expedition," *Journal of the United States Cavalry Association*, XIX (October 1905), 280 *et seq.*

5 "From a Tucson paper, about April 24 or 25, 1930," Gatewood Collection.

6 *Senate Report 756*, 53 Cong., 3 Sess., Serial 3288, 1.

7 See "Papers Relating to the Foreign Relations of the United States . . . December 6, 1886 (Mexico)," *House Exec. Doc. 1*, 49 Cong., 2 Sess., Serial 2460, 570-691. For the Sonoran investigation, see "Apache Folder, 1856-1886," Archive of Sonora.

8 "Apache Folder, 1856-1886," Archive of Sonora; and Betzinez, *I Fought With Geronimo*, 133.

9 Lieutenant James Parker later recalled, "We didn't go around taking snap shots then—photography was a tedious process, and nobody photographed except professional photographers." Parker to C. B. Gatewood, Jr., Newport, Long Island, August 27, 1925, Gatewood Collection. Fly was a professional photographer from Tombstone.

10 Bourke, *On the Border with Crook*, 474-476. His account of the surrender proceedings occupy pages 474-479 of his great narrative.

11 Davis, *The Truth About Geronimo*, 196-212, contains a complete transcript of the conference, along with copies of Crook's letters regarding it.

12 Schmitt (ed.), *General George Crook*, 261.

13 Barrett (ed.), *Geronimo's Story of his Life*, 139.

14 Quoted in Charles F. Lummis, *General Crook and the Apache Wars* (Flagstaff: Northland Press, 1966), 16; for details about Tribollet's life, see Thrapp, *Conquest of Apacheria*, 345-345n.

15 This telegram, as well as those that follow, are quoted in Davis, *The Truth About Geronimo*, 214-217. Crook's comments on these events is contained in George Crook, *Resume of Operations Against Apache Indians, 1882 to 1886* (NP: privately printed, 1886).

## CHAPTER VI

1 Virginia Weisel Johnson, *The Unregimented General: A Biography of Nelson A. Miles* (Boston, 1962), 7.

2 These details of Miles's life are from *ibid.*; Newton F. Tolman, *The Search for General Miles* (New York, 1968); and from Miles's two autobiographical efforts, *Personal Recollections and Observations* (Chicago: The Werner Company, 1897), and *Serving the Republic* (New York, 1911).

3 Quoted in Johnson, *The Unregimented General*, 230.

4 A copy of the order is in the Gatewood Collection; see also Miles, *Serving the Republic*, 221-222.

5 William H. Leckie, *The Buffalo Soldiers* (Norman: University of Oklahoma Press, 1967), 243-244.

6 H. C. Benson, "The Geronimo Campaign," *Army and Navy Journal* (July 3, 1909); copy in the Gatewood Collection.

7 Miles, *Serving the Republic*, 224.

8 Henry Creelman, "Leonard Wood—The Doctor Who Became a General," *Pearson's Magazine*, XXI (April 1909), 361-383.

9 Benson, "The Geronimo Campaign."

10 Miles, *Serving the Republic*, 225-226.

11 Lawrence R. Jerome, "Geronimo Campaign as Told by a Trooper of 'B' Troop," Gatewood Collection. See also William Stover, "Uprising of Apaches Under Geronimo," Washington *National Tribune*, April 23, 1925.

12 Quoted in Johnson, *The Unregimented General*, 236.

13 For copies of this correspondence, see Part III, *Senate Ex. Doc. 117*, 49 Cong., 2 Sess., Serial 2449, 49-77.

14 Copy in Gatewood Collection.

15 Much of the rest of this chapter is based on Charles B. Gatewood's reminiscence, entitled "An Account of the Surrender of Geronimo," written about 1895; an abbreviated version of this paper, edited by Gatewood's son, appeared as "The Surrender of Geronimo," in *Proceedings of the Annual Meeting and Dinner of the Order of Indian Wars of the United States* (Washington, 1929).

16 Dr. S. M. Huddleson, "An Interview with Geronimo and his Guardian Mr. G. M. Wratton," Gatewood Collection.

17 See James B. Parker, "Service with Lieutenant Charles B. Gatewood, 6th U.S. Cavalry," Gatewood Collection; also, Parker, *The Old Army: Memories 1872-1918* (Philadelphia: Dorrance & Company, 1929).

18 Lawrence R. Jerome, "Geronimo Campaign as Told by a Trooper of 'B' Troop," Gatewood Collection; Jerome had enlisted under the name Lawrence Vinton.

19 "Apache Folder, 1856-1886," Archive of Sonora.

20 Gatewood, "An Account of the Surrender of Geronimo," Gatewood Collection.

21 *Ibid.*

22 Copies of this message and all correspondence from Lawton's command to Miles's headquarters are in the Gatewood Collection, copied from originals at the headquarters, Division of the Pacific, in San Francisco by Charles B. Gatewood, Jr.

23 Gatewood, "An Account of the Surrender of Geronimo," Gatewood Collection.

24 Geronimo's embrace was an *abrazo* in the Spanish manner and was merely a greeting; however, it gave the troops the impression that the two were old friends when in reality they were meeting for the first time.

25 Gatewood to his wife, August 26, 1886, Letter no. 21, Gatewood Collection; a printed copy is in Charles Byars (ed.), "Gatewood Reports to his Wife from Geronimo's Camp," *The Journal of Arizona History*, VII (Summer 1966), 76-81.

### Chapter VII

1 Gatewood, "An Account of the Surrender of Geronimo," Gatewood Collection.

2 R. D. Walsh to C. B. Gatewood, Jr., Washington, May 3, 1926, Letter no. 255, Gatewood Collection.

3 "Apache Folder, 1856-1886," Archive of Sonora; a copy is in the Gatewood Collection.

4 T. J. Clay to C. B. Gatewood, Jr., Lexington, Kentucky, June 14, 1924, Letter no. 93, Gatewood Collection.

5 Leonard Wood Diary, quoted in Miles, *Personal Recollections,* 513-514.

6 Copies of this message and those that follow were copied from the originals at the headquarters, Division of the Pacific, San Francisco, by C. B. Gatewood, Jr., and are in the Gatewood Collection.

7 Quoted in Johnson, *The Unregimented General,* 247.

8 Miles, *Personal Recollections,* 520-522.

9 Barrett (ed.), *Geronimo's Story of His Life,* 158-159.

10 M. Doyle to C. B. Gatewood, Jr., Bisbee, Arizona, July 15, 1926, Letter no. 272, Gatewood Collection. See also Thomas J. Clay, "Some Unwritten Incidents of the Geronimo Campaign," *Proceedings of the Annual Meeting and Dinner of the Order of Indian Wars of the United States* (Washington, 1929) 62-65.

11 These telegrams were copied from the originals at the headquarters, Division of the Pacific, San Francisco, by C. B. Gatewood, Jr., and are in the Gatewood Collection.

12 Doyle to Gatewood, Letter no. 272, Gatewood Collection; Leckie, *The Buffalo Soldiers,* 245.

13 Quoted in Johnson, *The Unregimented General,* 250.

14 Barrett (ed.), *Geronimo's Story of His Life,* 159.

15 Miles, *Personal Recollections,* 527-529.

### Chapter VIII

1 All documentation in this chapter, unless otherwise footnoted, is from Part III, *Senate Ex. Doc. 117,* 49 Cong., 2 Sess., Serial 2449, 49-77, which contains all correspondence relative to the Chiricahua and Warm Springs Apache removal to Florida.

2 Quoted in Johnson, *The Unregimented General,* 242.

3 *Ibid.,* 243.

4 Stover's account, entitled "The Last of Geronimo and his Band," appeared in the Washington *National Tribune* on July 24, 1924; copy in the Gatewood Collection.

5 Miles, Personal Recollections, 529; Betzinez, *I Fought with Geronimo*, 143-145, tells the story of "Massai" in considerable detail. Paul Wellman wrote a novel of Massai's heroic journey back to Arizona; see his *Bronco Apache* (New York, 1936).

6 Leonard Wood Diary, quoted in Lockwood, *The Apache Indians*, 309.

7 This and all other correspondence relating to the particular terms under which Geronimo surrendered are quoted in *Senate Ex. Doc. 117*, 40 Cong., 2 Sess., Serial 2449, Parts I and II, 2-48.

8 Johnson, *The Unregimented General*, 252.

9 *Ibid.*, 252-253.

10 "Apache File, 1856-1886," Archive of Sonora.

11 Miles, *Personal Recollections*, 530.

## CHAPTER IX

1 Copy in the Gatewood Collection; all subsequent details of Gatewood's life are contained in the Biographical File, Gatewood Collection.

2 For additional details, see Helena Huntington Smith, *The War on Powder River* (New York, 1966).

3 For a copy of this report, as well as other documentation relating to the Apache captivity, see *Senate Ex. Doc. 83*, 51 Cong., 1 Sess., Serial 2686, 53 pp.

4 Bourke, *On the Border with Crook*, 486. Biographical material for Crook in this chapter came mainly from Schmitt (ed.), *General George Crook*, although the Gatewood Collection has considerable material on Crook in it.

5 Miles, *Personal Recollections*, 523-524.

6 C. A. P. Hatfield, "Expeditions against the Chiricahua Apaches, 1882 and 1883, and The Geronimo Campaign of 1885 and 1886," Gatewood Collection.

7 Johnson, *The Unregimented General*, 262-264; much of the biographical material in this chapter, relating to Miles, is from this book. The Gatewood Collection contains many documents not cited in Johnson's book which shed much light on his character.

8 *Senate Ex. Doc. 117*, 49 Cong., 2 Sess., 45-48, contains the full text of Lawton's revised report.

9 Benson, "The Geronimo Campaign."

10 Horn, *Life of Tom Horn*, 204-210.

11 Owen White, "Talking Boy," *Colliers* (February 18, 1933) 18, 38; copy in the Gatewood Collection.

12 Quoted in Eve Ball, "The Apache Scouts: A Chiricahua Appraisal," *Arizona and the West*, VII (Winter 1965), 327.

13 See Letters no 194, 231, 307, 308, and 399, Gatewood Collection, and C. B. Gatewood, Jr., "Memorandum: Subject: Enlisted service . . . of Kayitah and Martine," Gatewood Collection.

NOTES

## Chapter X

1 Barrett (ed.), *Geronimo's Story of his Life,* 177. For additional details on Geronimo's life in captivity, see *Senate Ex. Doc. 83,* 51 Cong., 1 Sess., Serial 2686.

2 Barrett (ed.), *Geronimo's Story of his Life,* 180.

3 See various newspaper clippings in the Gatewood Collection relating to Geronimo's later life, especially "Old Indian Geronimo Joins Wild West Show," *The Washington Times,* April 4, 1906; "Geronimo's Body Buried," from an unnamed Baltimore paper of February 18, 1909; and "General Nelson A. Miles Tells How He Captured the Indian Chief Geronimo," *New York Herald,* February 21, 1909.

4 Huddleson, "An Interview with Geronimo and his Guardian, Mr. G. M. Wratton," Gatewood Collection.

5 "Grave of Indian Warrior Empty," from an unnamed Los Angeles newspaper, datelined Fort Sill (Okla.) Feb. 16, 1930 (AP).

6 M. Salzman, Jr., "Geronimo: The Napoleon of Indians," *The Border* (March 1909), and reprinted in *The Journal of Arizona History,* VIII (Winter 1967), 215-247.

228

# BIBLIOGRAPHY

ANYONE who would read more about the final Geronimo campaign should begin with John Gregory Bourke's *On the Border with Crook* and Britton Davis's *The Truth About Geronimo*. These two firsthand accounts not only are factual and relatively unbiased, but also are filled with the soldiers' spirit of adventure, their willingness to endure hardships, and their knowledge that the Indian was not altogether wrong. The best secondary source is Dan Thrapp's *The Conquest of Apacheria*, which details the long and bloody Apache wars of the Southwest in truthful, readable fashion. In the field of fiction, two novels stand out: Paul Wellman's *Bronco Apache*, which tells the story of Massai, the Apache who jumped the train east of St. Louis and made his way back to Arizona, and Paul Horgan's *A Distant Trumpet*, which is a thinly disguised account of Gatewood and Crook's roles in the final Geronimo campaign.

## MANUSCRIPT MATERIALS

Arizona Pioneers' Historical Society, Tucson. Biographical files for most of the participants in the campaign.

Arizona State Department of Library and Archives, Phoenix. Newspapers.

Gatewood Collection, Arizona Pioneers' Historical Society, Tucson. Collected by Charles B. Gatewood, Jr., these eight archival boxes consist of more than six hundred letters by Gatewood and his wife, family correspondence, copies of all official correspondence taken mainly from the files of the Division of the Pacific at San Francisco, reminiscences by Gatewood about the campaign, clippings from newspapers, copies of articles relating to participants, unpublished and published firsthand accounts by soldiers and scouts involved in the campaign, and thousands of photographs.

National Archives and Records Service, Record Group 94.

Sharlot Hall Historical Museum, Prescott, Arizona. Documents, clippings, and newspapers.

Sonoran Archives, microfilm copy at Arizona Pioneers' Historical Society. Apache File, 1856-1886. Principally reports by Prefects to the governor concerning Apache depredations, letters from the governor relating to Apache activities, and scalp bounty claims.

University of Arizona Library, Tucson. Maus Collection.

University of New Mexico Library, Albuquerque. John G. Bourke, Diary, microfilm copy of original at the United States Military Academy Library.

## GOVERNMENT DOCUMENTS

"The Apache Indians," *Senate Ex. Doc. 83*, 51 Cong., 1 Sess., Serial 2686, 53 pp.

*Chronological List of Actions &c., with Indians, from January 1, 1866, to January, 1891.* Washington: Adjutant General's Office, 1891.

"Correspondence between Lieut. Gen. P. H. Sheridan and Brig. Gen. George Crook regarding the Apache Indians," *Senate Ex. Doc. 88*, 51 Cong., 1 Sess., Serial 2686, 18 pp.

Crook, George. *Resumé of Operations Against Apache Indians, 1882-1886.* Washington: Government Printing Office, 1887.

"Emmet Crawford, Deceased," *Senate Report 756*, 53 Cong., 3 Sess., Serial 3288, 5 pp.

Heitman, Francis B. *Historical Register and Dictionary of the United States Army, from its Organization, September 29, 1789, to March 2, 1903.* 2 vols. Washington: Government Printing Office, 1902.

"Indian War History of the Army During the Years 1865-1886, Compiled from War Department Records," *House Report 1084*, 1914.

*Medal of Honor Recipients: 1863-1963.* Washington: Government Printing Office, 1964.

"Papers Relating to Foreign Relations of the United States (Mexico)," *House Exec. Doc. 1*, 49 Cong., 2 Sess., Serial 2460, 570-691, for the Crawford affair.

"The Surrender of Geronimo," *Senate Ex. Doc. 117*, 49 Cong., 1 Sess., Serial 2449, 77 pp.

*U.S. Statutes.* Washington: Government Printing Office, various dates.

PRIMARY SOURCES

Barrett, S. M. (ed.). *Geronimo's Story of His Life*. New York: Duffield & Company, 1906.

Benson, H. C. "The Geronimo Campaign," *Army and Navy Journal*, July 3, 1909.

Betzinez, Jason. *I Fought with Geronimo*. Ed. by W. S. Nye. Harrisburg, Pa.: Stackpole Company, 1959.

Bigelow, John Jr. *On the Bloody Trail of Geronimo*. Ed. by Arthur Woodward. Los Angeles: Westernlore Press, 1958.

Bourke, John G. *An Apache Campaign in the Sierra Madre*. New York, 1886.

———. "General Crook in the Indian Country," *Century*, XLI (March 1891), 643-660.

———. *On the Border with Crook*. New York, 1891, and reprints.

Byars, Charles (ed.). "Gatewood Reports to his Wife from Geronimo's Camp," *The Journal of Arizona History*, VII (Summer 1966), 76-81.

"The Capture of Geronimo," *San Dimas* (California) *Press*, April 21, 1927.

Carter, R. G. "Lawton's Capture of Geronimo," *Collier's Weekly*, XXIV (January 27, 1900). 8ff.

Clay, Thomas J. "Some Unwritten Incidents of the Geronimo Campaign," *Proceedings of the Annual Meeting and Dinner of the Order of Indian Wars of the United States* (Washington, 1929), 62-65.

Clum, John. "Apache Misrule," *New Mexico Historical Review*, V (April, July 1930).

———. "Geronimo," *New Mexico Historical Review*, III (January, April, July 1928).

Crook, George. *General George Crook: His Autobiography*. Ed. by Martin F. Schmitt. Norman: University of Oklahoma Press, 1946.

Cruse, Thomas. *Apache Days and After*. Caldwell, Idaho: Caxton, 1941.

Daly, Henry W. "The Geronimo Campaign," *Journal of the United States Cavalry Association*, XIX (July 1908), 68-103.

———. "Scouts Good and Bad," *American Legion Monthly*, V (August 1928), 24-25, 66-70.

Davis, Britton. "The Difficulties of Indian Warfare," *Army-Navy Journal*, October 24, 1885.

———. *The Truth About Geronimo*. New Haven: Yale University Press, 1929.

Elliott, Charles P. "The Geronimo Campaign of 1885-6," *Journal of the United States Cavalry Association,* XXI (September 1910), 212ff.

Forsyth, George A. *Thrilling Days in Army Life.* New York, 1900.

Gatewood, Charles B. "Campaigning Against Victorio in 1879," *The Great Divide,* no volume, no number (April 1894), 102-104.

———. "The Surrender of Geronimo," *Proceedings of the Annual Meeting and Dinner of the Order of Indian Wars of the United States* (Washington 1929) ; this account was abbreviated from the longer, original manuscript, "An Account of the Surrender of Geronimo" (MSS, Gatewood Collection), by Charles B. Gatewood, Jr.

Hanna, Robert. "With Crawford in Mexico," *Arizona Historical Review,* VI (April 1935), 56-65.

Horn, Tom. *Life of Tom Horn: A Vindication.* Denver: The Louthan Company, 1904.

"The Killing of Captain Emmet Crawford," Prescott *Morning Courier,* March 24, 1886.

Miles, Nelson A. *Personal Recollections and Observations.* Chicago: The Werner Company, 1897.

———. *Serving the Republic.* New York, 1911.

Opler, Morris E. "A Chiricahua Apache's Account of the Geronimo Campaign of 1886," *New Mexico Historical Review,* XIII (October 1938), 360-386.

Parker, James. *The Old Army: Memories 1872-1918.* Philadelphia: Dorrance & Company, 1929.

Rope, John, as told to Grenville Goodwin. "Experiences of an Indian Scout," *Arizona Historical Review,* III (January, April, 1936).

*Roster of Troops, Department of Arizona, Operating Against Hostile Chiricahuas, July 14, 1885.* NP, ND, copy in Gatewood Collection.

Shipp, W. E. "Captain Crawford's Last Expedition," *Journal of the United States Cavalry Association,* XIX (October 1905), 280ff.

Stover, William. "The Last of Geronimo and his Band," Washington *National Tribune,* July 24, 1924.

———. "Uprising of Apaches Under Geronimo," Washington *National Tribune,* April 23, 1925.

Wood, Leonard. "Diary, 1886," Library of Congress, Washington; portions of this were printed in Miles, *Personal Recollections,* 506-517.

SECONDARY SOURCES

Arnold, Elliott. *Blood Brother.* New York, 1947. This work of fiction stays very close to the true story of the surrender of Cochise.

Ball, Eve. "The Apache Scouts: A Chiricahua Appraisal," *Arizona and the West,* VII (Winter 1965), 315-328.

Barnes, Will C. "The Apaches' Last Stand in Arizona," *Arizona Historical Review,* III (January 1931), 36-59.

Barney, James M. *Tales of Apache Warfare.* Privately printed, 1933.

Brandes, Ray. Frontier Military Posts of Arizona. Globe, Arizona: Dale Stuart King, 1960.

Carter, W. H. *From Yorktown to Santiago with the Sixth Cavalry.* Baltimore: The Lord Baltimore Press, 1900.

Clum, John. "The Apaches," *New Mexico Historical Review,* IV (October 1929).

Clum, Woodworth. *Apache Agent.* Boston, 1936.

Creelman, Henry. "Leonard Wood—The Doctor Who Became a General," *Pearson's Magazine,* XXI (April 1909) 361-383.

Cullum, George W. *Biographical Register of the Officers and Graduates of the U.S. Military Academy at West Point, N. Y.* 8 vols. Boston, 1891-1910.

*Dictionary of American Biography.* 22 vols. New York, 1958.

Forbes, Jack D. *Apache, Navaho, and Spaniard.* Norman: University of Oklahoma, 1960.

Glass, E. L. N. (comp. and ed.). *The History of the Tenth Cavalry, 1866-1921.* Tucson: Acme Printing Company, 1921.

Goodwin, Grenville. *The Social Organization of the Western Apache.* Chicago: University of Chicago Press, 1942.

Hagedorn, Herman. *Leonard Wood: A Biography.* 2 vols. New York, 1931.

Horgan, Paul. *A Distant Trumpet.* New York, 1960. This novel, with reasonable accuracy, tells of the efforts of Charles B. Gatewood and George Crook.

Johnson, Virginia W. *The Unregimented General: A Biography of Nelson A. Miles.* Boston, 1962.

King, James T. *War Eagle: A Life of General Eugene A. Carr.* Lincoln: University of Nebraska Press, 1963.

Leckie, William H. *The Buffalo Soldiers: A Narrative of the Negro Cavalry in the West.* Norman: University of Oklahoma Press, 1967.

Lockwood, Frank C. *The Apache Indians.* New York, 1938.

Lummis, Charles F. *General Crook and the Apache Wars.* Flagstaff: Northland Press, 1966.

Mazzanovich, Anton. *Trailing Geronimo.* Privately Printed, 1926.

*Memorial and Affidavits Showing Outrages Perpetrated by Apache In-*

*dians in the Territory of Arizona for the Years 1869-1870.* San Francisco: Francis & Valentine, Printers, 1871.

Nalty, Bernard C., and Strobridge, Truman R. "Captain Emmet Crawford: Commander of Apache Scouts," *Arizona and the West,* VI (Spring 1964), 30-40.

Ogle, Ralph H. *Federal Control of the Western Apaches, 1848-1886.* Albuquerque: University of New Mexico Press, 1940.

Opler, Morris E. *An Apache Life-Way.* Chicago: University of Chicago Press, 1941.

Price, George F. *Across the Continent with the Fifth Cavalry.* New York, 1883.

Reid, Mayne. *The Scalp Hunters: A Romance of Northern Mexico.* London: Seeley and Co., Ltd., ND

Rickey, Don. *Forty Miles a Day on Beans and Hay: The Enlisted Soldier Fighting the Indian Wars.* Norman: University of Oklahoma Press, 1963.

Sacks, B. "New Evidence on the Bascom Affair," *Arizona and the West,* IV Autumn 1962), 261-278.

Salzman, M., Jr. "Geronimo: The Napoleon of the Indians," *The Journal of Arizona History,* VIII (Winter 1967), 215-247.

Santee, Ross. *Apache Land.* New York, 1956.

Smith, Cornelius. "The Fight at Cibecu," *Arizona Highways,* XXXII (May 1956), 2-5.

Smith, Helena H. *The War on Powder River.* New York, 1966.

Smith, Ralph A. "The Scalp Hunter in the Borderlands," *Arizona and the West,* VI (Spring 1964), 5-22.

Sonnichsen, C. L. *The Mescalero Apaches.* Norman: University of Oklahoma Press, 1958.

Stevens, Robert C. "The Apache Menace in Sonora, 1831-1849," *Arizona and the West,* VI (Autumn 1964), 211-222.

Thrapp, Dan L. *Al Sieber: Chief of Scouts.* Norman: University of Oklahoma Press, 1964.

———. *The Conquest of Apacheria.* Norman: University of Oklahoma Press, 1967.

———. "Dan O'Leary, Apache Scout," *Arizona and the West,* VII (Winter 1965), 287-298.

Tolman, Newton F. *The Search for General Miles.* New York, 1968.

Tyler, Barbara A. "Cochise, Apache War Leader," *The Journal of Arizona History,* VI (Spring 1965), 1-10.

Utley, Robert M. "The Bascom Affair: A Reconstruction," *Arizona and the West,* III (Spring 1961), 59-68.

———. "The Surrender of Geronimo," *Arizoniana,* IV (Spring 1963), 1-9.

Weigley, Russell F. *History of the United States Army.* New York, 1967.

Wellman, Paul I. *Broncho Apache.* New York, 1936. A novel, but good.

———. *Death in the Desert.* New York, 1935.

———. *The Indian Wars of the West.* New York, 1947.

Welsh, Herbert. *The Apache Prisoners in Fort Marion, St. Augustine, Florida.* Philadelphia: Indian Rights Association, 1887.

Wharfield, H. B. *Apache Indian Scouts.* El Cajon, California: privately printed, 1964.

White, Owen. "Talking Boy," *Colliers,* February 18, 1933, 18ff.

Williamson, Dan R. "Al Sieber: Famous Scout of the Southwest," *Arizona Historical Review,* III (January 1931) 60-76.

Woodward, Arthur. "Side Lights on Fifty Years of Apache Warfare, 1836-1886," *Arizoniana,* II (Fall 1961) 3-14.

Wormser, Richard. *The Yellowlegs: The Story of the United States Cavalry.* New York, 1966.

# INDEX

237

Miles, Mary Hoyt Sherman, noted, 100; marries Miles, 99; letters to, 111, 143-4, 148, 150, 156, 158, 170, 191, 192

Miles, Nelson A., pictures of, 101, 149; noted 175, 203, 204, 210-11, 218, 220; early life of, 97-100; commands Department of Arizona, 100-02; plan to capture hostiles, 102-3; campaigns against hostiles, 103-31; and surrender of hostiles, 133-47; at Fort Bowie, 147-51; and removal of Apaches to Florida, 152-73; claims credit for surrender of Geronimo, 176-91; later life of, 191-3; and Tom Horn, 199-200

Mimbreño Apache Indians, 20

*Mining Journal* (Frostburg), quoted, 39-40

Missouri, 28

Mobile (Alabama), 186-7

Mogollon Mountains (New Mexico), 61, 62

Montana, 99, 189

Montoya, picture of, 89; noted, 86

Moore, Isaiah N., 11

Moore, Tom, picture of, 89; noted, 86

Morenci (Arizona), 58

Morrison, J. T., 108

Morrison, Pitcairn, 10-11

Morrow, A. P., 38

Mount Vernon Barracks (Mobile), Apaches at, 186-7, 207-8

Mud Springs (Arizona), 86, 92

Mule Mountains (Arizona), 68

Nachez, pictures of, 19, 89, 151, 172, 210; noted, 46, 152, 155, 190, 210; chief of Chiricahua Apaches, 18-19, 24-5; at San Carlos, 48-50; and outbreak of 1885, 58-70; Crawford campaigns against, 76-82; surrenders to Crook, 83-92; flees to Mexico, 92-3, 96; Miles campaigns against, 103-21; confers with Gatewood, 121-31; escorted to Arizona, 133-41; surrenders to Miles, 141-51; sent to Florida, 165-75; in Alabama, 186; in Oklahoma, 187

Nachi, 8

*Nacionales,* fight hostiles, 79-82

Nacori (Sonora), 82, 114

Nakaidoklini, and Cibecu Revolt, 24, 43

Nana, picture of, 89; noted, 86; at San Carlos, 48-50; and outbreak of 1885, 52-6; surrenders, 83

Natiotish, 24

Navajo Indians, 5

Navajo Scouts, 70, 73

Nelson, ——, 145

New Hampshire, 106

New Mexico, noted, 4, 5, 10, 14, 17-18, 22, 38, 152, 154, 155, 158, 167, 168, 169, 171, 176, 208, 216; Chatto raids, 36; and outbreak of 1885, 61-3; Josanie raids, 70-73

New York, 28, 167

New York City, 188, 192

Nez Percé Indians, 99

Ninth Cavalry, 18

Noche, picture of, 89; noted, 86, 92

No-doyohn Canyon (Arizona), 20

Nogales (Arizona), 105, 108

Nolgee, 17

Nonquit (Massachusetts), 148

No-po-so, 20-21

Nordstrom, Charles E., 71

North Carolina, 186

Officers, status during Indian wars, 30-31. *See also* individual names

Ohio, 28, 32, 99, 106

Ojo Caliente (New Mexico), Geronimo surrenders at, 17-18

Oklahoma, noted, 111, 155, 158; Apaches in, 208-20

Omaha (Nebraska), 184

Omaha Exposition, Geronimo in, 210

Oposura (Sonora), 115

Opunto (Sonora), noted, 65; described, 66

Oregon, 4

Otis, E. S., 194

Oury, Granville H., 72

Pack animals, used by Crook, 32-4

Papago Indians, noted, 5, 14; and Camp Grant Massacre, 12-13

Papanosas (New Mexico), 73

Parker, James, noted, 61; quoted, 114-15

Parker, Quanah, 211

Patagonia Mountains (Arizona), 61

Peaches (Apache), 36

Peck, ——, 104

Peck Ranch (Arizona), 104

Pennsylvania, 158

Perrico, picture of, 210; noted, 56, 137; surrenders, 141

Philadelphia (Pennsylvania), 36

Pierce, Francis C., and lost telegram, 52-5

Pima County (Arizona), 146